VOICES & VISIONS

A Television Course in Modern American Poetry

Produced by
The New York Center for Visual History
and Presented by
South Carolina ETV Network

An Annenberg/CPB Project

Study Guide

Alice Rabi Lichtenstein

KENDALL/HUNT PUBLISHING COMPANY
2460 Kerper Boulevard   P.O. Box 539   Dubuque, Iowa 52004-0539

Advisory Board Chairman
Alan C. Purves

Associate Editor
Robert Carnevale

Contributors
Robert Carnevale
Wendy Flory
Tony Eprile
Kendra Kopelke
Sue Standing

Copyrights and Citations appear on pages 231-233.

The 'Voices & Visions' Telecourse

Voices & Visions is a landmark television course in modern American poetry. Films for the course were produced by the New York Center for Visual History which with the South Carolina ETV Network created the telecourse. Programs in the course were initially broadcast on PBS in the spring of 1988.

The New York Center for Visual History is a not-for-profit independent film production company founded in 1978 to develop stimulating and original programs on American culture, particularly its neglected aspects. The Center links educators, writers and filmmakers for the production, distribution and promotion of projects involving the humanities and media. New York Center project director for **Voices & Visions** is Lawrence Pitkethly who also served as executive producer for the films. Jill Janows was senior producer and Robert Chapman series executive for the films.

The South Carolina ETV Network, founded in 1958, is one of the major producers of public and educational television and radio programming for use throughout the United States. Programs produced range from energy education for junior high school students to presentations on **Great Performances**. The S.C. ETV Network has been producing college credit courses since 1970. S.C. ETV project director for **Voices & Visions** is Ruth Sproat, director of higher education.

Major funding for **Voices & Visions** has been provided by The Annenberg/CPB Project and the National Endowment for the Humanities. Series funding has also been received from the National Endowment for the Arts and The Arthur Vining Davis Foundations. Program funders include the Corporation for Public Broadcasting, The Pew Memorial Trust, The Geraldine R. Dodge Foundation, Soft Sheen Products, Inc., the New Jersey Committee for the Humanities, The Ohio Humanities Council, Hartford Insurance Group, The Massachusetts Foundation for Humanities and Public Policy, the Vermont Council on the Humanities and Public Issues, The Witter Bynner Foundation for Poetry, The Rockefeller Foundation, the Connecticut Humanities Council, The George Gund Foundation, the New York Council for the Humanities, and The Seth Sprague Educational and Charitable Foundation.

Curriculum Committee

Jane Donahue Eberwein
Professor of English
Oakland University

William Howarth
Professor of English
Princeton University

Herbert Leibowitz
Professor of English
Graduate Center, CUNY

A. Walton Litz
Professor of English
Princeton University

Kathleen Jordan Mallory
Assistant Professor of English
Southern Arkansas University

Ron Marostica
Director for Affiliate
and Member Services
National Council of
Teachers of English

William G. McBride
Professor of English
Colorado State University

Harriet Susskind
Professor of English
Monroe Community College

Alan Purves
Professor of Education
SUNY, Albany
Committee Chairman

Frederick Grossberg
Associate Professor of English
George Mason University
Curriculum Consultant

Table of Contents

Acknowledgements 1

Introductory Unit 3

Robert Frost 14

Ezra Pound 28

Langston Hughes 44

Walt Whitman 61

Hart Crane 76

William Carlos Williams 94

Emily Dickinson 108

Marianne Moore 124

T.S. Eliot 142

Wallace Stevens 161

Elizabeth Bishop 177

Robert Lowell 192

Sylvia Plath 208

Glossary 223

Self Test Answers 226

Copyrights and Citations 231

Acknowledgements

First, I would like to thank Alan Purves and Robert Carnevale for their considerable help and support. This study guide could not have been written without them. As curriculum committee chairman, Alan Purves contributed his guidance, intelligence, and astute criticism (not to mention his excellent turkey barley soup) to keep the entire project on track. Associate Editor Robert Carnevale contributed in just about every way possible: through his editing, writing, researching and unflappable commitment to getting the job done.

I would also like to thank the many other people who contributed their time and support: A. Walton Litz, Princeton University; Jane Eberwein, Oakland University; William Howarth, Princeton University; Herbert Leibowitz, City University of New York; Harriet Susskind, Monroe Community College; Kathleen Mallory, Southern Arkansas University; and Patricia Willis, curator of the Rosenbach Museum and Library. Their expert advice was invaluable. I would like to thank the wonderful people at S.C. ETV: Ruth Sproat, project director, who had the vision and took an active role in making it a reality; Andrea Lo Piccolo, Ruth's amazing assistant; Pat Dressler, publications director, and her assistant, Michele Reap—a very special thanks. These people were the lifeline.

The New York Center for Visual History staff contributed in many important ways. In particular, I would like to thank Lawrence Pitkethly, executive director; Jill Janows, senior producer; Jonathan Kovel, researcher; Minda Novek, series coordinator; and all the filmmakers who took the time to screen the films for me and to provide me with up-to-date information.

Hy Field of the Annenberg CPB Project helped to steer the project.

I want especially to thank the study guide contributors who managed to convey in their individual chapters their considerable knowledge and love of their poets. These writers were dedicated to communicating this love to students who will use this guide.

Finally, I would like to acknowledge my husband Jim Bercovitz, for his putting up with the reams of paper taking over the apartment and his endless support.

Introductory Unit

This unit includes some suggestions on how to read poetry, a note on poetic forms, and a brief history of American poetry. For this course you will need:

- A volume (or volumes) that contains the poems that will be discussed;
- A dictionary that gives etymologies;
- A notebook in which you can make a variety of journal entries;
- Access to a library or an encyclopedia;
- A willingness to explore the poems as well as your responses to them.

An Overview of the Units

Each of the units on the poets contains the following:

1. A brief biographical sketch of the poet, followed by an essay on the world of the poems and an essay on a key "theme" in the poet's work.

2. Brief biographies of the various speakers you will see in the film.

3. A study plan for the unit, including a list of the featured poems. You should read all these poems once before doing any of the exercises and before watching the film. Do not worry if you do not understand the poems; read them to get a feel for the poet and the poems.

4. One of the most important aspects of this course is the journal-notebook. Writing a journal-notebook is an informal way of keeping track of your thoughts, feelings, and responses to the poems and a way to practice writing about poetry without the pressure of worrying about style, grammar, or grades. It also helps you to focus. Try setting a certain time to write in your journal. The more of a habit writing becomes, the easier it is to do.

Many of the poets in the series kept journals or notebooks (much like artists' sketchbooks) to record striking observations, details, phrases, dreams, images, rhymes. Some of the poets, such as Dickinson and Crane, expressed their ideas in letters to friends. (You may want to think of your journal entries as self-addressed letters or letters to a friend about what the poems mean to you.) As the weeks go by, you will probably see changes in your thinking about poetry. It's a good idea to look back on previous entries to see how your opinions have changed about particular poems and poets. These entries may also reveal themes to develop into essay topics.

Above all, remember that the journal is a place where you should feel free to express yourself.

Some tips on keeping a journal:

- Find a notebook that you really like. Think of this notebook as "your book."
- Write on every other line. You may want to add comments to previous entries.
- Date your entries. Although the journal should not be confused with a diary, you do want to have a sense of continuity.
- Write freely. Don't worry about revising or correcting. Don't worry about the length of your entry but try to write for at least 15 minutes.

In each week's section of the study guide, there are listed suggestions for journal entries before viewing the film, after viewing the film, and while reading certain of the featured poems. The next section will present some general journal exercises.

5. A guided reading of a featured poem. This reading presents one way of reading a poem. It asks questions about details as well as about the overall meaning of the poem. Answers are presented. You should answer the questions yourself first, but feel free to read the answers provided. These represent one person's understanding of the poem.

6. A set of exercises and assignments. Your instructor will ask you to do particular ones.

7. A self test to let you get a sense of how well you know the poet. This also has answers provided.

8. A list of suggested further readings, including the works of the poet and works about the poet.

Some Ways of Reading Poems and Using Your Journal

There are a number of different ways of reading poems so as to get an understanding of them and a sense for how they are making themselves felt. We shall list a number of ways, some of which work better with certain poems and poets and with certain kinds of readers. Try several of them as you go through the course; each time record the results in your journal. Then look over the journal entries when you return to the poem or the poet for further study.

1. **Take free reading notes.** As you read the poem, simply write down whatever comes into your head. You may use phrases or words or even doodles. Keep doing this, starting over each time you read the poem. You might have a dozen separate trips through the poem, not always reading it from beginning to end but going back or skipping forward. Keep doing this until you feel comfortable with the poem. Look over your notes and see where you were consistent and where you changed your mind.

2. **Read the poem aloud.** As you read it, notice any occasions where you were not sure how to phrase a line or a sentence. Jot down those occasions and note what it was that caused you to stumble. When you read the poem again, you will have to make a decision about that segment so that the reading will go smoothly.

You will also need to decide what tone the poem projects, and how that affects you. How did you come to that decision? What about the poem led you to it?

In hearing the readings in the various films, you may notice that many of the readings are not dramatic. Others are quite forceful. Why do you think this variation might occur?

3. **Underline any striking words or phrases.** Often these words will need to be explored. You should look them up in your dictionary and see which of the various meanings might apply. Do these words seem to be keys to the poem? Do they set the tone or the mood of the poem? Are they deliberately ambiguous? Look at the various proper names and refer to the notes as well as to an encyclopedia or dictionary that might give more information. Why did the poet insert these words? What memories or recollections of prior reading or prior knowledge of history, society, art, music or general culture do they trigger?

With some of the poets in this course, you will find many allusions to other poems, artworks, myths and legends, and historical events, many of which are referred to in footnotes. Look at those references and determine why you are being asked to refer to them. What connection do you think the poet wants you to make?

4. **Look for repetitions.** These might be repetitions of sound such as alliteration, rhyme, or rhythm and cadence. They might be repetitions of words or phrases. There might be repetitions of whole images or segments of the poem. Poets often use repetition to help the reader connect items that might not otherwise appear to be connected, to emphasize a particular image or idea, to make associations between parts of the poem, or to point out comparisons and contrasts.

5. **Look for contradictions or oppositions.** In many poems oppositions might be established, often signalled by adjectives that pair some of the more traditional oppositions such as square and round, light and dark, here and there, male and female, me and them, or high and low. Jot down these oppositions in two columns in your journal and see what other elements in the poem can be put in one of the two columns. Do the opposites appear to balance each other out? Do they remain in tension? Are they somehow resolved? Often poets present an ambiguous meaning or feeling in their poems. As a reader, you are not necessarily supposed to find a resolution to that ambiguity, but to note its existence and realize that sometimes ideas and feelings have no solutions.

6. **Treat the poem as a little drama.** In many cases, you can view a poem as taking a situation and making it into a small scene. Often the speaker of the poem appears to be engaged in part of a dialogue with someone else. You might jot down the answers to these questions:

- Who is the speaker? What sort of a character is presented? What sort of tone or attitude is the speaker adopting towards the listener or the subject?
- Where is the speaker? Is there a suggested scene or setting?
- Is there any way of picturing the audience or the person or people to whom the speaker is talking?
- Is there a plot? That is, does there appear to be a rising action and a climax and resolution? What is the climax?

7. **Draw a picture of the poem or outline a filmed version.** Look at the visual set-up of the poem on the page. Many poems have a shape, in that they give more or less attention to certain parts, so that we may envisage the words and stanzas as making up boxes of various sizes. You can draw a schematic of a poem in this way, or you may draw a line graph illustrating your sense of the progression of tension or emotion. This sort of graph may also emerge from the use of the scales suggested in the next section.

Other graphic representations might include colors, sets of pictures or illustrations. You might consider that you have been asked to put the poem in an illustrated volume. What size type would you use? What sort of page? Would you use line drawings? Photographs? Black and white? Color? Each of these decisions represents an interpretive presentation of the poem. After you make your decision, write a brief justification of the choices you have made.

In the telecourse you will be seeing many filmed presentations of poems. You should think of these as one person's interpretation. Is there an alternate visualization? How would the alternate change the reading of the poem?

8. **Use a scale to chart your response.** Here are two examples:

For a poem with two characters, read the poem and then fill out the following set of scales to indicate your reaction to the poem and the people in it. On each scale rank the person or the poem from 1 (low in that quality) to 5 (high in that quality).

	Speaker	Second Character	Poem
Good	_____	_____	_____
Strong	_____	_____	_____
Active	_____	_____	_____
Smooth	_____	_____	_____
Clever	_____	_____	_____
Rugged	_____	_____	_____
Difficult	_____	_____	_____
Simple	_____	_____	_____
Evil	_____	_____	_____
Passive	_____	_____	_____
Moral	_____	_____	_____
Humorous	_____	_____	_____

Look over the ratings that you have made. In a page for each of the two people and for the poem, write a rationale for your ratings. What in the poem and what in your understanding of the situation led to your ratings?

Below is a set of scales and the marked off sections of a sonnet. After you finish each section, rate that section on each of the scales. Do not spend a lot of time with each scale but record your first impression. When you have finished, enter the results on a graph. On the basis of that graph, write a paragraph in which you explain for yourself the direction of each graph. In what ways does the mood of the poem shift or remain stable?

Graph of Response to a Poem

The grading system runs from 1-5; treat 1 as low in the quality and 5 as high in the quality.

Lines	Good	Active	Smooth	Forceful	Strong	Pleasing
1-4	____	____	____	____	____	____
4-8	____	____	____	____	____	____
9-12	____	____	____	____	____	____
13-14	____	____	____	____	____	____

Note: This should be set up so that you can draw a line graph for each column.

9. **Look for unusual uses of grammar or syntax.** You should be aware that a poet will often change normal word order to draw attention to something in the clause or phrase. A poet may also turn what is normally a noun into a verb or an adjective in order to create a fresh image and help the reader to see things just a little bit differently from normal. Jot down these instances in your journal and then come back to them to see what they might be affecting in the tone or meaning of the poem.

10. **Look for any persistent metaphor or image.** Many poems employ imagery, which is best defined as word pictures (even though imagery can appeal to the other senses as well). Often poets will use metaphor, which is the equation of one thing with another. In some cases an image or a metaphor may recur several times in a poem; such repetition suggests its importance. In other cases, the poet may extend a metaphor and make several points of comparison within it. In this case the whole poem needs to be seen in a "double" fashion.

11. **Look at the line breaks.** Often a poet will use the break between lines to call attention to a word, an image, or an idea. Although the sense of the phrase or clause will not end where the line does, by putting the break at an "unusual" place in the sentence, the poet may be inviting you to reconsider the normal state of affairs in what's being said.

12. **Write an imitation of the poem.** Try to capture the sense of the poem with an imitation of the tone and voice but writing about a different subject. Or try to use the same form and structure, or the same sorts of rhythm and rhyme. In that way you will get some sense of the kinds of problems the poet was facing in making the poem. You will probably gain some sort of an insight into the way the poem is constructed, and therefore, into its sense or feeling.

A Note on Meter

> "Some meter by accent
> Some meter by tone
> But the best way to meter
> Is to meter alone"

One of the devices most common to poetry is its use of various forms of repetition. Repetition is a way by which a poet may make the poem seem melodic or rhythmic. What is repeated may vary from poet to poet. Some poets repeat words and phrases at regular intervals. Walt Whitman is one of the poets whom you will encounter during this course who uses this form of repetition.

> Have you reckon'd a thousand acres much?
> Have you reckon'd the earth much?
> Have you practis'd so long to learn to read?
> Have you felt so proud to get at the meaning of poems?

> ("Song of Myself" 2)

Another form of repetition is that which is based on a particular sound. If the sound is at the beginning of words, the repetition is called alliteration; if it is at the end of words, it is called rhyme. Ezra Pound uses alliteration in some of his poems, particularly those which imitate the patterns of early English poetry. Many of the poets use rhyme, which we shall take up a bit later.

One of the most common forms of repetition in poetry in English is called meter, the repetition of alternating stressed and unstressed syllables, much like the beat of a piece of music. A particular meter is usually established as the basic pattern for a given poem, but often the poet will alter the actual sequence of beats in some lines in order to emphasize a word, to create a mood, or to establish a change or syncopation in the rhythm.

> Maybe it just sags
> like a heavy load.

> (Hughes, "Harlem")

The rhythm shifts from stressed before unstressed in the first line and the beginning of the second to a rise from unstressed to stressed at the end of the second line.

When people talk about meter, they usually use as the basic term the foot, which is like the bar in music; that is to say, it is the basic building block of the metrical pattern of a poem. A foot is usually defined as a stressed syllable, and the unstressed syllables before or after it. In English poetry, there are four common basic feet:

- iambic: a **wake**
- trochaic: **soft** ly
- anapestic: all the **rest**
- dactylic: **ten** der ly

These four types of feet are the basic building blocks of metrical poems. Other kinds of feet exist as substitutions, as does the possibility of lopping off or adding an unstressed syllable. The most common substitutions are the pyrrhic (two unstressed syllables) and the spondee (two stressed syllables).

Of the four basic feet, the most common metrical patterns in English and American metrical poetry are based on the iambic. The majority of metrical lines have either four or five iambic feet as the starting pattern from which different kinds of variation might occur. The iambic five-foot measure is called iambic pentameter, and it is the line used in Shakespeare's plays and in many of the poems of such writers as Pope, Swift, Wordsworth, Keats, and Browning. It is popular with Robert Frost as well. Most of these poets do not follow the meter strictly; often they will employ variations, the most common of which are as follows.

Inversion. To reverse the order of stressed and unstressed syllables, particularly at the beginning and in the middle of the line (this has a dramatic effect).

> **Some**thing/there **is**/that **does**/not **love**/a **wall**.
> (Frost, "Mending Wall")

Truncation. To eliminate the unstressed syllable, particularly at the beginning of the line (this makes the line sound more like a chant).

. . . **Foot**/it **feat**/ly **here**/and **there**;
And, **sweet**/**sprites**/, the **bur**/den bear.
(Shakespeare, The Tempest)

Substitution. To put in, for example, an anapestic foot rather than an iambic one (this speeds up the line) or to put in two stressed syllables (this slows the line down).

Of **man's**/**first dis**/obed/ience, **and**/the **fruit**
(Milton, "Paradise Lost")

In the iambic five-foot line, there is frequently a pause, called a caesura, which usually occurs after the fourth, fifth, or sixth syllable.

. . . Nothing that is not there//and the nothing that is.
(Stevens, "The Snow Man")

When you are determining the meter of a particular poem, read it aloud naturally and see if you can hear whether the stressed syllables occur in a regular pattern. If they do, that is the meter. As you read a poem aloud, you should not try to force the reading to match the abstract meter; there will always be tension between the abstract pattern and the actual words. It is that tension that you will be examining in part when you read Frost's poetry and listen for "the sound of sense" which he discusses in the film, and which is the theme of the Frost unit. Read the next line from William Wordsworth's "It Is a Beauteous Evening" aloud and notice that the shift in emphasis demonstrates a strong attachment between the people.

Dear child!/**Dear girl!**/That **walk**/est **with**/me **here**.
(Wordsworth, "It Is a Beauteous Evening")

The beginning fall sets the tone of one speaker, and the repeated rise sets the tone of the other speaker.

Rhyme

The other frequent form of repetition which characterizes much poetry is rhyme, which is the repetition of sounds at regular intervals in the poem. Usually the rhyming words are at the ends of the lines, but occasionally there will be additional rhymes between the middle and end of the line or at other points. In many cases the regular rhymes occur in patterns or rhyme schemes which are themselves repeated through the course of the poem. These repeated rhyming groups are called stanzas, and are often noted with an alphabetic pattern to indicate which lines are rhymed. If the rhymes are in repeated pairs, such as *aa bb cc dd* etc., the rhyme scheme is called a couplet. A four-line stanza is called a quatrain. Often a stanza pattern is marked by a combination of letters and numbers, the letters to indicate the rhyming words and the numbers to indicate the number of feet. Emily Dickinson's stanza is usually indicated *a4 b3 c4 b3*.

> Experiment escorts us last (a4)
> His pungent company (b3)
> Will not allow an axiom (c4)
> An Opportunity (b3)

Not all rhymes are exact repetitions; in some of the poems you will encounter what is called slant rhyme, such as "mind/send," or eye rhyme, such as "bead/dead."

Some of the Patterns You Will Encounter

Robert Frost has two favorite forms. One is unrhymed iambic pentameter, called blank verse. This is the same meter that Shakespeare used in his plays and that poets like Milton, Wordsworth, and Robert Browning used in their narrative and epic poems. It is a meter that is close to the natural rhythm of speech, and Frost uses it extensively in his narrative and dramatic poems. Blank verse is made dramatic and varied by using metrical variation, by moving the caesura around in the line, and by not always stopping the flow of the phrase or clause at the end of the line. The lack of a pause indicated by punctuation or syntax (such as the end of a clause) at the end of a line creates what is called enjambment or the run-on line.

> *Why* do they make good neighbors? Isn't it
> Where there are cows? But here there are no cows.
> (Frost, "Mending Wall")

Frost's other favorite form is the sonnet, a 14-line iambic pentameter poem, which is of two sorts, the Shakespearean, which has a rhyme scheme of *abab cdcd efef gg*, and the Petrarchan or Italian, which has a more varied rhyme scheme, usually a variation of the following: *abba abba cdecde*. Often there is a break or turn of thought after the 12th line of a Shakespearean sonnet and after the eighth line of a Petrarchan one. The sonnet is a very popular traditional form for many poets who enjoy working out variations within this relatively fixed structure.

Emily Dickinson's favorite stanza form is the hymn stanza, which we have described earlier. It is a four-line stanza a4 b3 c4 b3 and is also called common measure or ballad stanza. Many of the hymns in Protestant hymnals use this stanzaic form, which was also a popular form for traditional ballads and is used today in folk ballads.

Walt Whitman does not use a metrical pattern or a stanza. Instead he created what is known as the long line, a line without traditional meter, but with 15 to 20 syllables and a variable number of accents. These accents occur in phrases or cadences. Many have claimed that the rhythm is modelled on the King James translation of the Bible and, indeed, there are resemblances. Whitman's lines employ repetition of words and phrases, but there is no rhyme scheme.

Several of the poets, such as Pound, Eliot, and Williams, use an unmetrical and unrhymed verse form with varied line lengths. This is called free verse, and became popular in the 20th century. There may be individual rhythms and patterns for particular poems, but in many cases the arrangement of words into lines is to establish a visual pattern on the printed page, rather than to establish an oral pattern. When read aloud in the exact pattern of their visual presentation, some of the poems, such as those of Williams, seem almost nonsense; on the page as something to look at, they make a great deal of sense.

Marianne Moore's poetry is based on a syllabic principle, rather than a metrical one. Syllabic verse goes back to the Greeks and the Romans whose language had what are known as long and short syllables dependent on the particular vowel or vowel-consonant combinations. English does have long and short vowels as in "bite" and "bit." But in English speech, accent or stress appears to do more to make up the rhythm than does the relationship of long to short vowels. Much of Moore's poetry, nonetheless, bases its lines and stanzas on syllabic rather than stress patterns.

Many of the other poets you will encounter use a variety of meters and stanza forms. These poets seem not to be as particular about adhering to one specific verse form. Some, like Lowell and Plath, work to create what to them is an "organic" union of content and form. Some, like Williams, care most particularly about the visual impression of the poem and try to have the words on the page take on a distinctive shape that suggests how the poem is to be read but in some cases is hard to render orally. Pound incorporates words and even lines from other languages and in various script systems to attract the eye as well as the mind.

American Poetry Before Whitman

The first English settlers on the Atlantic seaboard brought with them a habit of writing poetry that resulted in a remarkable flowering of early American verse. When Anne Bradstreet's *Tenth Muse* was published in London in 1650, it won attention not only as the first volume of poetry written by an American colonist, but also as the first such book ever published by an English-speaking woman. Bradstreet displayed an exceptional wit and range of learning while providing warm personal insight into the values and conflicts of Puritan life. Another New England poet, Edward Taylor, created powerful verse meditations on his religious experiences—always the primary topic among Puritan writers. His poems, however, remained unpublished until the 20th century.

By the mid-18th century, poets showed greater interest in public themes than in personal experiences. They began to explore local landscapes in topographical poems. From the physical prospect of the land as viewed from natural elevations, they moved naturally to the new world's temporal prospects in such long celebratory poems as "On the Rising Glory of America" by Philip Freneau and Hugh Henry Brackenridge and "Greenfield Hill" by Timothy Dwight. The American Revolution stimulated the production of verse satire as well as more conventionally patriotic poetry. Among the most interesting poets of this period was Phillis Wheatley, a black slave who learned English as a young girl after being transported from Africa to Boston and who enjoyed a brief celebrity both in America and England. During and after the Revolution, some poets attempted to create epic poems to demonstrate American nationalism. Best known among these efforts was Joel Barlow's *Columbiad.*

The romantic movement of the early 19th century brought with it a more reflective, inward-directed sort of poetry and a new sense of nature as something kindred to man: a source of insight and comfort. William Cullen Bryant's poems reflected this change of style and values with his emphasis on the soothing and restorative calm of wilderness as a corrective to the faults of civilization. Poets considered themselves as exercising a special role in society by expressing sensitive feelings. Much poetry of this period was sentimental in nature, purposely evoking feelings of compassion, pity, and sometimes anger at such moral horrors as slavery and child labor abuses. John Greenleaf Whittier may have been the best-loved writer of such socially conscious verse. Early 19th-century writers also gave us many familiar hymns and some of our most popular patriotic songs such as Francis Scott Key's "Star-Spangled Banner" and Julia Ward Howe's "Battle Hymn of the Republic."

The most popular American poet of this period, on both sides of the Atlantic, was Henry Wadsworth Longfellow; his work epitomized the taste of his era. Longfellow became famous for his long narrative poems based on incidents from American history, among them *Evangeline*, *The Song of Hiawatha*, and *The Courtship of Miles Standish*. He also wrote a number of inspirational poems like "A Psalm of Life" that offered encouragement and support to persons who felt overburdened with the pressures of life. In this way he made himself a friend to the general reader. He was also an accomplished metrist who experimented with a wide variety of poetic forms borrowed from such languages as German and Finnish, which he taught at Harvard.

Although Longfellow's achievements made him a preeminent literary figure in his own day, it was Ralph Waldo Emerson and Edgar Allan Poe's writing that influenced the modern American poets whom you will meet in **Voices & Visions**. Emerson separated himself sharply from Longfellow's tradition when he declared that "it is not meters, but a meter-making argument that makes a poem—a thought so passionate and alive that like the spirit of a plant or an animal it has an architecture of its own, and adorns nature with a new thing." Although he is better known today for his powerful essays, Emerson experimented often with verse and tended to produce a distinctively condensed, cryptic, and riddling poetry that unsettled things rather than providing formulaic answers to life's questions. In "Uriel," he declared: "Line in nature is not found;/Unit and universe are round;/In vain produced, all rays return;/Evil will bless, and ice will burn." Robert Frost once alluded to this poem as "the greatest Western poem yet." Other modern poets strongly influenced by Emerson, although in strikingly different ways, included Emily Dickinson and Walt Whitman, who once declared "I was simmering, simmering. Emerson brought me to a boil."

Poe's poetic aims diverged sharply from Emerson's. Poe disregarded the subject matter of poetry and all concern with the paraphrasable message to emphasize evocation of mood in the reader. He created symbolic landscapes like that of "Dream-Land," which takes place in "a weird clime that lieth sublime,/Out of SPACE—out of TIME," and he produced strange stories narrated by speakers so obsessed with personal griefs that they verged on madness in such immensely popular poems as "Annabel Lee" and "The Raven." Unlike Emerson, who was satisfied with roughness and even fragmentation in his verse forms, Poe cultivated the art of style. He experimented with novel meters and cultivated haunting sound effects. Through the French *Symboliste* poets whom he strongly influenced, Poe exercised a force on the writings of such 20th-century American poets as Hart Crane, T.S. Eliot, and Ezra Pound.

When Whitman sent Emerson a copy of his 1855 *Leaves of Grass*, the older poet responded with prophetic enthusiasm: "I greet you at the beginning of a great career, which yet must have had a long foreground somewhere, for such a start." Part of that foreground came from the existing heritage of American poetry on which Whitman and his successors proceeded to build.

For Further Reading

Nims, John Frederick. *Western Wind: An Introduction to Poetry*. New York: Random House; 1974.

Williams, Miller. *Patterns of Poetry: An Encyclopedia of Forms*. Baton Rouge: Louisiana State University Press; 1986. (This new volume is one of the best introductions to poetic meters and rhyme schemes, having mostly examples from modern and contemporary American poets.)

Robert Frost (1874-1963)

Robert Frost was one of the most popular poets of all time and the only poet to read at a presidential inauguration. An athletic man who was still vigorous into his white-haired eighties, Frost's image was of the celebrator of American virtues, the man who builds poems as well-wrought and solid as a New England farmhouse. His best known poems—"Stopping by Woods on a Snowy Evening," "The Road Not Taken," "Mending Wall,"—present a moment in rural life, a moment that has wider implications about life itself. Frost appeared to be the cheerful and honest New England farmer. However, critic Lionel Trilling has reminded the literary world of Frost's darker side. A demanding though loving husband and father, Frost was dogged by personal tragedy: the death of his father when Frost was young, the deaths of three of his children (one by suicide) and of his wife, whom he survived by twenty-five years. A sense of lurking tragedy informs the brightness of his poetic vision.

"The Poet of New England" lived in San Francisco until he was eleven, when he moved to Lawrence, Massachusetts. There he met Elinor Miriam White, his co-valedictorian in high school, who was to become his wife. After a term at Dartmouth, he spent two years at Harvard and then dropped out to farm in New Hampshire and take various odd jobs. In later years, Frost received so many honorary degrees that he was wryly to remark that he received his education by degrees. Frost continued to farm and teach school into his late thirties, writing many of his greatest lyric poems during this period but remaining largely unrecognized.

In 1912, he sold his farm and moved to England to experience firsthand the land described by Keats, Wordsworth, and the other poets he loved. This move proved to be the launching of his career. He quickly found a publisher for his first two books—*A Boy's Will* and *North of Boston*—and came to meet many influential poets of the day, including Ezra Pound and William Butler Yeats. Pound's favorable reviews of the books appeared in American publications, and when Frost returned to the United States in 1915, it was with a firmly established reputation.

Frost continued to write poems and became a well-loved teacher at Amherst College. With the publication of his next two books, *Mountain Interval* (1916) and *New Hampshire* (1923), which won a Pulitzer Prize, his reputation grew. In the ensuing years, he received three more Pulitzer Prizes, a Bollingen Prize for poetry and a Congressional Gold Medal. He was also made a goodwill emissary to cultural missions in South America and the Soviet Union.

Frost's enormous popularity with the public, his stress on traditional forms ("Writing free verse is like playing tennis with the net down," he once said) and his deceptively simple language at times caused the critics to ignore him in favor of more "difficult" poets such as Pound and Eliot. Trilling's 1958 reassessment, however, helped to revive his place in the eyes of the critics, and Frost died in 1963 recognized as one of his century's greatest poets.

The World of the Poems

As you watch the program, remember that Frost's poems, especially the early ones, describe the world as it was seventy years ago. There were few gas-powered mowers and balers for cutting hay; people still used scythes, hand-held cutting tools with long, curved blades. Imagine cutting hay all day with such a tool. You would need to swing the scythe back and forth with a regular, steady rhythm; otherwise, you would soon tire. Try to imagine the sound it would make as it cut the grass.

The world was much quieter seventy years ago, and people were more isolated from each other. Living on a small farm way out in the country in a time when there were no television sets, few paved roads and cars, people commonly lived and died in the same place where they were born. Loneliness could be very intense in this isolation, but it could also make for greater intimacy.

Even with a radio, you wouldn't be so aware of places and events around the world and the possibilities of your own life might seem more limited and simple to you. In any event, life would go on in this relative isolation and so would death. You might very well have your own family graveyard near your house, and when someone in your family died you might bury them yourself.

Notice this sense of solitude as you watch the Robert Frost program. Conversations, talk and the sound of the human voice become especially important in this solitude, and Frost was a master at capturing the sound of a voice talking. As you view the program, listen closely to the voices in the poetry and try to imagine them speaking out of a place like this.

Robert Frost: The Sound of Sense

In 1913, Frost sent to a friend what may be his first written statement of "the sound of sense," Frost's theory of how to make poetry dramatic. You will also hear it in the film:

> Now, it is possible to have sense without the sound of sense (as in much prose that is supposed to pass muster but makes very dull reading) and the sound of sense without sense (as in *Alice in Wonderland** which makes anything but dull reading). The best place to get the abstract sound of sense is from voices behind a door that cuts off the words. Ask yourself how these sentences would sound without the words in which they are embodied:
>
> > You mean to tell me you can't read?
> > I said no such thing.
> > Well read then.
> > You're not my teacher.

One way to catch on to this notion is to test it. You and someone you know should each think of five to six sentences that have a definite tone and intent, such as, "Don't tell me how to drive," or "I wish you could have seen him." But don't tell each other what they are.

---

*For example, the opening lines of "Jabberwocky":

> 'Twas brillig, and the slithy toves
> Did gyre and gimble in the wabe;
> All mimsy were the borogoves,
> And the mome raths outgrabe.

Then try speaking them as you would in a real situation while the other person listens from another room. (You will have to experiment with the volume so that your voice can be heard but not each word.) Afterward the listener should give his impression of the speaker's tone and attitude and see how close he comes. (Was it a tone of defiance or anger? Or was it teasing or affectionate?) Then the roles can be reversed.

Another way to detect the sound of sense is to pay attention to muffled conversations you overhear from other apartments or rooms. See how much you can tell without making out the words.

As you listen to the readings of Frost's poems in the film, in particular "Home Burial," see how many times you can "catch" the sound of sense. Listen to the combination of where the emphasis falls, where there are pauses, and the rise and fall of intonation that makes the sound dramatic.

When we talk to people, we use many devices beside words to get across our concern and intent. Gestures and facial expressions, postures and movements, volume and pitch, pacing and pauses all may come into play. Actors on stage and screen have the same array of devices. But when a poet wants to create dramatic effects in a book, as Frost does, almost all he has at his disposal are those aspects of the speaking voice which he can direct from the printed page.

This is why sentence sounds are so important. They embody dramatic attitudes that people commonly take. In Frost's theory, it is as though the sound of the voice were being maneuvered into various poses, a threatening or placating one, a teasing or reverent one. Under the pen of a skilled craftsman, the voice can strike an attitude of defiance, say, as clearly as the body can. Then the words can flesh out what is being defied, how much so and why; but no matter how much is added, without the sentence sound there is no drama in the words.

Meet the Speakers

Seamus Heaney is one of Ireland's foremost living poets. He has in common with Robert Frost a firsthand knowledge of rural life and a gift for crossing the speaking voice with the musical structures of poetry. Among his works of poetry are *Death of a Naturalist*, *North* and *Station Island*.

Richard Poirier is one of America's most respected critics. His 1977 study *Robert Frost: The Work of Knowing* is widely regarded as the best book ever written on Frost. Poirier is Marius Bewley Professor of English at Rutgers University and edits a leading intellectual journal *Raritan*.

Joseph Brodsky is one of the greatest living poets in the Russian language. Forced to leave the Soviet Union in 1972, he has rapidly become a central figure in the Western cultural world. Brodsky's major collection of poems in English translation is called *A Part of Speech*, and his essays (most of which were written in English) can be found in *Less Than One*.

Richard Wilbur is a distinguished American poet and translator who is known for the grace and formal perfection of his work in both of those fields. Among his books of poems are *Things of This World*, which won the National Book Award and the Pulitzer prize, and *The Mind Reader*.

Alfred C. Edwards met Robert Frost in the 1940s when he joined the staff of Henry Holt and Company, Frost's publisher. The two men soon started a friendship that lasted until Frost's death in 1963. Edwards took over Holt's dealings with Frost in 1946 and eventually became president of the company. He has now retired from Holt but still continues as the executor of Robert Frost's estate.

Jan Marsh is a British author best known for her biography *Edward Thomas*, published in 1978 for the centennial of Thomas' birth.

William Pritchard is Henry Clay Folger Professor of English at Amherst College. His recent book *Robert Frost: a Literary Life Reconsidered* has inspired a major reevaluation of the relationships between Frost's life, his public image and his art.

Study Plan for This Unit

1. Complete the section **Before Watching the Film: Journal-Writing and Other Activities**.

2. Read the Frost poems that will be featured in the film. A good idea is to find someone to whom you can read the poems aloud. Read through these poems at a moderate speed without stopping. Don't worry if you don't understand them completely.

Mowing
Mending Wall
Home Burial
After Apple-Picking
The Wood-Pile
The Road Not Taken
"Out, Out—"
Acquainted with the Night
Provide, Provide
Never Again Would Birds' Song Be the Same
The Gift Outright
Away!

3. Watch the film.

4. Complete the section **After Watching the Film: Journal-Writing and Other Activities**.

5. Go through the **Guided Reading**.

6. Complete the **Exercises and Assignments** as specified by your instructor.

7. Take the **Self Test**.

Before Watching the Film: Journal-Writing and Other Activities

1. In your journal, write a response to this statement: "Good fences make good neighbors."

2. Reread the one or two poems you liked the best from the list of poems featured in the film. When you hear the poem in the film, jot down the lines that sound different from the way you imagined them. Put down a key word or two as a reminder.

While Watching the Film

1. As you're watching the film, jot down any images that leap out at you.

2. Jot down anything you find confusing.

3. Listen closely to all the voices you hear in the film, especially when someone is reading poetry.

After Watching the Film: Journal-Writing and Other Activities

1. What did you like about the film? What did you dislike? Record your observations in your journal.

2. What poems did you like best from the film presentation? Were there any poems you liked more than before you watched the film? Were there any you liked less?

3. Reread "After Apple-Picking." Now write a dialogue between you and Frost in which you ask questions about the poem and he responds.

4. Reread "Home Burial." Did you sympathize more with Amy or her husband? How did the treatment of the poem in the film differ from what you imagined when you read the poem? What do you think will happen after the end of the poem? Write the answers to these questions in your journal.

5. Read "Desert Places." What kind of desert places would you film and why?

6. If you haven't yet tried the "sound of sense" experiment suggested in the essay **The Sound of Sense**, try it now.

Guided Reading

First read "Mending Wall" printed below. Then answer the questions and do the activities for each section. Remember that the only purpose of these questions is to guide you through the poem. Most of them call for simple, straightforward answers. Don't ponder too long over any of them. Do keep referring back to the poem as you consider each question. The answers to each set of questions are printed below them. These answers are one person's ideas. If you don't agree with a particular answer, that's fine. But make sure you can support your own answer with evidence from the poem.

Mending Wall

Something there is that doesn't love a wall,
That sends the frozen-ground-swell under it,
And spills the upper boulders in the sun;
And makes gaps even two can pass abreast.
The work of hunters is another thing: 5
I have come after them and made repair
Where they have left not one stone on a stone,
But they would have the rabbit out of hiding,
To please the yelping dogs. The gaps I mean,
No one has seen them made or heard them made,   10
But at spring mending-time we find them there.

I let my neighbor know beyond the hill;
And on a day we meet to walk the line
And set the wall between us once again.
We keep the wall between us as we go.   15
To each the boulders that have fallen to each.
And some are loaves and some so nearly balls
We have to use a spell to make them balance:
'Stay where you are until our backs are turned!'
We wear our fingers rough with handling them.   20
Oh, just another kind of outdoor game,
One on a side. It comes to little more:
There where it is we do not need the wall:
He is all pine and I am apple orchard.
My apple trees will never get across   25
And eat the cones under his pines, I tell him.
He only says, 'Good fences make good neighbors.'
Spring is the mischief in me, and I wonder
If I could put a notion in his head:
'Why do they make good neighbors? Isn't it   30
Where there are cows? But here there are no cows.
Before I built a wall I'd ask to know
What I was walling in or walling out,
And to whom I was like to give offense.
Something there is that doesn't love a wall,   35
That wants it down.' I could say 'Elves' to him,
But it's not elves exactly, and I'd rather
He said it for himself. I see him there
Bringing a stone grasped firmly by the top
In each hand, like an old-stone savage armed.   40
He moves in darkness as it seems to me,
Not of woods only and the shade of trees.
He will not go behind his father's saying,
And he likes having thought of it so well
He says again, 'Good fences make good
          neighbors.'   45

Lines 1-4

1. Put the first line in normal English word order.

2. What is "the frozen-ground-swell"?

Answers

1. "There is something that doesn't love a wall" is the normal word order.

2. The stone walls that run between farmers' fields in New England are made of rocks that are placed on top of one another without any cement or mortar to hold them together. In winter the moisture in the ground under the wall freezes and expands. The

wall buckles and the top stones fall off. Sometimes gaps form in the wall that are big enough for two people to pass through walking side by side.

Now say the word "frozen-ground-swell." The physical sensation of saying "frozen-ground-swell" imitates the swelling of the ground.

Lines 5-12

1. Write a sentence using "another thing" in the same way that Frost does.

2. Are these hunters hunting rabbits? Why do they demolish the wall?

3. Look at line 9. Is there another kind of gap in this line other than the ones mentioned? Search through the poem for these unmentioned gaps.

4. What is the difference between the gaps mentioned in lines 9-11 and the gaps the hunters make?

Answers

2. The hunters mentioned are not rabbit hunters; they are really out after deer or maybe even bears. But every so often their dogs start chasing a rabbit who dashes into a crevice under a wall to hide himself. The dogs gather around the spot, yelping. The hunters tear the wall apart to find the rabbit for their dogs so they can get back to their main business.

3. The end of the sentence in the middle of line 9 creates a gap. Notice that Frost creates gaps in the poem where he wants pauses. Sometimes breaks at the ends of lines also create pauses, but not always.

4. The gaps mentioned in lines 9-11 are not caused by people; they happen silently, gradually, almost mysteriously, and one doesn't find them until long afterwards. "These are the gaps I mean," the ones the speaker refers to in the first four lines of the poem and the ones that concern him "at spring mending-time."

Lines 12-20

1. What does Frost mean by "walk the line" in line 13?

2. Read lines 12-16 aloud, listening to the rhythm. What happens to this rhythm in line 16? How does this line act out what it describes?

Answers

1. There is a New England custom in the spring of "walking the line" between towns or properties. In "Mending Wall," the speaker and his neighbor meet to repair the wall that marks the property line. Frost's choice of this phrase emphasizes the ritual aspect of their behavior and the extent to which it is embedded in regional culture.

2. Lines 12-15 have a strictly regular rhythm—da-DA/da-DA/da-DA/da-DA/da-DA—just as the two men follow the same pattern and procedure year after year. Line 16, however, has a dramatically different rhythm: "To each the boulders that have fallen to each." Here there are four heavy stresses instead of the five that are normal in blank verse, and these four stresses are grouped symmetrically at either end of the line, just like the stones that have fallen on either side of the wall. The repetition of the phrase "to

each" at either end of the line reinforces this symmetry. The very structure of the line diagrams the scene it describes.

Lines 21-27
1. In these lines, the speaker tells you what was said but not in the exact words. Write out their dialogue.

2. Paraphrase line 24: "He is all pine and I am apple orchard." What are you?

3. Apart from tone and rhythm, why did Frost make this direct equation between the two men and their property?

Answers
2. One paraphrase might go like this: "He has pine trees on his land, and I have an apple orchard on mine."

3. Saying one *is* something closes the gap between *who* one is and *what* one owns. This, in turn, highlights the sharp contrast between the two men.

Lines 28-38
1. Line 31 consists of ten one-syllable words. At this point in the poem, what does this reveal about the speaker's attitude toward his neighbor?

2. What is the difference between "walling in" and "walling out"?

3. Why does the speaker think of elves?

Answers
1. Spring brings out the mischievousness in the speaker. He feels like rebutting his neighbor's statement that "Good fences make good neighbors," and he imagines what he would say to him. He would talk to him as if he were talking to a child, very slowly and deliberately, in words of one syllable: "Isn't it / Where there are cows? But here there are no cows."

2. By "walling in," you're setting a limit to your ambitions and fears. By "walling out," you're protecting yourself from attack or competition whether real or imagined. But notice how hard it is in any particular instance to tell which motive is the dominant one.

3. Traditionally, elves are known for playing pranks on humans or spirits who invade their territory. The speaker may be suggesting that the humans are creating boundaries where the elves do not recognize any. So the speaker thinks, whimsically, that it's the elves who want the wall down.

Lines 38-45
1. What is an "old-stone savage"? What does the speaker imagine his neighbor doing with the stones he is carrying?

2. Read lines 39-40 aloud. How do the sounds of the words and the rhythm pattern reinforce the visual image?

3. What is the other kind of "darkness" the speaker mentions in line 41?

4. Why won't the neighbor "go behind his father's saying"? Why did Frost choose the phrase "go behind" rather than, for example, the word "contradict"?

Answers

1. & 2. Seeing his neighbor advancing to the wall with a large stone grasped in each hand, the speaker fantasizes that he is a cave man coming to attack him. The three heavy accents in the phrase "a stone grasped firmly" thump down like three blows to the head; the consonant sequences (n-gr) and (sp-t-f) are extremely hard to say and slow the phrase down even further. The speech rhythm of line 40 is similarly ponderous and clumsy: "In each hand, like an old-stone savage armed." The line seems to move in slow motion.

3. According to the speaker, his neighbor "moves in darkness" both literally and metaphorically. Not only does he work in the shade of his pine trees, but he sees things in the shade of received ideas and opinions.

4. The phrase "go behind" immediately conjures the image of a wall. Frost, therefore, presents us with yet another kind of "wall," the wall of outmoded folk wisdom, or empty phrases passed down from generation to generation. Can you think of any of these kinds of sayings that you've inherited without examining? More important than the saying itself may be the sentiment behind it.

Further Questions

Now think back over the poem as a whole and try to answer the following questions.

1. Why do you think Frost wrote "Mending Wall" as one continuous stream of verse running down the page rather than breaking it into stanzas?

2. Notice the speaker is the one who initiates mending the wall. Why does he do this if he isn't in favor of a wall? Can you think of some tasks that you perform seasonally, year after year? What are your reasons for doing them?

3. Now that you've studied "Mending Wall," go back to your original journal entry. Has your attitude changed toward "Good fences make good neighbors"?

Answers

1. & 2. There seems to be a contradiction between the speaker's opposition to the wall and the fact that he takes the initiative in repairing it every year. If you think about it, there are other contradictions in the poem as well.

The wall which brings the two men together each year is the same wall that separates them. The activity of mending the wall unites the men for a brief time. Although the speaker of the poem questions the necessity of the activity, he wouldn't dream of actually forgoing mending the wall.

Throughout the poem, Frost emphasizes the themes of ritual and tradition in life and convention in relationships. Notice that the shape and structure of the poem reinforce this theme. The lines continue one after another methodically, predictably, except in a few places where the speaker calls attention to his inner thoughts.

Before long, however, the narrative, that is, the telling of the "mending wall" story, takes over again. There's a feeling that as long as "something" (nature) destroys a wall, the two men will repair it. The fact that the speaker accepts the ritual of mending the wall does not preclude him from reflecting on the ritual, and, indeed, on the meaning of the wall itself.

Final Question

The poem ends with the neighbor's proposition, just as it opened with the speaker's. In between, each of the statements has been repeated one time. So the bare bones of the poem look like this:

> Something there is that doesn't love a wall
> . . .
> Good fences make good neighbors
> . . .
> Something there is that doesn't love a wall
> . . .
> Good fences make good neighbors

Why did Frost give the neighbor the last word?

Exercises and Assignments

1. a. Reread "After Apple-Picking." Notice that Frost used a variety of line lengths. Which is the longest line? Which is the shortest?

   b. Now look at Frost's irregular rhyme scheme, that is, the irregular rhyme pattern in the poem. Give at least two reasons Frost varied the line lengths and used an irregular rhyme scheme.

2. Compare "Mowing" and "Out, Out—." Describe the differences in tone and form. How do these differences reflect the two different kinds of work described in these poems? Comment on Frost's use of sound in the poems. **(Note**: Frost's title comes from a famous speech in Act V, Scene v of Shakespeare's *Macbeth*. Macbeth has just learned of the death of his wife. "Out, out, brief candle," he laments.)

3. Imagine a dramatic situation such as the one Frost uses in "Home Burial" and write some dialogue, as though you had eavesdropped on an interesting conversation. Try to capture the tension and conflict or tenderness of the situation. See how much information you can withhold from the reader and still create the scene; feel free to present the beginning, the middle, or the end.

4. During the course of the poem "The Wood-Pile," the speaker notices first the bird and then the wood-pile. What similarities are there between the speaker's attitude toward the bird and toward the wood-pile? What do the similarities suggest about Frost's view of nature?

5. Read "Provide, Provide." There are three lines in a row that contain alliteration or near alliteration:

   "beauty Abishag"

"picture pride"
"great and good"

What tone of voice do these alliterations suggest? Does this tone contrast with or complement the rest of the poem?

6. After having read Frost's poems a few times, where do you stand on the "Trilling controversy"? Was Frost a "poet of terror," or a "gentle New England poet"? Both? Or neither? Write a brief defense. Use evidence from the poems to support your thesis.

7. Think of several sayings that people use today that illustrate the sound of sense. Write a short scene or poem set in the 1980s using one of these examples of the sound of sense.

8. In the film, we hear the opening lines of "Out, Out—," but not the entire poem. After you read the poem, how do you feel? Does it bring up any personal memories, images, or feelings? Could the poem have been filmed for family viewing? What would have been gained or lost by making it explicit?

9. Read "Acquainted with the Night." Notice that the first half of the poem is built on verbs using the auxiliary "have" and the first person.

"I have been one acquainted"
"I have walked"
"I have outwalked," etc.

Now write your own poem using the same repetitive subject-verb pattern. (If you want, you can use second- or third-person subjects instead of "I.")

10. In "Stopping by Woods on a Snowy Evening," Frost originally wrote the first line of the last stanza with two commas, one after "lovely" and one after "deep." The line looked like this:

The woods are lovely, dark and deep,

After Frost's death, however, his editor made numerous changes in punctuation and spelling throughout the poems to produce a consistent edition. To the above line, the editor added a third comma after "dark." The line looked like this:

The woods are lovely, dark, and deep,

Read the lines aloud to yourself with the extra comma and without. Do the two versions mean the same thing? Read through the entire poem at least once.

11. Frost once said:

The Founding Fathers didn't believe in the Future. . . .they believed it *in*. You're always believing ahead of your evidence. . . .the most creative thing in us is to believe a thing in, in love, in all else.

Read "The Gift Outright." The last line reads:

Such as she was, such as she would become.

President John F. Kennedy asked Frost to read this poem at his inauguration with one change: "will" instead of "would." Frost complied with the President's request only for Kennedy's inauguration; all printed copies retain the "would." In a brief paper, explore the reasons President Kennedy requested the change and Frost went back to the original word choice. See if you can tie in the quote above.

Self Test

1. Read the following poem by Maxine Kumin, a contemporary poet from New Hampshire, and then answer the multiple choice question.

The Woodlot in Winter

To come among the hardwoods
in a high wind is to enter
a long-empty house of many chambers
whose doors fly open and clap shut
scraping on dry lintels. Cupboards
complain to their hinges and windows
rise and fall, teeter and fall.

Oak here breaks its heart.
Hickory drops its shagbark
and the woman-smooth beech tree
pushes nine legs through the floorboards.
Fat stones rub under the snow crust.
The rafters drink in their birds.
Only, in the inglenook the ghost
of a rabbit is having its throat cut.

Kumin's subject resembles many found in Frost's poems. Yet there are many instances in the poem of technique and style that are clearly her own. Which of the following is an argument for how Maxine Kumin's poem resembles Frost?

a) The poem uses extended simile.
b) The writer uses free verse.
c) The poem reveals the underlying violence in nature.
d) The human presence is minimized.

2. The following poem by Frost has a stanza omitted. Following the poem are three alternate stanzas, one of which is by Frost. Without looking at the poem in your anthology, see if you can identify the Frost version. In a paragraph, explain why it must be by Frost.

Neither Out Far nor In Deep

The people along the sand
All turn and look one way.
They turn their back on the land.
They look at the sea all day.

As long as it takes to pass
A ship keeps raising its hull;
The wetter ground like glass
Reflects a standing gull.

. . . .
. . . .
. . . .
. . . .

They cannot look out far.
They cannot look in deep.
But when was that ever a bar
To any watch they keep?

a) The shore may shift around;
But whate'er the reason they follow—
As the sea hurls at the ground,
The watchers stare at the billow.

b) The land may vary more;
But wherever the truth may be—
The water comes ashore,
And the people look at the sea.

c) The sailors on the deck,
Return the gaze of the others—
Who hope to see a wreck,
Mindless of their brothers.

3. Read the parody below of Frost's "Mending Wall."

Mending Sump

"Hiram, I think the sump is backing up.
The bathroom floor boards for above two weeks
Have seemed soaked through. A little bird, I think,
Has wandered in the pipes, and all's gone wrong."
"Something there is that doesn't hump a sump,"
He said; and through his head she saw a cloud
That seemed to twinkle. "Hiram, well," she said,
"Smith is come home! I saw his face just now
While looking through your head. He's come to die

26

Or else to laugh, for hay is dried-up grass
When you're alone." He rose, and sniffed the air,
"We'd better leave him in the sump," he said.

Kenneth Koch

a) List at least three Frost poems referred to in the parody.

b) List at least three ways in which the style of the parody is like Frost's.

c) Write your own parody of a Frost poem.

4. In "Never Again Would Birds' Song Be the Same," which line refers specifically to the sound of sense? How does the poem generally work to convey the concept?

Answers to Self Test
Answers to Self Tests begin on page 226.

For Further Reading
Books by Robert Frost

Selected Prose of Robert Frost. Cox, Hyde, and Lathem, Edward Connery, editor. New York: Collier; 1966.

Selected Letters of Robert Frost. Thompson, Lawrance, editor. New York: Holt, Rinehart and Winston; 1964.

Selected Poems of Robert Frost: Introduction by Robert Graves. New York: Rinehart Paperbacks; 1963.

The Poetry of Robert Frost. New York: Holt, Rinehart and Winston; 1969.

Books about Frost

Cox, James Melville, editor. "Robert Frost: A Collection of Critical Essays," *20th Century Views.* Englewood Cliffs, NJ: Prentice-Hall; 1962.

Lathem, Edward Connery, editor. *Interviews with Robert Frost.* New York: Holt, Rinehart and Winston; 1969.

Poirier, Richard. *Robert Frost: The Work of Knowing.* New York: Oxford University Press; 1977.

Thompson, Lawrance and Winnick, R.H. *Robert Frost* (A one-volume condensation of the authorized three-volume biography). New York: Holt, Rinehart and Winston; 1982.

Ezra Pound (1885-1972)

At 15, Ezra Pound decided that by the time he was 30 he would know more about poetry than anyone alive. The painter and novelist Wyndham Lewis, speaking of Pound as he was in his twenties, said that all Pound's busy social life had some bearing on "Letters" or the business of writing. "He was," Lewis said, "a man of letters, in the marrow of his bones and down to the red follicles of his hair. . . He breathed Letters, ate Letters, dreamt Letters. A very rare kind of man."

Pound was born in the frontier town of Hailey, Idaho, where his father, Homer, ran the government land office. The rough and ready life did not agree with his rather genteel mother so, when Pound was still an infant, the family moved to the Philadelphia area where Homer worked as assistant assayer at the United States Mint. Pound enrolled in the University of Pennsylvania and later transferred to Hamilton College, from which he graduated. He then returned to the University of Pennsylvania for graduate work in Romance languages. While he enjoyed his studies, he found the life of a college teacher too stifling and, in 1908, went to Italy and then settled in London to be a full-time man of letters.

Pound's first book of poems, *A Lume Spento*, was published in Venice in 1908, when he was 22. By April, 1909, when his *Personae* appeared, he had already made a name for himself in London literary circles. He founded a new "school" of poetry which he called "Imagism," and was involved in publicizing a new movement in painting and sculpture— "Vorticism." He brought to public attention the works of previously unknown or little known major writers—T.S. Eliot, James Joyce, Robert Frost, H.D. (Hilda Doolittle) and Marianne Moore—and he so impressed W.B. Yeats with his talent, energy and critical judgement that the older poet even made some changes in his own poetic style at Pound's suggestion.

Pound, with good reason, had high hopes for a new London-based renaissance in the arts, but the First World War dashed these hopes and the mood of post-war Britain was so dispiriting that Pound moved to Paris. Here he was in contact with Hemingway, Joyce and many French writers and artists. Helped by the young American composer George Antheil and by Olga Rudge, a violinist who would become his life-long companion and the mother of his daughter Mary, Pound composed an opera. Pound's main poetic achievement, however, was his 800-page poem *The Cantos* which would eventually include 117 separate sections or "cantos." Pound had known since his college days that he wanted to write a long poem of this kind. In 1917 he published "Cantos 1-3," but at that time the poem was still at the experimental stage. It was not until 1922, after he had written *Hugh Selwyn Mauberley*, another poetic sequence, that he could see more clearly what direction to take with his Cantos.

In 1924 Pound moved to Rapallo, near Genoa in Italy, where he found the way of life congenial. He was interested in Italian culture not only because of the great works of art and architecture of the past, but also because of the economic and social reforms that Mussolini was instituting. Pound had been absorbed in economic theory since 1919 and saw, in the ways in which Mussolini had improved the standard of living for most of the Italians, evidence that economic policies that Pound himself argued for could be made to work. Yet by the 1930s his economic ideas had become an obsession. He came to see himself as an economic theorist and reformer as much or more than a poet and literary innovator.

Pound assumed that Mussolini, like himself, was anti-war, but in 1935 Mussolini invaded Abyssinia (Ethiopia) and in 1939 became Hitler's ally. Pound, unable to accept the idea of Mussolini as a "warmonger," convinced himself that the Second World War was started by Churchill and Roosevelt. They were tricked into this, he claimed, by the "Usurers," a secret conspiracy of mainly Jewish international financiers.

In a series of very confused and rambling broadcasts over Rome Radio, Pound tried to "educate" his listeners by "explaining" his original economic theories and his new paranoid one. Because some of his broadcasts were made after America was at war with Italy, Pound was arrested on a charge of treason in 1944, detained in a prison camp for U.S. military criminals and then flown from Italy to Washington. Declared mentally unfit to stand trial, Pound was incarcerated for twelve and a half years in St. Elizabeths Hospital for the Criminally Insane. Here he continued to write cantos, as he had in the prison camp near Pisa. Yet his paranoia persisted, and he still clung to his belief in a conspiracy of usurers. In 1949 he was awarded the Bollingen Prize for his *Pisan Cantos*, but there was strong protest against this by some writers and critics because of the anti-Semitic tirades in his radio speeches.

After his release in 1958 and his return to Italy, Pound was finally able to break out of his delusion about the "Usurers," but the shock of this self-confrontation was devastating. He became severely depressed, and his physical condition deteriorated. The obsessiveness with which he had earlier committed himself to his poetic and then to his economic goals was now to show itself in the intensity of his self-blame and remorse. After 1961, he rarely spoke. He died on November 1, 1972, and was buried on the Venetian cemetery island of San Michele.

The World of the Poems

It is to be expected that a film on the life and poetic career of Ezra Pound would begin with the poet arrested on a charge of treason. For many people, the issues of Pound's alleged treason, his wartime broadcasts over Rome Radio, and the anti-Semitic views he expressed in them almost eclipse the issue of the extent and nature of his poetic achievement in *The Cantos*. Many others feel that, no matter how skilled a poet Pound was, it is not possible to admire him as a poet without reservation, given the objectionable nature of opinions he expressed during the war. For this reason it is important to understand how Pound's views about Mussolini developed directly out of his views about poetry and about the duty of the American poet.

Pound believed that it was the duty of patriotic poets to make their societies more civilized. This meant not only producing excellent literature, but also encouraging precision in the use of language among educators and legislators as well as poets. If language was kept clear and accurate, students and the general public would not be misled with distortions of the facts. Yet he felt that a society that failed to make it possible for all its citizens to feed, clothe and house their families decently could not be considered truly civilized, and he believed it his duty to instigate economic measures which would correct such a situation.

In 1919, Pound had become interested in Social Credit, an economic theory which argued that the true wealth of a country was its productive capacity. The Social Creditors did not want to make changes in the capitalist system of production, but they thought it was wrong that privately-owned banks should be in charge of the nation's money and that they should make large profits for themselves by lending out at interest "money" ten times in excess of deposits which they held.

By the 1930s the collapse of the economies of America and the European countries during the Great Depression made Pound feel that his economic views were being proved right. In the U.S. and Europe there were consumers wanting goods, factories that could make these goods, raw materials to make them from, people wanting to work, but no productive activity actually taking place: all because the financial system had broken down.

In Italy Mussolini had set up many economic programs which were similar to those the Social Creditors advocated. His aim was to remove an enormous deficit, double industrial productivity, increase government control of the banks and of prices and to improve housing, health care and educational opportunities. In fact, Mussolini was very popular in England and America where his social programs were widely praised in the press. Yet this was to change suddenly and completely when he decided to invade Abyssinia.

Where before Pound had taken the reasonable position that economic problems persisted because reforms had not been carried out, he now adopted the paranoid view that these problems were being deliberately created by the "Usurers" as a way of sabotaging the economies of individual nations. As he increasingly lost contact with the realities of the political situation, he began to speak as though all international bankers were Jewish and to refer to paranoid anti-Semitic theories that had been current in America in the late 1800s and in America and Europe at the time of the First World War. He spoke of an international group of specifically Jewish bankers and arms-sellers which had tried to ruin American prosperity, undermine Western culture and brought about both world wars for its own profit.

Interestingly, by the time that he was fully in the grips of these paranoid delusions, he no longer included them in the Cantos. In "Cantos 52-71" (1940) Pound turned abruptly away from the subject of the usurers' sinister purposes and concentrated on two subjects which would keep him in a much calmer state of mind—Chinese History ("Cantos 52-61") and the career and political wisdom of John Adams ("Cantos 62-71"). It was only after his release from St. Elizabeths that he could finally allow himself to see that, although there is grave economic injustice, it is not the result of the plotting of a secret group of bankers, but the consequence of a vice which is a fundamental part of human nature, greed. As he wrote in his 1972 Foreword to his *Selected Prose*, "re usury: I was out of focus, taking a symptom for a cause. The cause is AVARICE."

Ezra Pound: The "Live Tradition"

In "Canto 81," having taken himself to task for his past mistakes and trying to think of those positive achievements of his which might offset his errors, Pound credited himself with having "gathered from the air a live tradition." His "gathering" of this "live tradition" took two somewhat different yet related forms. First, there was the extraordinary way in which the great literary works of the past "lived" for him. When Wyndham Lewis called Pound "a man in love with the past," he was recognizing how vividly and readily for Pound the past became the present.

In addition, Pound saw the work of talented contemporary writers as being a part of the "live tradition." Much of Pound's energy went into the "gathering" of the tradition in both of these ways. He familiarized himself with the best that had been written in the past to learn as much as possible about poetic technique. He also did what he could to ensure that those young writers who could shape the tradition for future generations would have the opportunities to realize their potential, and he worked hard to bring their works to public attention.

Pound believed that serious American poets should set themselves the highest possible artistic standards. They should study the best poetry of the past and not just that written in English. At the University of Pennsylvania and at Hamilton College, Pound chose to make a careful study of poetry written in the "Mediterranean languages"—Greek, Latin, Italian, French, Spanish, and Provencal. He also studied Anglo-Saxon and later would work on Chinese. His aim was to learn as much as possible about the "music" of poetic cadences and rhythms and how effectively to make the sound of the poetry complement its meaning.

William Carlos Williams, who first came to know Pound when they were students together at the University of Pennsylvania and who was to remain Pound's close friend until his death, would say of Pound that he had "the most acute ear for metrical cadences, to the point of genius, that we have ever known." As part of his poetic training, Pound made many translations from the Italian of Dante and of Dante's contemporary, Cavalcanti. He particularly liked the challenge of working from an original with an intricate stanza form and rhyme scheme. In his translations of the poems of the Provencal troubadours, he tried to preserve, not just the rhyme scheme, but some of the onomatopoeic effects within the lines.

Many of Pound's earliest poems, even when they were not translations, were written "in the manner of" poetry of an earlier period or presented as though they were being spoken by a poet or personage from the past. Even though Pound's behavior in public was often flamboyant, he was somewhat self-conscious about speaking or writing too intimately and seemed to be more at ease adopting a mask or "persona" for the purposes of "speaking" his poems. In fact, his third book of poems was called *Personae* and he decided to keep this title for his *Collected Poems*.

Pound argued strongly for simplicity, clarity, and directness of poetic expression. He saw that, if poetic rhythms were more flexible than the rigid metrical schemes of most of the 19th century poets, the "music" of the lines could adapt itself more specifically to the sense or "shade of emotion" being expressed. He felt that it was never justifiable to distort normal word-order for the sake of getting a line to end with a word that would fit the rhyme scheme.

Pound discussed these ideas with the poets Hilda Doolittle (H.D.) and Richard Aldington and, in the spring of 1912, they agreed on three requirements for this new kind of poetry: direct presentation of the subject, no unnecessary words, a musical and flexible rhythm. Pound labelled this new poetic school Imagism. He realized how detailed and intense a sensitive reader's response to a single poetic image could be. If the poet placed images side by side, without specifying a relationship between them, readers would make the connection on their own in accordance with whatever particular connotations the words held for them.

T.S. Eliot wrote of how much effort Pound put into helping others with their writing and into getting their work published. He did this not only for H.D. and Aldington and other "Imagistes," but for James Joyce, Marianne Moore, Robert Frost and Eliot himself who said that "For [Pound] to discover a new writer of genius is as satisfying an experience as it is for a lesser man to believe that he has written a great work of genius himself." It took Pound six months of virtual harrassment to persuade

Harriet Monroe to publish Eliot's "The Love Song of J. Alfred Prufrock" in *Poetry* magazine. Of all Pound's helpful suggestions to writers, the most famous are the changes he made to the original manuscript of Eliot's *The Waste Land*.

In 1913, Pound was chosen as literary executor of Ernest Fenollosa, an American who had been Imperial Commissioner of Art in Tokyo. Working from Fenollosa's literal translations from the Chinese and Japanese, Pound prepared his own very beautiful translations of several Japanese Noh plays and *Cathay* (1915), a volume of poems translated from the Chinese so impressively that it prompted Eliot to call Pound "the inventor of Chinese poetry for our time."

Yet Pound's interests ranged far beyond poetry. He was closely involved with a group of innovative painters and sculptors which had formed around the writer and artist Wyndham Lewis. Pound gave this new school of art its label—"Vorticism"—and felt that its experimental techniques were similar in spirit to his own poetic innovations. Vorticist art and sculpture encouraged him to think of using a wider field of composition in his own poetry as he would do in his *Cantos*. Pound thought of the individual poetic image as functioning like a vortex or whirlpool in miniature—and described it as a "radiant node or cluster. . .a VORTEX, from which, through which, and into which, ideas are constantly rushing."

In their painting and sculpture, the Vorticists simplified forms, leaving out smaller details to emphasize major planes and "lines of force" and to suggest moving energies. They wanted to see some of the "clutter" of old-fashioned, lethargic social attitudes "blasted" away too, to provide scope for the more dynamic and innovative approaches of younger people.

Of all the Vorticists, it was the young French sculptor, Henri Gaudier-Brzeska, to whom Pound felt the closest. He saw signs of real genius in Gaudier's art and believed that in time Gaudier would produce unquestionably great sculpture. The combined sense of personal loss and loss to the arts that Pound felt when Gaudier was killed in action in 1915 was a severe shock. It made the destructiveness of the First World War seem to him not only an international tragedy, but also a personal affront.

To Pound, war was an outrage. He was angry at the stupidity and callousness of politicians who had allowed this war to happen, and he decided that he must find out all he could about the causes of wars to see what would be required to prevent future ones. *Hugh Selwyn Mauberley* shows his reactions to the war and his realization that, in these times, to concern himself only with producing beautiful poetry would be irresponsible.

In 1925 his first group of Cantos in book form was published as *A Draft of XVI Cantos*. By now he was deeply involved both in working on his Cantos, and in publicizing his economic theories. He would continue writing Cantos, and finally fragments of Cantos, until 1960. He had hoped that, like Dante concluding his *Divine Comedy* with a section called "Paradise," he would finally be able to close his poem on a positive note with a group of Cantos that would celebrate the order and harmony of the world. This plan was ruined by the war and the mental confusion into which it threw him. As we see from "Canto 81," he found himself, in the prison camp at Pisa, writing a group of Cantos that was more like Dante's "Purgatory" than his "Paradise."

Meet the Speakers

Olga Rudge was Ezra Pound's life-long companion. A member of the Paris avant-garde, she was also an accomplished concert violinist.

James Laughlin is a publisher and poet who has played a key role in the history of the literary avant-garde in this country. He is best known for founding and heading New Directions, a press which has published some of the most experimental and original writers of this century, including Ezra Pound, Henry Miller, George Oppen, Kenneth Patchen and William Carlos Williams.

Alfred Kazin is one of America's most widely respected literary critics. In such books as *An American Procession*, and *On Native Grounds*, he offers in-depth analyses of modern American writers.

Mary de Rachewiltz is the daughter of Ezra Pound. A literary figure in her own right, she is, among other things, the Milan editor of *The Paris Review* and the author of *Ezra Pound, Father and Teacher: Discretions*.

Boris de Rachewiltz, a noted Egyptologist, is the husband of Mary de Rachewiltz and the son-in-law of Ezra Pound. The appearance of hieroglyphs in Pound's Cantos is attributed to his influence.

Basil Bunting, who died in 1986, had a distinguished literary career. His books of poetry include *First Book of Odes*, *Briggflats* and *What the Chairman Told Tom*, among others. A close friend of Pound when they both lived in Rapallo, he credited Pound with being one the most important influences on his work.

Hugh Kenner is a highly acclaimed literary critic and scholar who has written detailed studies of writers such as Joyce, Beckett, and Pound. His books on Pound include *The Poetry of Ezra Pound* and *The Pound Era*.

John Drummond was a personal assistant to Ezra Pound.

John Greusen was an American G.I. in World War II who observed Ezra Pound during his incarceration in the U.S. Disciplinary Training Center, an American military prison outside Pisa.

Study Plan for This Unit

1. Complete the section **Before Watching the Film: Journal-Writing and Other Activities**.

2. Read the following Pound poems, many of which are featured in the film. As you first read them through, try to visualize the images in the poems as much as possible. Allow the words on the page to suggest to you, where possible, a "picture"—some object that you can see the shape and color of "in your mind's eye." Often you will find that the "images" that come into your mind will be of specific objects that you remember having seen in the past. Next read the poems out loud. Try rereading some passages in different ways and decide which kind of emphasis or rhythm seems to fit with the sense of these lines.

Sestina: Altaforte
In a Station of the Metro
The Return
Exile's Letter
Homage to Sextus Propertius
Hugh Selwyn Mauberley
Cantos: 1, 45, 74, 80, 81, 91, 99

3. Watch the film.

4. Complete the section **After Watching the Film: Journal-Writing and Other Activities**.

5. Go through the **Guided Reading**.

6. Complete the **Exercises and Assignments** as specified by your instructor.

7. Take the **Self Test**.

Before Watching the Film: Journal-Writing and Other Activities

1. Keep a record in your journal of those images which, as you read the poems, were easiest to visualize or had the strongest emotional associations for you. See if any of these images can be classified in groups. Are they natural or man-made objects; are they associated with water, light, certain colors? Do the kinds of images vary from poem to poem?

2. Choose a persona for yourself, an historical person whom you have always thought of as particularly interesting. Write a poem or prose sketch in which you speak in this person's voice and describe those things which this person would be particularly interested in or likely to comment on.

3. Reread "Sestina: Altaforte." Does this poem rhyme? Write down in seven columns, side by side, the concluding words of each line in each of the seven stanzas. What pattern do you see?

4. Memorize "In a Station of the Metro." As the title tells you, the setting of the poem is the Paris subway system. The petals, Pound tells us elsewhere, are beautiful faces of passersby. If you were a filmmaker, how would you recreate the poem in visual images?

While Watching the Film

1. Notice the filmmaker's use of images. Which objects or details of a scene are given particular emphasis through close-ups, or because the camera fixes on them for longer than on other details around them, or because they are shown in an unusual lighting? You can list these as you watch the film.

2. Notice the animated sequence which has been chosen to illustrate "In a Station of the Metro." Does it correspond to your own visualization of the poem?

3. Notice what Pound's voice sounds like as he comments on the Chinese characters while drawing them. How is his voice different from the voice he uses when he reads his poems?

After Watching the Film: Journal-Writing and Other Activities

1. Look at the list of images you made as you watched the film. Compare this list to the images that you singled out in your journal from your reading of the poems. Can

you suggest images which you would have made a point of including had you been the filmmaker?

2. With a felt-tipped pen (or brush and ink) practice copying the following five Chinese charcters that Pound made in the film:

日　jih, the sun.

旦　tan, the dawn, the morning. (The sun over the horizon.)

木　muh, a tree.

東　tung, the east, eastern, eastwards. (The sun seen through the branches of a tree.)

杲　kaou, brightly. (The sun seen above the tree, i.e., as Pound says in the film, "later in the day.")

If you are working with or have access to the paperback *Selected Poems of Ezra Pound* you could also copy the characters you will find on pages 145, 146, 147 and 151.

Note: Chinese characters are written from top to bottom on the page and in columns that begin on the right hand side of the page.

3. In the film, Hugh Kenner says that Pound in "Homage to Sextus Propertius" gives the speaking voice of his Propertius persona "a tone of aloof and ironic superciliousness" partly by having him use so many formal words of Latin origin. Pick out eight or ten words that seem particularly formal and "aloof" and use a dictionary to see if they do come from Latin. Can you think of simpler and less formal synonyms or substitutes for these words?

4. If Pound were alive today, what problems in the American economy would he probably point to as examples of how the financial system makes it much easier for people to make money by manipulating money than by working to produce goods and foodstuffs? Is there any sense in which it is still true to say that "wool comes not to market/sheep bringeth no gain," "weaver is kept from his loom," and "no man can find site for his dwelling?"

Guided Reading

The concluding section of "Canto 81," written while Pound was being held in the U.S. Army Disciplinary Training Center outside Pisa, is one of the most frequently quoted sections of *The Cantos*. As you can see from this passage, he was no longer in the cement-floored, wire mesh, maximum security "cage" where he had at first been confined, but was now in a tent, which gave him some privacy and where he had a cot to sleep on. This passage describes the visionary apparition in his darkened tent of several human forms, of which only the eyes are clearly visible. The expression of the eyes has a strong effect on the poet and makes it possible for him to understand more clearly some important truths about himself and about the people he loves.

Ed ascoltando al leggier mormorio   1
    there came new subtlety of eyes into my tent,
whether of spirit or hypostasis,
    but what the blindfold hides
or at carneval   5
                nor any pair showed anger
    Saw but the eyes and stance between the eyes,
colour, diastasis,
    careless or unaware it had not the
    whole tent's room   10
nor was place for the full Εἰδὼσ
interpass, penetrate
    casting but shade beyond the other lights
        sky's clear
        night's sea   15
        green of the mountain pool
        shone from the unmasked eyes in
            half-mask's space.
What thou lovest well remains,
                        the rest is dross
What thou lov'st well shall not be reft from thee   20
What thou lov'st well is thy true heritage
Whose world, or mine or theirs
                    or is it of none?
First came the seen, then thus the palpable
    Elysium, though it were in the halls of hell,   25
What thou lovest well is thy true heritage
What thou lov'st well shall not be reft from thee.

The ant's a centaur in his dragon world.
Pull down thy vanity, it is not man
Made courage, or made order, or made grace,   30
    Pull down thy vanity, I say pull down.
Learn of the green world what can be thy place
In scaled invention or true artistry,
Pull down thy vanity,
                    Paquin pull down!   35
The green casque has outdone your elegance.

"Master thyself, then others shall thee beare"
    Pull down thy vanity
Thou art a beaten dog beneath the hail,
A swollen magpie in a fitful sun,   40
Half black half white

Nor knowst'ou wing from tail
Pull down thy vanity
        How mean thy hates
Fostered in falsity,   45
        Pull down thy vanity,
Rathe to destroy, niggard in charity,
Pull down thy vanity,
        I say pull down.

But to have done instead of not doing   50
        this is not vanity
To have, with decency, knocked
That a Blunt should open
        To have gathered from the air a live tradition
or from a fine old eye the unconquered flame
This is not vanity.
        Here error is all in the not done,
all in the diffidence that faltered.

Lines 1-11

1. "Ed ascoltando al leggier mormorio" is Italian for "and listening to the light murmur." Read the line aloud. How does the sound of the line reflect its meaning?

2. Just as the meaning of line 1 is veiled from the reader by being in Italian, so is the meaning of "hypostasis" ("something that underlies something else; a foundation" or "the essence or principle of something") because it is a word of Greek origin with a specialized philosophical meaning. "Eιδωσϛ" (Greek for "knowing or insight"), in line 11, is veiled both in these ways and by being written in a different alphabet. Only the spirits' eyes appear to the speaker, but they seem to represent the essence of these spirits. Why is the fact that the meanings of "hypostasis" and "Eιδωσϛ" are obscure to the reader appropriate to the poet's experience in this excerpt?

Answers

1. The sound of the line is itself a "murmur," the meaning of which is not yet revealed to the reader. Similarly, at the stage of hearing this light murmur, the poet does not yet know what significant apparition it is a prelude to.

2. The meanings of these Greek words are first of all hidden and then difficult to interpret and fully understand. The same could be said of the poet's own visionary experience which begins in "obscurity" (the darkness of the tent) then is seen only partially and turns out to have a meaning which only gradually becomes clear to him.

Lines 4-5

1. How do these lines tell us exactly what part of each face the poet can see clearly? (Hint: Think of "carneval" as an outdoor Italian carnival where the participants wear masks.)

2. Since the expressions of these eyes encourages the poet to understand with a new depth of thought that "What thou lovest well remains" and "shall not be reft from thee," what can we deduce about their expression?

Answers

1. The poet can see clearly the part of each face which would be covered if the person were wearing a blindfold or a carnival mask.

2. The eyes seem to be looking at him with a calm and reassuring expression. He seems to have expected that they would have looked at him with some degree of anger. Since they do not, their expression is, presumably, forgiving, understanding and loving.

Lines 14-17

1. We know that more than one pair of eyes appears since the poet says "nor any pair showed anger." What clue is there in these lines as to how many pairs of eyes appear?

Answer

1. There seem to be three pairs since three different colors are mentioned.

Lines 18-27

1. Which words would you pick out from this section as being archaic or "old-fashioned"? Give the less formal and more modern equivalents for these words.

2. What effect is created by Pound's use of these archaic words?

3. What kinds of repetition occur in the section and what patterns does the repetition form?

4. What effects are created by these patterns which you have identified?

Answers

1. "thou lovest" (you love); "dross" (worthless remnants or left-overs); "reft" (snatched away from); "thee" (you); "heritage" (inheritance); "the palpable" (what can be touched); "Elysium" (Heaven).

2. These archaic words create a distance between the poet and the reader, yet the effect is not to make this section seem impersonal, but rather very authoritative and solemnly earnest. The poet presents these insights as an important revelation of profound wisdom and of universal truth. "What thou lovest" sounds like poetry of an earlier period and, to some extent, like Shakespearean diction. It also sounds somewhat like the language of the King James version of the Bible, although Pound's use of "Elysium" rather than "Heaven" modifies its Biblical associations somewhat.

Altogether, Pound has done something quite impressive in this passage. He has managed to express very movingly sentiments which we feel to be sincere and heartfelt, yet he has done this in the kind of archaic diction that could have produced an impersonal and detached impression. The explanation for this, in part, is Pound's uneasiness about communicating directly and confidingly those emotions which he feels most strongly. On several occasions in the *Pisan Cantos* we see him finding some indirect way of "masking" his most intimate observations, either, as here, through archaic expression, or, on occasions, through his use of foreign languages, as, when he says, in French, "The tears which I have created are drowning me," or "I have felt pity for others, but not enough, not enough." The strength of emotion with which he is writing registers itself even through these "masks."

3. The following could be thought of as "patterns": a)Lines 18,20,21,26, and 27 all begin with "What thou lovest (or lov'st) well." b) Lines 20 and 21 are repeated, in reverse sequence, in lines 26 and 27. c) "or mine or theirs/or is it of none?" makes a group of three "or" phrases. d) "the seen" and "the palpable" make a contrasted pair as do "Elysium" and "the halls of hell" in the following line.

4. The repetition in pairs produces an effect of definiteness and emphasis. When the same thing is said twice it presents the issue as settled or "closed." The fact that lines 20 and 21 are repeated in reverse sequence at the end of this section (lines 26 and 27) gives the whole section a closed or resolved shape. When "or mine" and "or theirs" is followed by the third "or phrase"—"or is it of none?"—this opens up the structure. The earlier half line—"the rest is dross"—has a falling cadence and is emphatic and definite, but this half line—"or is it none?"—has a rising inflection and opens up the issue, largely because it is a question. But the question is followed by the two sets of assertions in paired lines (lines 24-25 and 26-27) giving this section a definite conclusion. (The "closedness" of this ending is further emphasized by what follows it—double spacing and then a change of subject.)

Line 28-36

1. Why does Pound focus on the ant at this point? How does the "ant allegory" relate to the motif "Pull down thy vanity"?

2. What does Pound think that man needs to learn about his place in the universe?

3. Who is "Paquin"? What has "outdone" his elegance?

Answers

1. The ant is magnified in his own world just as we regard ourselves as powerful or dominant in our own. But if we shift our perspective, we can see the "vanity" of assuming that everything is on the human scale.

2. Pound instructs man to "learn from the green world" or from the natural world about beauty, and about acting appropriately, with neither arrogance nor timidity.

3. Paquin was a Parisian dress designer. Pound is saying that nature's creation, the "green casque" (the shell of an insect), is more elegant than a man-made creation.

Lines 29-49

1. Reread this section aloud. What other lines or phrases in this section particularly echo the refrain "Pull down thy vanity" both in sound and in rhythm?

2. How would you describe the tone of the "vanity" section?

3. What is the poet suggesting about himself when he accuses himself with: "Thou art. . ./A swollen magpie in a fitful sun,/ Half black half white/Nor knowest'ou wing from tail"? What similarity is there between the fact that the sun is "fitful" and the fact that the bird is "half black half white"?

Note on line 37: Pound derived this line from a line in the medieval "The Ballad of Good Counsel."

Answers

1. "Fostered in falsity," "niggard in charity," and "This is not vanity."

2. The tone here is stern, challenging and condemnatory. It is a little like a sermon in which a preacher is forcing a congregation to confront all their shortcomings, but in fact the poet uses the singular "thou" and "thy" rather than the plural "ye" and "your." We realize that Pound here is preaching first and foremost to himself. He is accusing himself of pride or failing to "master" or control himself, or having been carried away by anger so that he thought destructive thoughts rather than compassionate ones.

3. The magpie is easy to think of as "vain" because it is loud and noisy. A person who is constantly talking is said to "chatter like a magpie." Pound is probably thinking of how he ranted on in his talks over Rome Radio and how he endlessly "lectured" his friends (in letters and in person) and his readers (in articles on economic subjects). The fact that this magpie is "swollen" suggests that it is doubly "puffed up" with pride. This magpie is a person who is confused as well as vain. It doesn't distinguish what its wings should do (make it fly) from what its tail should do (give direction to its flight and give it balance). This should certainly apply to Pound's uncontrolled state of mind in the late '30s and early '40s when his mood became increasingly frenetic, and he was flailing around with less and less sense of direction or sense of perspective.

The part black and part white plumage of the magpie is like alternating sunny spells and dull spells when the sun is shining "fitfully." The poet's hopelessly divided state of mind could well be represented imagistically by the two-tone or "pied" plumage of the bird alternately brightly lit by sunlight or dulled when the sun is not shining.

Lines 50-58

1. How does the shift in tone beginning with line 50 mirror the shift in content?

Answer

1. The poet is now speaking more quietly and reflectively. Notice how "this is not vanity" (lines 51 and 56) does not have the forward momentum that "Pull down thy vanity" has in the earlier section. "This is not vanity" is presented as a firm, assured, decisive statement, but calmly. Pound is saying that, although so much of his recent behavior is worthy of strong criticism, his efforts, particularly in the past, have led to some positive achievements also. He is remembering going with other artists to present to Wilfrid Scawen Blunt (1840-1922), then an old man, one of Gaudier's carvings in recognition of Blunt's poetry and his opposition to British imperialism and support of Irish nationalism.

Pound is also remembering the way in which, during his London years, he was able to recognize and encourage artistic talent among his contemporaries, to gather "from the air a live tradition" by seeing in this new generation of artists the potential to create actual works of art which would then become part of an ongoing literary and artistic tradition for following generations.

Exercises and Assignments

1. In "Canto 1," Pound retells Homer's account in the *Odyssey* of Odysseus' journey into the world of the dead to ask advice from the ghost of the prophet Tiresias. Read a translation of Homer's version of this episode in *The Odyssey*, Book IX. Comment on the ways in which Pound's version differs from its original. What has Pound most emphasized and what has he left out? What difference do these changes make to the overall impression that the "Canto 1" version creates?

40

2. If you are working with Pound's *Selected Poems*, read Acoetes' story in "Canto 2" and compare it to its source in Ovid's collection of myths, *Metamorphoses* (Book III, lines 584-692).

3. In "Canto 1," although Pound is translating Homer's Greek verse, he has chosen to use a poetic form from a completely different culture and time period. He is using an imitation of Anglo-Saxon meter in which the lines vary a good deal in the number of syllables, but can be read with four strongly stressed words in every line and with a pause between the first and the second halves of the line. Read "Canto 1" out loud, deciding, at first by trial and error, which four words in each line can best be given strong stresses. In some lines you are helped in deciding by the fact that Pound has been able to duplicate the second characteristic of Anglo-Saxon meter—alliteration of the first, second, and third words on which the strong stresses fall (e.g., from Pound's poem "The Seafarer": "weathered the winter, wretched outcast/. . ./Hung with hard ice-flakes, where hail-scur flew.")

4. List, in your own words, all the things mentioned in "Canto 45" as having been made or accomplished because of "Usura." What is the effect of all the negatives in the canto? Say why it is particularly appropriate for there to be so many of them.

5. Try writing a poem in the sestina form (as in "Sestina: Altaforte"). Since you will have to use the same group of six words for the line endings of each stanza, have your theme in mind as you choose the six words. A sestina traditionally has six stanzas of six lines each, just one set of six words for the line-endings in all the stanzas (although the order in which the words are used can vary from stanza to stanza), and a seventh three-line stanza (or tercet) which either uses just three of the six words or all six of them, two to a line.

6. Read "Exile's Letter" and write a poem of your own in a similar mood. For your subject choose a former close friendship with someone with whom you are no longer physically in contact because you are living at a distance from each other. Focus very specifically, in your poem, on things you did or places that you went with each other and, in particular, on an object or objects that are particularly associated with this friendship in your memory.

7. Read parts IV and V of the first section of *Hugh Selwyn Mauberley* ("These fought in any case," and ""There died a myriad"). Comment on the way in which, in both poems, Pound is simultaneously writing a tribute to those killed in the First World War and an anti-war poem.

8. Work your way carefully through "The Return," looking for all the ways in which the ideas of return, hesitation and slowness are emphasized. List the words in the poem whose meaning is connected to these three ideas and also describe the ways in which the forward movement of the poem is slowed or interrupted both within the individual lines and by breaks at the end of the lines.

9. Pound, from early in his career, valued the wisdom of Confucius and came increasingly to rely on it as a stabilizing influence as the circumstances of his life became increasingly chaotic. Read "Canto 13" carefully and, taking Confucius' words and his reactions to others as your data, say as exactly as possible, in your own words, what values Confucius seems to be advocating, how he feels people should behave and what kind of a person he seems to be himself.

10. How would you describe the tone of "Canto 13"? In what ways has Pound created this tone in the canto? The final three lines of the canto could stand on their own as a haiku-like imagist poem. (A haiku is a Japanese poetic form made up of three lines of five, seven, and five syllables in that exact order. The aim of the haiku is to convey the poet's impression of a natural scene or object.) What could these lines mean and why do they make a particularly effective ending to the Canto?

11. Study Pound's diction (word choice) in "The Garden." Make two lists—the first of the simple and straightforward words and phrases and a second of the more formal ones. To what extent do the two kinds of diction correspond to two different viewpoints? Notice that there is a difference, not only between the poet's point of view and the woman's, but also between two sides of the woman.

12. Notice the patterns of repetition in "Salutation" and the rhythms these create. In what ways can you relate these back to rhythms in Whitman's poetry and forward to passages in *The Cantos*?

13. As the title tells you, "Ballad of the Goodly Fere" is written in the very regular metrical form and rhyme scheme of the old Scottish ballad. Pound's persona here is the apostle, Simon the Zealot, but Pound has Simon speak in the Scottish dialect in which the ballads were written. (Many of the ballads tell the stories of brave lords who are doomed.) Make a list of words, phrases or idioms that suggest a Scottish dialect or are archaic in other ways. What kind of a person is Christ characterized as in the poem?

Self Test

In *The Women of Trachis*, Pound's translation of Sophocles' play about the death of Hercules, the dying Hercules realizes that the oracle's prophecy that he would finally be "released from trouble" after all his labors meant not, as he had assumed, that he would live out the end of his life in comfort, but that he would die. Although he is dying in agony from the centaur's poisoned blood that is eating into his flesh, he is finally reconciled to his fate and can accept that his life followed the course it was intended to. The climax of the play is his triumphant exclamation: "what/SPLENDOR,/IT ALL COHERES."

Bearing this in mind and also the fact that Pound frequently uses light imagery to represent the most profound kinds of truth or insight, discuss the following passage from "Canto 116" as Pound's commentary on what has happened in his life and what he feels about it. Say also how far you can relate this commentary to what he had said in the "Canto 81" passage. [Note: "the elms" he is remembering would be those in the grounds of St. Elizabeths and the "beauty" under them would be beautiful women who had come to visit him there.]

Note: Pound wrote "Canto 116" as an old man, after he was released from St. Elizabeths and was living with his daughter in Italy.

> I have brought the great ball of crystal;
> who can lift it?
> Can you enter the great acorn of light?
> But the beauty is not the madness
> Tho' my errors and wrecks lie about me.

And I am not a demigod,
I cannot make it cohere.
If love be not in the house there is nothing.
The voice of famine unheard.
How came beauty against this blackness,
Twice beauty under the elms—
To be saved by squirrels and bluejays?
. . . . .
. . .it coheres all right
even if my notes do not cohere.
. . . . .
To confess wrong without losing rightness:
Charity I have had sometimes,
I can not make it flow thru.
A little light, like a rushlight
to lead back to splendour.

Answers to Self Test
Answers to Self Tests begin on page 226.

For Further Reading
Books by Ezra Pound
The Cantos of Ezra Pound. New York: New Directions, 1973.

Personae: The Collected Poems of Ezra Pound. New York: New Directions, 1949.

Selected Cantos of Ezra Pound. New York: New Directions, 1970.

Selected Poems of Ezra Pound. New York: New Directions, 1957.

Books About Ezra Pound
Alexander, Michael. *The Poetic Achievement of Ezra Pound.* Berkeley and Los Angeles: University of California Press, 1979.

Davie, Donald. *Ezra Pound: Poet as Sculptor.* New York: Oxford University Press, 1964.

Flory, Wendy Stallard. *Ezra Pound and the Cantos: A Record of Struggle.* New Haven: Yale University Press, 1980.

Froula, Christine. *A Guide to Ezra Pound's Selected Poems.* New York: New Directions, 1983.

Kearns, George. *Guide to Ezra Pound's Selected Cantos.* New Brunswick, NJ: Rutgers University Press, 1980.

Kenner, Hugh. *The Poetry of Ezra Pound.* New York, New Directions, 1951.

Ruthven, K.K. *A Guide to Ezra Pound's Personae(1926).* Berkeley and Los Angeles: University of California Press, 1969.

Stock, Noel. *The Life of Ezra Pound.* New York: Pantheon, 1970.

Witemeyer, Hugh. *The Poetry of Ezra Pound: Forms and Renewal 1908-1920.* Berkeley and Los Angeles: University of California Press, 1969.

Langston Hughes (1902-1967)

Langston Hughes, often called "Poet Laureate of the Negro Race," wrote poems that celebrated the richness of black language and culture and that spoke to the poor black man. Born February 1, 1902, in Joplin, Missouri, Hughes spent his early years shuttling between various households, but was mainly looked after by his grandmother in Lawrence, Kansas. Hughes' grandmother, who had once served on the Oberlin station of the underground railroad, told Hughes stories of men and women who fought to end slavery. Wrapped in his grandmother's shawl, Hughes listened to the brave deeds of her husbands—Lewis Sheridan Leary, killed in the attempt by John Brown to free slaves at Harpers Ferry, and Charles Howard Langston, a passionate abolitionist, arrested and tried for rescuing a fugitive slave. Charles Langston's younger brother, John Mercer Langston, had been elected to Congress from Virginia and represented the United States in Haiti. Through these stories, his grandmother instilled in Hughes a sense of duty toward his people.

When asked how he became a poet, Hughes would tell the story of his being elected "class poet" in the seventh grade. He had never written a poem, but the white students, reasoning that all blacks had a good sense of rhythm, elected him unanimously. At graduation, when Hughes read his poems praising the school, the applause was thunderous. Hughes went on to attend Central High School in Cleveland (a prestigious school whose best known alumnus was John D. Rockefeller) where he became editor of the year book and class poet.

Hughes' earliest poems reflected the influence of the poets Paul Laurence Dunbar, who used black dialect; Walt Whitman, whom Hughes revered for his democratic vision; and Carl Sandburg, whom Hughes once called "my guiding star." Yet, as his biographer Arnold Rampersad has remarked, "The key to his (Hughes') release as a poet was his discovery of the significance of race, as well as his final, full admission of aloneness in the world." Hughes' parents separated soon after his birth. His mother, a minor actress, was often away. His lawyer father moved to Mexico to become a successful businessman. Hughes' earliest experiences with his fellow black people were in attending church. Though not religious, he was entranced by the congregation's abundance of faith and hope. He was also influenced by the hymns and the rhythms of the sermon. Later, he discovered the blues, another form of powerful rhythmic expression of the black man's capacity for survival.

Hughes' sense of identity was honed by a visit to his father in the summer of 1919 when Hughes was 17. His father openly despised blacks. He also hated poets and insisted that his son become an engineer. Hughes flatly refused; their differences were never resolved. Hughes wrote three of his most famous poems after this confrontation: "The Negro Speaks of Rivers," a poem of racial pride; "When Sue Wears Red," a love poem; and "Mother to Son," a poem rooted in the black experience. Finding his parents lacking in love, Hughes turned to the black masses, which he reached through his poetry, for love.

In June 1922, after attending Columbia University for one year, Hughes dropped out to gain "life experience." Aboard a ship to Africa, he threw all of his books—except for Whitman—overboard. During the next four years, he worked on shipboard to Africa and Europe, washed dishes in Paris and in Washington, D.C., and began publishing poems in such magazines as *Crisis*, *Opportunity*, and *Vanity Fair*. In 1925, Hughes, a busboy at the Wardman Park Hotel in Washington, was "discovered" by the poet Vachel Lindsay, after he left some poems by Lindsay's plate. Lindsay circulated the poems and advised Hughes to "hide and write and study and think." In 1926, Hughes enrolled in Lincoln University in Pennsylvania, from which he eventually graduated. This was also the year he published his first volume of poetry, *The Weary Blues*.

From this point on, Hughes embarked on his prolific career which covered a 40-year span. Aside from 16 volumes of poems, Hughes produced novels, short stories, historical works, plays, musicals, operettas, children's books, radio and television scripts, and two volumes of autobiography. Indeed, Hughes was the first black writer to support himself entirely by his craft. His work in the '20s established him as one of the leading figures of the Harlem Renaissance, the literary and cultural movement of the '20s that created a new black art.

In the 1930s, Hughes covered the Spanish Civil War as a correspondent for the *Baltimore Afro-American*. He identified strongly with the anti-Fascists and wrote poems praising the Spanish peasants and the soldiers of the International Brigade. Clearly, Hughes saw in this cause a reflection of his own people's struggles for freedom.

During the 1940s and '50s, Hughes wrote a weekly column for the *Chicago Defender* which became one of his lasting contributions. He often devoted this column to the tales of Simple, a sort of black Everyman who, although uneducated, perceived the world with great wisdom and humor. Through Simple, Hughes used comedy to express the conflict between black and white America. (In the film you will see an enactment of one of his Simple stories.)

Hughes died May 22, 1967, but his influence on many of today's poets is still evident. He opened up a new territory for poetry by expanding it to include black language, style and experience. He paved the way for poets both black and white, by bringing the jazz, blues and gospel traditions into American poetry.

The World of the Poems

From 1915 through the 1920s, hundreds of thousands of blacks moved from the rural South into the Northern cities. This demographic shift called, "The Great Migration," grew out of a combination of economic and social pressures. In the South, low wages, floods, soil exhaustion, the destruction of the cotton crop, and agricultural mechanization, combined with racist violence and injustice, forced blacks to begin the journey north. During World War I, the North offered jobs for blacks in railroad-building, ship-building, coal mining, and in soldiering.

By the 1920s, over one million blacks had arrived in New York, Chicago, Detroit, Philadelphia, and other cities. By the end of the 1920s, Harlem's population had tripled, making it the most densely populated black area in the world. The Great Migration, in spite of the hardships, caused a sense of excitement, opportunity, and drama. Above all, it began to foster a sense of community among blacks, a collective awareness, heightened by other events of the time.

One of these events was the war itself. Black soldiers fought valiantly, despite the discouraging obstacles of Jim Crow laws in the military, preventing blacks from obtaining equal status to whites, and continued reports of racist violence at home. In France, the black soldiers were treated as comrades which heightened their frustration with their country. Ironically, the blacks were fighting to preserve democracy and to make the world safer while they continued to suffer injustice at home.

By the early 1920s, a heightened feeling of racial identity and solidarity arose among blacks. Two important magazines served as forums for black political thought and culture: W.E.B. Du Bois' *Crisis*, sponsored by the National Association for the Advancement of Colored People (NAACP), and the social scientist Charles S. Johnson's *Opportunity*, sponsored by the Urban League. (Both magazines helped Hughes' writing career. His first major poem, "The Negro Speaks of Rivers" was published in *Crisis* the year he left Columbia.)

Another expression of solidarity was the rise in support for Marcus Garvey, the native Jamaican whose goal was to create a "free Africa" controlled by the world's 400 million blacks. In August 1920, 25,000 blacks crowded into Madison Square Garden to hear him speak. His message was one of racial assertiveness: he wanted the black people to be proud of their race in a world where blacks were despised. Hughes shared this theme.

This growing pride and nationalism among blacks led to an explosion of literary and cultural expression by black artists, writers, musicians, and social scientists that came to be called the "Harlem (or Negro) Renaissance." The four principal writers were: Langston Hughes, Claude McKay, Jean Toomer, and Countee Cullen. Other writers included novelists Zora Neale Hurston, Jessie Fauset, Walter White, Nella Larsen, George Schuyler, Wallace Thurman, and Eric Walrond, and poets Arna Bontemps, Waring Cuney, Sterling A. Brown, Frank Horne, Gwendolyn B. Bennett, and Helene Johnson. Although these writers differed in subject and point of view, all engendered racial self-awareness and pride. In their ways, they encouraged liberation from white literary standards and values.

Yet it wasn't only from white critics that some black writers needed to become liberated. Many black intellectuals of the day genteelly promoted white traditional standards for art. These critics intensely disliked Hughes' work which, in their eyes, portrayed blacks in an unflattering light. Hughes responded to his critics both white and black in his essay, "The Negro Artist and the Racial Mountain":

> We younger Negro artists who create now intend to express our individual dark-skinned selves without fear or shame. If white people are pleased we are glad. If they are not, it doesn't matter. We know we are beautiful. And ugly, too. The tom-tom cries and the tom-tom laughs. If colored people are pleased we are glad. If they are not, their displeasure doesn't matter either. We build our temples for tomorrow, strong as we know how, and we stand on top of the mountain, free within ourselves.

The excitement and importance of the Harlem Renaissance succeeded in attracting the white world. For the first time white publishers were interested in publishing black writers. Black writers' works began to appear in white magazines. A number of important white writers such as Eugene O'Neill were fascinated by black themes and characters. Although somewhat naive, O'Neill's plays, *Emperor Jones* (1920) and *All God's Chillun Got Wings* (1935), created multi-dimensional black characters and gave Paul Robeson and Charles Gilpin the opportunity to appear in starring roles.

Black culture, indeed, became a fad among whites who visited Harlem's jazz clubs, danced Harlem's dances, and watched Harlem's entertainers. However, the black virtues were seen as "primitive": spontaneity, joy, energy, sensuality. If black artists overstepped this line, the whites were no longer interested. Then came the Great Depression. The black community was hit as hard if not harder than the white community by the economic crisis. Many of the established black writers, including Hughes, responded to the crisis by turning to the left. Much of the literature of the period from 1930 to 1945 could be characterized as a literature of protest.

Langston Hughes: Voice of the Dream Deferred

Unlike many of his contemporaries who wrote in the formal, heightened language of traditional poetry, Hughes chose to mine the richness of black culture and to reach a wider audience by using the language (or idiom) of working-class blacks as the basis of his work. To him, this language effectively conveyed the black experience. Through it, he communicated the true voice of the speaker: a voice that was rich both in the experience of hardship and suffering, and in the experiences of love, joy, and worship.

For the structural and rhythmic basis of his work, Hughes turned to the musical forms of the blues, jazz, and spirituals. Hughes recognized that these forms, arising from the folk culture, spoke directly to black people. His decision to treat black themes with resources from the black tradition was revolutionary. His influence is found in the work of contemporary black poets such as Michael Harper, Amiri Baraka, Don L. Lee, Gwendolyn Brooks, Nikki Giovanni and Sonia Sanchez.

Hughes' Blues

Mostly, Hughes modelled many of his poems on the classic blues stanza. The blues stanza (with some variation) consists of three lines of lyrics, the second line a repetition of all or part of the first line, and the third line rhymes with the first two. Hughes often broke the three lines in half so that he had a six-line stanza, the third line repeating all or part of the first, and the fourth line repeating all or part of the second. Look, for example, at the first stanza from Hughes' "Morning After":

> I was so sick last night I
> Didn't hardly know my mind.
> So sick last night I
> Didn't know my mind.
> I drunk some bad licker that
> Almost made me blind.

The blues singer sings about his sorrows and uses repetition to reinforce the sense of a story told. The repetition also creates suspense that is usually resolved in the rhyming line. By transforming the oral form to a written one, Hughes calls attention to the poetic language of the blues as in "Lover's Return":

> *Oh, men treats women*
> *Just like a pair o'shoes—*
> *You kicks 'em round and*
> *Does 'em like you choose.*

Hughes also chose the blues form for its themes and tone. Traditionally, the blues addresses themes of suffering and hardship. Yet its tone of sorrow is always leavened with some irony and humor. Hughes celebrates this attitude that makes survival possible.

Read, for example, the last stanza of "Early Evening Quarrel." The woman's man has gambled her "sugar money" away.

> Lawd, these things we women
> have to stand!
> I wonder is there nowhere a
> Do-right man?

Hughes' Jazz Poems

Hughes explored another aspect of black idiom in his jazz poems. The language of jazz is quick, hip, spontaneous, often dissolving into the nonsense sounds called "scat." Read the following stanzas from "Children's Rhymes":

> *What's written down*
> *for white folks*
> *ain't for us a-tall:*
> *"Liberty And Justice—*
> *Huh—For All."*
>
> *Oop-pop-a-da!*
> *Skee! Daddle-de-do!*
> *Be-bop!*
>
> *Salt'peanuts!*
>
> *De-dop!*

Like the blues, the jazz idiom is built on the language people actually speak, rather than on the language they write. Hughes' jazz poems, like jazz itself, rely on quick changes, juxtapositions and reversals to convey various daily rhythms. One of the best examples is Hughes' book-length poem "Montage of a Dream Deferred," made up of individual poems arranged in contrasting pairs. Throughout the poem, Hughes sounds his motif of the dream deferred as though it were a musical motif in jazz. Reading the poem is like listening to a long jazz solo. In fact, Hughes intended the poem to be accompanied by jazz.

In the preface to "Montage of a Dream Deferred," Hughes wrote:

> . . . this poem on contemporary Harlem, like be-bop, is marked by conflicting changes, sudden nuances, sharp and impudent interjections, broken rhythms, and passages sometimes in the manner of the jam session, sometimes the popular song, punctuated by the riffs, runs, breaks, and disc-tortions of the music of a community in transition.

Our **Guided Reading** for this unit, covers three poems from "Montage of a Dream Deferred." You can read a larger selection from this work in *Selected Poems* by Langston Hughes.

The Idiom of the Church

Although Hughes was not religious, he liked listening to spirituals and sermons. To Hughes, spirituals, which incorporate repetition ("Jesus, won't you come by here; Jesus, won't you come by here; Jesus, won't you come by here? Jesus, we're in need of prayer"), deep feeling, and spontaneous composition, provided another form and language through which he could reach the masses and convey the black experience. In the following excerpt from "Sunday Morning Prophecy," listen for the minister's call and the congregation's responsive shouts:

> You will turn back
> And look toward the mountains.
> You will turn back
> And grasp for a straw.
> You will holler,
> *Lord-d-d-d-ah!*
> *Save me, Lord!*
> *Save me!*
> And the Lord will say,
> *In the days of your greatness*
> *I did not hear your voice!*
> The Lord will say,
> *In the days of your richness*
> *I did not see your face!*
> The Lord will say,
> *No-oooo-ooo-oo-o!*
> *I will not save you now!*

In leading the way in acknowledging folk culture (black idiom and forms) as the basis of black art, Hughes effected an historic change in poetry. His poetry compelled both blacks and whites to admit the power of black language. Hughes, like Whitman, saw himself as the representative poet of the people. He once said, "I believe that poetry should be direct, comprehensible, and the epitome of simplicity."

Exercise: To get an even better idea of what Hughes was doing in his poetry, listen to your friends the next time you're speaking in an informal situation. Then write down a few of their sentences to compare with sentences from a textbook, newspaper, or TV newscaster. The difference between the way your friends speak informally and the standard characterizes their idiom. Next, use your idiom in a blues stanza or a jazz poem. Or, perhaps, you can find another musical form that suits your idiom.

Meet the Speakers

Leopold Sedar Senghor served in the French National Assembly and later became president of newly independent Senegal, his birth place and a former French colony. A major poet in his own right, he shared with Langston Hughes a devotion to a poetry of social consciousness. During the 1920s and '30s, he was a leading proponent of Negritude, a cultural movement that sought to unite black people all over the world in an awareness of their common African heritage. Senghor credited Hughes with providing a major inspiration for the Negritude movement.

James Baldwin is one of America's most talented writers, known for his novels, short stories, plays, and essays. Baldwin's major works, such as *Go Tell It On The Mountain*, *Another Country*, and *Just Above My Head* probe the complex issues of racial and sexual identity.

Raoul Abdul was a personal assistant to Langston Hughes and has authored several books on black culture, including *Blacks in Classical Music: A Personal History*, and *Famous Black Entertainers of Today*. In addition he has edited *The Magic of Black Poetry* and *3000 Years of Black Poetry*.

Faith Berry is the author of *Langston Hughes: Before and Beyond Harlem*, a biography which concentrates on the first half Hughes' career.

George Houston Bass is the Executor-Trustee of the Langston Hughes Estate. He is also the co-author, with Phil Winchel Petric, of *Who Am I? A Manual of Negro History Written Especially for the Youth of Harlem* and a professor of Afro-American Studies at Brown University.

Amiri Baraka is a poet and political activist. In addition to his books of poetry, such as *The Dead Lecturer* and *The Sidney Poet Heroical*, he has written and produced many Off-Broadway plays. Like Langston Hughes, he has been a persuasive voice for the liberation of black people everywhere.

Arnold Rampersad, a professor of English at Rutgers University, is author of *The Life of Langston Hughes*. In addition to his work on Hughes, Rampersad has written *The Art and Imagination of W.E.B. DuBois*.

Gwendolyn Brooks is an imaginative and accomplished poet whose poems center around themes of black life in Chicago. Some of her best known books are *In the Mecca*, *Beckonings*, and *A Street In Bronzeville*.

Louise Thompson Patterson is a political activist and was a secretary and lifelong friend of Langston Hughes.

Rowena Woodham Jelliffe is the co-founder, along with her husband Russell, of Karamu House, a community center for minority and under-privileged children and adults in Cleveland. Hughes attended classes there as a young boy. Later on in his life, Karamu House staged the premieres of several of Hughes' plays.

Study Plan for this Unit

1. Complete the section **Before Watching the Film: Journal-Writing and Other Activities**.

2. Read the Hughes poems, many of which are featured in the film. Hughes' poems, which are based on the rhythms of jazz and the blues, as well as spirituals and sermons, must be read aloud for full enjoyment. Unlike some of the other poetry you've encountered so far, Hughes' poems are often accessible on first reading. They are also relatively short.

In addition, we recommend that you listen to some of the music that Hughes admired: for the blues, listen to Lightning Hopkins, Muddy Waters, or Blind Lemon Jefferson; for be-bop, listen to Charlie "Yardbird" Parker, Miles Davis, Lester Young, or Ben Webster. Another record you might enjoy is "The Weary Blues," a recording of Langston Hughes reading his poetry to jazz accompaniment.

Afro-American Fragment
My People
The Heart of Harlem
Aunt Sue's Stories
The Negro Speaks of Rivers
To a Negro Jazz Band in a Parisian Cabaret
When Sue Wears Red
Madrid 1937
Still Here
Consider Me
Feet o' Jesus
Note on Commercial Theatre
Genius Child
Listen Here Blues
Young Gal's Blues
Negro Ghetto
From *Montage of a Dream Deferred*:
    Dream Boogie
    Movies
    Tell Me
    Harlem ("Dream Deferred")
Morning After
I, Too
Dream Variations
Mother to Son
Madam and Her Madam
Mulatto
Cross
Blue Bayou
Let America Be America Again

3. Watch the film

4. Complete the section **After Watching the Film: Journal Writing and Other Activities**.

5. Go though the **Guided Reading**.

6. Complete the **Exercises and Assignments** as specified by your instructor.

7. Take the **Self Test.**

Before Watching the Film: Journal-Writing and Other Activities

1. Write about an experience you've had of a "dream deferred."

2. Read aloud the lyrics of one of your favorite songs. Look for places where the rhythm of the lyrics may have suggested the rhythm of the melody to the songwriter. Is there anything else in the words that suggests the sound of the melody?

While Watching the Film

1. Note the images of urban life in Harlem in the past and in the present. How has

life in Harlem appeared to change?

2. Pay attention to the images of black women in the film.

After Watching the Film: Journal-Writing and Other Activities

1. After watching the film, what images remain in your mind that further illuminate the phrase "a dream deferred"?

2. In Hughes' "Theme for English B," the poet responds to the instructor's assignment: *"Go home and write/ a page tonight/ And let that page come out of you—/Then, it will be true."* Read the remainder of Hughes' prose poem and then write your own prose poem in response to the same "assignment."

3. Which visual presentations of the poems did you like best and why?

4. Write a few blues verses based on a phrase people commonly say such as "Why did you say that?" or "I haven't got the time."

Guided Reading

The following **Guided Reading** is based on sections from Hughes' book *Montage of a Dream Deferred* (1951). This book was conceived as one continuous poem, although it was organized in titled sections, and used poems that had been previously published. The poems are arranged in thematic clusters; within the clusters, poems are arranged in contrasting pairs. The main subject and setting of the poem is Harlem. Although we only treat three short poems in this **Guided Reading**, we strongly recommend that you read the entire sequence which can be found in *Selected Poems*. It is particularly important to read these poems aloud since the themes are carried out in musical motifs that are hard to detect if read silently. Remember, we present here only one person's interpretation. Our questions and answers are only starting points for your own "variations."

Dream Boogie

Good morning, daddy!
Ain't you heard
The boogie-woogie rumble
Of a dream deferred?

Listen closely: 5
You'll hear their feet
Beating out and beating out a—

    You think
    It's a happy beat?

Listen to it closely: 10
Ain't you heard
something underneath
like a—

    What did I say?

Sure,   15
I'm happy!
Take it away!

Hey, pop!
Re-bop!
Mop!   *20*

Y-e-a-h!

Lines 1-4

1. What does the first line imply?

2. How does the rhythm of the first stanza help to establish the tone of the poem?

3. What is "the boogie-woogie rumble/of a dream deferred?"

Answers

1. The implication of "Good morning, daddy!" is that the reader/listener is "asleep." The speaker of the poem rouses both "daddy" and the reader to the new day and to the main theme of the poem: a dream deferred. It's not until we wake up to the fact that blacks are socially and economically deprived that we can hope to usher in a "new day" of change.

2. Using line breaks and a combination of long and short syllables, Hughes creates syncopation: the jumpy rhythm that forms the basis of jazz. "Good morning, daddy!/Ain't you heard/The boogie-woogie rumble/Of a dream deferred?" The rhythm, in effect, starts up the "boogie-woogie rumble" of the poem. The tone is lively, charged with energy, insistent.

3. Boogie-woogie is a style of jazz piano that is characterized by a repeated rhythmic and melodic pattern in the bass, a kind of "rumble." (If you aren't familar with boogie-woogie, we suggest you borrow a record from the library.) In black culture, the "rumble" is also a rumor, a fight, or any trouble. Someone might ask, "What was the rumble about?" The narrator of this poem tries to spread the rumble of the dream deferred, just as musically, the boogie-woogie with its deep "rumble" expresses the restlessness, the frustration, and the energy of blacks whose social and economic dreams have yet to be fulfilled.

Lines 5-7

1. Who does "their" refer to in line 6?

2. What connotations does the "beating out" have in line 7?

Answers

1. & 2. Although the filmmakers used footage of some important marches of the civil rights period to illustrate this line, "their feet" refers more immediately to the pianist's or the drummer's foot tapping out the beat. The "beating out" could also refer, however, to the black ancestors, the slaves and elders, who beat drums to send distant

messages from tribe to tribe. One always has to listen closely to the message of the drums since silent beating of drums or ideas is all that is allowed by society. Hughes implies that the rumble of a dream deferred has been "beating out" since the first slaves were captured.

Lines 8-13
1. What is the "something underneath" of line 12?

Answer
1. Underneath the gaiety of the music is the sad, ominous, rumbling of the dream deferred that someday may explode. Before the speaker can say what's underneath, he's interrupted—once again, the message is deferred, and the question is left open-ended.

Lines 14-21
1. To whom is the narrator speaking when he says "What did I say?"

2. What motivates the narrator to shift from spreading the word ("rumble") to dancing?

3. What does "Sure, I'm happy!/Take it away!" mean? Define "it."

Answers
1. "What did you say, boy?" was commonly asked by a white man who wanted to make sure he kept his slave or laborer in place. At that point in the confrontation, the black man usually had to back down to avoid serious trouble. Society here challenges the narrator's dream. "What did I say?" seems to be the narrator's way of avoiding a confrontation.

2. When the narrator is caught spreading the word of freedom, dignity, self-esteem, equality by the oppressor, he masks his message and keeps on dancing. In changing the topic back to what the oppressor understands, he avoids confrontation.

3. "Take it away" is a term in jazz used when one musician turns the solo spot over to another—the equivalent of "your turn." "It" refers to the boogie solo, but also to the dream. The speaker's cry to to take "it" away (actually giving it away) implies that once again the dream will be deferred.

Movies

The Roosevelt, Renaissance, Gem, Alhambra:
Harlem laughing in all the wrong places
        at the crocodile tears
        of crocodile art
        that you know   5
        in your heart
        is crocodile:

(Hollywood
laughs at me,
black—   10
so I laugh
back.)

Questions

1. What do the "Roosevelt," "Renaissance," "Gem," and "Alhambra" have in common?

2. What is "Crocodile art"?

3. Invent an example of "wrong places" to laugh that Hughes may be thinking of.

4. In what way does Hollywood "laugh" at the black man?

Answers

1. Names of movie theaters in Harlem, they also suggest a dream or a promise of a better way of life. Hughes looks back, for example, at Roosevelt's promise of bringing economic reform and stability to the country (which did not ultimately help the blacks), and the Harlem Renaissance's dream of enlarging black literary culture, a dream which petered out in the Depression. The Gem and Alhambra provide dreams of exotic escape in the movies—the celluloid American dream.

2. Because Hollywood movies do not depict reality (particularly in conveying the reality of life in Harlem), movie art is "crocodile art" evoking "crocodile tears"—fake or insincere tears.

3. What is serious to Hollywood is funny to blacks and vice versa. The black people depicted in movies, especially in Hughes' day, are usually stereotypes. (Think, for example, of Hollywood stereotypes of the loving black "mammies" on slave plantations.)

4. In *Montage of a Dream Deferred*, "Movies" is followed by a poem entitled "Not a Movie" in which Hughes tells the story of a black man who leaves the South after having been beaten up by the Ku Klux Klan (KKK). By making this contrast, Hughes points to the real life brutality that blacks are subjected to—a reality in which Hollywood, particularly in Hughes' day, was not interested.

Harlem

What happens to a dream deferred?

    Does it dry up
    like a raisin in the sun?
    Or fester like a sore—
    And then run?   5
    Does it stink like rotten meat?
    Or crust and sugar over—
    like a syrupy sweet?

Maybe it just sags
like a heavy load.   10

Or does it explode?

Questions

1. What form does this poem take and what is the significance of that form?

2. List the five similes in the poem. What do they have in common?

3. Where is the sixth simile?

Answers

1. The poem takes the form of a series of questions that sum up the possible consequences of deferring the dream. By posing these questions, Hughes demands the reader's participation. The repetition of "Does it. . ." builds to the ultimate question (which can be read as a challenge): "Or does it explode?"

2. Each of the similes contained at one time some promise, a "dream" of something life-enhancing. The raisin was once a juicy grape; the body was once healthy until through neglect it developed festering sores; the meat was once good; the sweet was once fresh; the load is causing someone or something to bend under its weight. In each case through inattention or neglect the grape, body, meat, sweet or true shape is gone. The elements of the deferred dream look insignificant from the outside, but if they are ignored the raisin, the sore, the meat, the candy, and the load become a threat.

3. The sixth simile is in the reader's head: "Or does it explode" like a . . .?

Further Questions

1. How does the dream shift in meaning through "Dream Boogie" and "Movies" to "Harlem"?

2. How has the Civil Rights Movement lent credibility to these poems, especially to "Harlem"?

Answers

1. The intensity and importance of the dream deferred build from the first poem in *Montage*, "Dream Boogie," through the poem, "Harlem" which comes close to the end of the series. Throughout the *Montage*, the message deepens in its seriousness as it reflects the Harlem dwellers' growing frustration with poverty, inequality, and bigotry. Indeed, by the time we read "Harlem," the cluster of deferred dreams and unfulfilled promises has become a bomb that threatens to explode any minute.

In "Dream Boogie," the speaker refers to the dream deferred, but seems more interested in survival. Rather than confront the problem head on, the speaker dons a "happy" mask and allows the musicians to "take it away." In "Movies," the tone is angrier, and more analytical: "Hollywood /laughs at me . . . so I laugh/back." The message is "I'm just as smart as my oppressor. You're not fooling me." Unlike the narrator in "Dream Boogie," who seems content to pretend that life's just one happy party, the speaker of "Movies" remarks the grotesque distortion of reality ("crocodile art") that white society promotes and accepts in the movies. The speaker of "Movies," in spite of his awareness of the dream deferred, takes refuge in his cynical "laughing back"—instead of taking action.

Finally, in "Harlem," Hughes compels the reader to take a sharp look at the reality of the dream deferred and to analyze the situation. The dream is not a mere pipe dream; the dream is serious business with serious consequences. Unless Harlem takes action, the dream will dry up, decay, grow rotten, and the black man will continue to live as a second class citizen. Hughes asks the reader to ponder the consequences, and by implication to reflect on the positions of black leaders such as Booker T. Washington, the president of Tuskegee Institute, who sought to involve recently freed blacks in America's expansion, but who also insisted on maintaining the status quo—he was, for example, against radical social change that would surely get the black man lynched; Marcus Garvey, the black nationalist; and W.E.B. Du Bois, the historian, who countered Booker T. Washington by stressing the need for higher education and full political and civil rights for blacks.

2. Hughes' question in "Harlem,": "*Or will it explode?*" was prophetic. The Civil Rights Movement led by Dr. Martin Luther King, among others, exploded on the scene in the early 1960s, and through nonviolent protest, brought down the state laws that made racial discrimination legal. The Civil Rights Movement also succeeded in making white society more aware of the reality of black experience. Sadly, the Civil Rights era ended in violence with the assassination of Dr. Martin Luther King, and the explosive riots of Watts and other cities.

For Further Consideration
Read Dr. Martin Luther King's famous speech, "I Have a Dream," in which he says: "I have a dream that one day this nation will rise up and live out the true meaning of its creed: 'We hold these truths to be self-evident; that all men are created equal.' " Is the dream alluded to in this speech and in these poems still deferred?

Exercises and Assignments
1. Hughes once described the blues as a form which contains "ironic laughter mixed with tears." Read "Young Gal's Blues" and "Morning After." What is it about human experience that the blues captures so well?

2. Hughes' particular world is the inner city and, specifically, Harlem. The people he writes about are the inhabitants of this world, the urban working classes. When Hughes' work first appeared, it was denounced by black critics of his time as "vulgar," "sordid," and "sensational." Why do you think this audience rejected Hughes' work? Do you think Hughes' work has universal qualities? What are they?

3. Both Whitman and Hughes searched for an American idiom to convey the American experience. In particular, Hughes sought a "black idiom" to convey the experience of working-class blacks. Both poets felt they were representing segments of the American population who had never been represented in poetry before. Read Whitman's "I Hear America Singing," and then read Hughes' "I, Too." Write a dialogue between Whitman and Hughes in which they discuss their roles as American poets and

their development of an American idiom. Be sure to include examples from each poets' work in the discussion (they, of course, have their works memorized!).

4. How does the narrator's attitude toward his dream change from "Dream Variations" and "Tell Me" to "As I Grew Older"? Analyze each poem and determine the age of the speaker. What could cause the speaker's attitude to change? What social situations could account for the existing attitude in each poem?

5. In "Mother to Son," Hughes develops an extended metaphor, comparing life to a worn-out staircase. Choose a metaphor for life and extend it through a short poem. You may want, as Hughes does, to look at life through the eyes of a character other than yourself.

6. Compare Hughes' poem "Madam and Her Madam" to Williams' poem "To a Poor Old Woman." How have the different poets tried to convey the experience of a poor person?

7. If you can, replay the sections of the film in which the poems are presented. What is lost in reading the poem silently from the page?

8. Write a blues song about studying poetry. Don't forget there are some happy blues!

9. Read "The Negro Mother," "Mother to Son," and "Aunt Sue's Stories." What roles did the mother figure fulfill in Hughes' poetry?

10. Read "Mulatto," "Cross," "Blue Bayou," "Madam and Her Madam." How did Hughes handle society's assault on black women?

11. Contrast the types of stories a modern elder (a grandparent or older family friend) would tell versus the ones told by Aunt Sue in the "Aunt Sue's Stories." What social changes have taken place? Then write a skit in which the two opposing aunts meet and compare notes about their lives: work, families, and other topics discussed by Hughes.

12. What ideas make "Let America Be America Again" a radical poem?

Self Test

Read the following poem written in 1969 by Don L. Lee. Write one or two paragraphs in which you discuss how Hughes' work may have influenced Lee consciously or unconsciously.

But He Was Cool
or: He Even Stopped for Green Lights

super-cool
ultrablack
a tan/purple
had a beautiful shade.

he had a double-natural
that wd put the sisters to shame.

his dashikis were tailor made
& his beads were imported sea shells
    (from some blk/country i never heard of)
he was triple-hip.

His tikis were hand carved
out of ivory
& came express from the motherland.
he would greet u in swahili
& say good-by in yoruba.
woooooooooooooo-jim he bes so cool & ill tel li gent
            cool-cool is so cool he was un-cooled by
                other niggers'
                    cool
            cool-cool ultracool was bop-cool/ice box
                cool so cool
                    cold cool
            his wine didn't have to be cooled,
                him was air
                    conditioned cool
            cool-cool/real cool made me cool—
                now ain't that cool
            cool-cool so cool him nick-
                named refrigerator.

cool-cool so cool
he didn't know,
after detroit, newark, chicago &c.,
we had to hip
            cool-cool/super-cool/real cool
        that
to be black
is
to be
very-hot.

Answers to Self Test
Answers to Self Tests begin on page 226.

For Further Reading
Books by Langston Hughes

Ask Your Mama: 12 Moods for Jazz. New York: Alfred A. Knopf; 1961.

The Best of Simple. New York: Hill & Wang; 1961.

The Big Sea. New York: Hill & Wang; 1984.

I Wonder As I Wander. New York: Hill & Wang; 1964.

Selected Poems. New York: Vintage Books; 1974.

The Ways of White Folks. New York: Vintage Books; 1962.

Books about Hughes

Jemie, Onwuchekwa. *Langston Hughes: An Introduction to the Poetry.* New York: Columbia University Press; 1977.

O'Daniel, Therman B., editor. *Langston Hughes: Black Genius.* New York: Morrow; 1971.

Rampersad, Arnold. *The Life of Langston Hughes, Volume I: I, Too, Sing America.* New York: Oxford University Press; 1986.

Walt Whitman (1819-1892)

Long Island was still part wild in 1819 when Walt Whitman was born in Huntington. One of his earliest memories was seeing the ocean across rolling fields from a high hill near his home. The ebb and flow of the Atlantic and its open horizon were to be prime inspirations for his great poem *Leaves of Grass*. In 1823 Whitman's family moved to Brooklyn. Here Walt, the second son of eight children, had five years of school before going out to work to help support the large family. He was lucky in his first employer, a Brooklyn lawyer who enrolled him in a lending library and set him to reading Sir Walter Scott. In 1831, at the age of 12, Whitman apprenticed to the printing trade, staying on alone in Brooklyn when the family moved back to Long Island.

After four years as a printer's devil, Whitman only worked a year as a printer before the whole printing district was destroyed by a fire. For two years he taught school in small towns on Long Island and began to be swept up in the age's political fevers, debating, writing editorials for local papers and then starting his own. At 19, he wrote, edited and printed his *Long Islander* himself and even delivered it, riding out on horseback and handing it to the farmers in their fields.

Whitman returned to New York as a compositor for the *New World* and was soon reporting, reviewing, writing features and editing for papers such as the *Aurora* and the *Evening Tattler*. The pugnacious journalistic style of those days seems to have spilled over into the newsrooms themselves. Most of Whitman's jobs ended after a few months in some quarrel with his employer over politics or work. The second time he left the *Star*, its editor described him in print as a "hectoring scrivener," and Whitman returned him tit for tat, writing up the *Star* as the "incarnation of nervelessness" and adding that it was so moribund it would need help just to "lean against the wall and die." Apparently this was customary, for Whitman was quickly taken on as editor of the *Daily Eagle*, Brooklyn's most popular paper, where he would stay almost two years, the longest stretch of his career.

In 1848 Whitman got to see some of the untamed frontier he had been celebrating in editorials. He set out for New Orleans to become the founding editor of a new daily. The two-week, 2000-mile stagecoach and riverboat ride filled his mind with sights and sounds that would later emerge in the pages of *Leaves of Grass*. At Cumberland he saw hundreds of Conestoga wagons taking on stores and forming parties for the long journey across the prairies. And in New Orleans he saw slaves on the auction block.

Whitman's stay in the South intensified his opposition to the extension of slavery to the new territories of the West. These "Free Soil" beliefs helped to precipitate Whitman's break with the New Orleans paper, and when he returned to Brooklyn he founded the *Freeman*, a paper devoted to the Free Soil cause. Soon after, the Democratic Party backed off from a strong Free Soil position. From now on Whitman's political drives were to center not on party politics but on his own social vision. He began to nourish dreams of being a charismatic orator who would inspire a great resurgence of democratic fervor.

Although it's something of a mystery how Whitman's ambitions came to focus on poetry and how he developed the radically new style of poetry that would emerge in *Leaves of Grass*, some influences are clear: Ralph Waldo Emerson's call for an American poet (in his 1842 lecture which Whitman reviewed); the plain-spoken eloquence of the Quaker orator Elias Hicks; the long cadences and parallel structure of the King James Bible; and the aria and recitative style of Italian opera which Whitman loved. By 1850 he had become an accomplished journalist, but his poetry and fiction were utterly conventional and unremarkable. Between 1850 and 1854 we see a few inklings of the new style—a few unrhymed poems in a kind of biblical cadence, trial lines in a notebook—but nothing to prepare us for the sweeping confidence and daring originality of the 1855 first edition of *Leaves of Grass*.

He printed 795 copies, helping to set the type himself, and sending it off to various literary men for review. Most were outraged or offended by the book, but a few saw its importance and the most influential of all, Emerson, sent a warm personal letter praising the book in the highest terms. Whitman revised *Leaves of Grass* in 1856, his ambition still on the upswing. He began to think of a vastly expanded edition that would be a sort of bible for the democratic future.

By 1859, however, Whitman had fallen into what he called a "slough." A number of factors combined to break his confidence and cause him to doubt the value of what he had done. He had fallen far behind in his plan for "The New Bible" (the expanded edition of *Leaves of Grass*); he was working hard to eke out a minimal living; and he found it hard to reconcile his physical desires with his idealization of them as the "dear love of comrades" that he held up in his poem. Out of this despair he wrote the "Sea-Drift" poems in the 1860 edition of *Leaves of Grass*, including the great "Out of the Cradle Endlessly Rocking."

Whitman was already pulling out of his "slough" when the outbreak of the Civil War in 1861 shook him out of it altogether. He began tending the wounded in New York Hospital and then worked as a volunteer in the military hospitals in Washington. He supported himself with part-time work so that he could visit the wards daily. He wrote letters for the men, talked to them and brought them gifts, and kept company with the dying.

Near the end of the war he became a clerk in the Department of the Interior, but was fired by his superior, who considered *Leaves of Grass* an obscene book. Whitman was able to transfer to the attorney general's office where he remained until suffering a paralytic stroke in 1873. Unable to care fully for himself, he had to move in with his brother George in Camden, New Jersey. Whitman never regained use of his legs but did recover enough to resume lecturing and to make a long dreamed-of transcontinental voyage in 1879-80.

He lived in Camden for the rest of his life, following the state of the nation, reminiscing with friends and admirers and expanding *Leaves of Grass*. Whitman had incorporated his Civil War poems into the fourth edition of *Leaves of Grass* in 1867 and continued to expand it in successive editions in 1870, 1876 and 1881. In 1884 he bought a small house on Mickle Street. A few months before he died in 1892, he sent to press the final version of *Leaves of Grass*.

The World of the Poems

It is hard to imagine the America of today as a young, half-formed republic, still trying out ways to put into practice the principles of its revolution. But during Walt Whitman's early years, the democratic experiment was in full swing, and many issues were being debated: how centralized should governments be, would European immigration alter the national character, were the banks a threat to democracy, should slavery be extended to the newly settled lands to the west? The nation was finding itself, under the skeptical, and sometimes hostile, eyes of a world dominated by autocratic and monarchic governments. Nor were such sentiments and opinions without their echo at home. But Americans, in general, were quite swept up in their democratic dream and very confident it would be realized.

Part of this optimism came from the new opportunities that had been created by technology and the new vistas opened by science. The steamboat, the telegraph, the Erie Canal, the steam-powered printing press and the transcontinental railroad were as revolutionary in Whitman's time as the radio, gramophone, automobile, antibiotics, airplane, movies and television have been in the 20th century. People envisioned a brave new era in which man would conquer the hardships of life and go on to create untold wealth.

Another aspect of America's optimism came from the country's steady expansion westward to the Pacific. Even more than its actual wealth in natural resources and land, the West represented a chance to start over, to give the imagination free rein, to work unhindered by old preconceptions and conventions in an entirely virgin soil. Americans came to believe it was their moral duty, their "manifest destiny" (to use a term coined at the time) to spread the gospel of material progress and democracy across all North America and even to evangelize the globe.

Whitman early found himself at the center of the stormy controversies of Jacksonian democracy, when the common people came to be the major force in American politics. He apprenticed at 14 to a printer and, before he was out of his teens, began writing for the colorful "penny presses." Here he joined heartily in the loud and often vituperative debates over immigration and slavery and the shape of "manifest destiny." As Justin Kaplan says in the film, "What's important about Whitman's journalist background . . . is that this, in a sense, is his bank account in experience. This is the way he learns the city . . . What he calls 'million-footed Manhattan.' This is the way he learns about violence and conflict, this is the way he learns about American society. It's a very direct exposure to experience: there's nothing bookish about Whitman's education."

Whitman's main interest was always in the American experience, the democratic experiment, and its spiritual meaning. He wanted his book to be original and open to suit the spirit of the times, and he wanted it to be American to celebrate the country he saw as the torchbearer of that spirit. Today, we are used to open, experimental art, to poems in free verse that sound the way Americans speak, but in 1855 such work was utterly revolutionary. Most readers were too startled by what Whitman *wasn't* doing—rhyming, counting the beats, using elevated language, treating "poetic" subjects—to see what he *was* doing.

Whitman also threw off social and sexual conventions. In an age when "men of fashion were dressed from head to toe like black tubes" and "women of fashion looked like tea cozies, jampots and other gently rounded objects of manufacture, their breasts, buttocks and legs . . . hidden by nearly one hundred yards of gown, petticoat and underclothing," Whitman celebrated the health of the uninhibited body and the beauty of its naked form. He announced the equality of man and woman and preached on the beauty and glory of sex. His contemporaries were not so much shocked by what he had to say about sex and the body as by his *treating them frankly at all*. Most readers didn't get far enough to see how this aspect of Whitman's writing fit into his larger scheme. Whitman's call for sexual liberation was part of his larger call for the liberation of the human spirit. It was a central part of his vision of a democratic society based on love. We today also run the risk of misunderstanding him if we separate his celebration of sex and the body from his love for humanity and its daily life.

Walt Whitman: An American

The roster of famous American poets of Walt Whitman's day included William Cullen Bryant, John Greenleaf Whittier, Ralph Waldo Emerson, Henry Wadsworth Longfellow, and James Russell Lowell. After these names, "Walt Whitman" sounds too colloquial, a nickname on the order of Kit Carson, Davy Crockett, Dan'l Boone, Andy Jackson. Whitman was always "Walt" to his family, but before 1855 he signed newspaper pieces "Walter Whitman" or "W. W." and on business documents used "Walter Whitman, Jr." That he introduced himself as "Walt Whitman" in the 1855 edition of *Leaves of Grass* is a clue to that book's originality, for these poems were intended to represent the direct and unfettered expression of a man of the people.

> Walt Whitman, an American, one of the roughs, a
>   kosmos,
> Disorderly fleshy and sensual . . . eating
>   drinking and breeding,
> No sentimentalist . . . no stander above men and
>   women or apart from them . . . no more modest
>   than immodest.

(Leaves of Grass, 1855)

But the "Walt Whitman" who speaks to us in this part of *Leaves of Grass* (the part later called "Song of Myself") turns out to be not so much a typical American working man as an archtypical one. He is a type of Free Man—ideal inhabitant of Whitman's ideal democracy. By producing such men and women, the democratic experiment will justify itself.

> I swear I begin to see the meaning of these things,
> It is not the earth, it is not America who is so great,
> It is I who am great or to be great, it is You up there,
>   or any one . . .
>
>   . . .
>
> . . . this America is only you and me,
> Its power, weapons, testimony, are you and me,
> Its crimes, lies, thefts, defections, are you and me,
> Its Congress is you and me, the officers, capitols, armies,
>   ships, are you and me . . .

("By Blue Ontario's Shore")

Whitman could speak for America because America *was* its people, and he saw himself as very much one of them. He saw that the true voice of democracy would not be that of a sympathetic aristocrat speaking for the people, but a voice of the people themselves, and that, to be convincing, it must not only take their part but also *sound like* the common speech. So, in "Song of Myself," he created "Walt Whitman," a man who was both his uncensored self and an ideal extension of himself. In this voice he could sing at the same time both America's dreams and realities.

Whitman doggedly refused to separate his public and private identities. There is nothing in "Song of Myself" (and little in *Leaves of Grass* as a whole) to distinguish Walt Whitman the author from Walt Whitman the working-class poet-hero of the poem. Whether Whitman did this deliberately or spontaneously out of sheer self-confidence is hard to say. But either way it expresses his faith in there being a bridge between the two. By making such claims, he challenges the reader to envision a bridge between the America you see around you and the one we could create. He challenges you to create a bridge between yourself and what you could be, and to cross it.

Meet the Speakers

Allen Ginsberg, poet, has been a lively, active force on the American literary scene over the past 30 years. He is the author of *Howl, Kaddish,* and *Mind Breaths,* among other works. Ginsberg says he has been influenced by Whitman ever since he was a young boy.

Galway Kinnell, poet, returned to Whitman when he decided to break with conventional poetic forms in such works as *The Book of Nightmares, Body Rags,* and *Mortal Acts, Mortal Words.* In addition to his own verse, he has made many translations. He has been the recipient of many literary awards, including a Guggenheim Fellowship.

Donald Hall, besides poetry, has written books on the sculptor Henry Moore, on baseball, and on Marianne Moore. In addition to his own books of verse such as *Kicking the Leaves* and *Exiles and Marriages,* he has edited *A Choice of Whitman's Verse.*

Justin Kaplan is the author of the highly acclaimed biography *Walt Whitman, A Life* which reconstructs Whitman's life in all its complexity and ambiguity. Kaplan has also written a biography of Lincoln Steffens, and one of Mark Twain for which he received the Pulitzer Prize and the National Book Award. He is currently writing a biography of Charlie Chaplin.

Harold Bloom is Sterling Professor of the Humanities at Yale University and one of America's foremost contemporary literary critics. In *The Anxiety of Influence* he examines the literary relationships between great writers and their predecessors.

Study Plan for This Unit

1. Complete the section **Before Watching the Film: Journal-Writing and Other Activities**.

2. Read the Whitman poems, many of which are featured in the film. These poems, among others, will be featured in the study guide. Some lines you should read aloud to catch the word-sounds and cadences. Read through the poems at a moderate speed without stopping. Don't worry if you don't understand them completely.

Song of Myself
Crossing Brooklyn Ferry
I Sing the Body Electric
Out of the Cradle Endlessly Rocking
A Glimpse
When I Heard at the Close of the Day
When Lilacs Last in the Dooryard Bloom'd
The Wound-Dresser

Reconciliation
Cavalry Crossing A Ford
As I Sit Writing Here
As I Ebb'd with the Ocean of Life

3. Watch the film.

4. Complete the section **After Watching the Film: Journal-Writing and Other Activities**.

5. Go through the **Guided Reading**.

6. Complete the **Exercises and Assignments** as specified by your instructor.

7. Take the **Self Test**.

Before Watching the Film: Journal-Writing and Other Activities

1. Read the following passage from *Song of Solomon* (the King James Bible):

Behold, thou art fair, my love; behold, thou art fair; thou hast doves' eyes within thy locks: thy hair is as a flock of goats, that appear from Mount Gilead.

Thy teeth are like a flock of sheep that are even shorn, which came up from the washing; whereof every one bear twins, and none is barren among them.

Thy lips are like a thread of scarlet, and thy speech is comely: thy temples are like a piece of a pomegranate within thy locks.

Thy neck is like the tower of David builded for an armory, whereon there hang a thousand bucklers, all shields of mighty men.

Thy two breasts are like two young roes that are twins, which feed among the lilies.

(Song of Solomon 4:1-5)

Note the use of repetition in this passage and the use of parallel structure, that is, the repetition of grammatical forms to reflect parallel meanings. Whitman was strongly influenced by the rhythms of the King James Bible and relied on repetition and parallel structure as the basis for his free verse. Now write a poem in which you use repetition and parallel structure to create rhythm. Try describing someone you love or hate: "Your teeth are like _____," "Your eyes are like_____," etc. (This can be a serious poem or a silly one. For example: "Your teeth are like charred marshmallows hanging off a burnt stick." Or "Your teeth are like small piano keys, the ivory of which, time has in places eroded.")

After Watching the Film: Journal-Writing and Other Activities

1. Read Whitman's descriptive poem, "Cavalry Crossing A Ford." This poem is like a "moving picture" or film of a scene. List the changes of points of view (camera angle and distance) within the film. How does Whitman shift us from one to the next? (**Note:**

Whitman puts in only one period at the end of the poem. However, you could put in five more periods. Where would they go?)

2. Pick one or two stanzas from "Song of Myself" that have long lines—this shouldn't be hard since most of them do. Read the stanzas aloud, paying attention to the length of the phrases. Now write the same passage out in lines of six to ten syllables. Read your new version aloud. What has been lost? Try to describe.

3. Turn to section 26 of "Song of Myself." Go through Whitman's catalogue and underline every element that is simply the name of a thing. Then go through the catalogue again. This time circle every element that involves some metaphoric comparison.

4. Jot down everything interesting you see, hear, taste, touch, or smell in 20 minutes. Next, make these observations into a list, using Whitman's lists as a model. Try to use some metaphoric comparison in your catalogue.

Guided Reading

First read sections 5 & 6 from "Song of Myself" printed below. Then answer the questions and do the activities for each section. Remember to keep referring to the poem as you consider each question. Our answers, not necessarily the only correct ones, are printed below them. After reading through these two sections, start at the beginning of the poem and read through it entirely. Keep asking yourself questions and answering them as you read. You may want to make note of these questions and answers in your journal to use later in completing the **Exercises and Assignments**.

5

I believe in you my soul, the other I am must not
    abase itself to you,
And you must not be abased to the other.

Loafe with me on the grass, loose the stop from
    your throat,
Not words, not music or rhyme I want, not custom
    or lecture, not even the best,   85
Only the lull I like, the hum of your valvèd voice.

I mind how once we lay such a transparent summer
    morning,
How you settled your head athwart my hips and
    gently turn'd over upon me,
And parted the shirt from my bosom-bone, and
    plunged your tongue to my bare-stript heart,
And reach'd till you felt my beard, and reach'd till
    you held my feet.   90

Swiftly arose and spread around me the peace and
    knowledge that pass all the argument of the
    earth,
And I know that the hand of God is the promise of
    my own,
And I know that the spirit of God is the brother of
    my own,
And that all the men ever born are also my brothers,
    and the women my sisters and lovers,
And that a kelson of the creation is love,   95
And limitless are leaves stiff or drooping in the fields,
And brown ants in the little wells beneath them,
And mossy scabs of the worm fence, heap'd stones,
    elder, mullein and poke-weed.

6

A child said *What is the grass?* fetching it to me with
    full hands;
How could I answer the child? I do not know what
    it is any more than he.   100

I guess it must be the flag of my disposition, out of
    hopeful green stuff woven.

Or I guess it is the handkerchief of the Lord,
A scented gift and remembrancer designedly dropt,
Bearing the owner's name someway in the corners,
    that we may see and remark, and say *Whose?*

Or I guess the grass is itself a child, the produced
    babe of the vegetation.   105

Or I guess it is a uniform hieroglyphic,
And it means, Sprouting alike in broad zones and
    narrow zones,
Growing among black folks as among white,
Kanuck, Tuckahoe, Congressman, Cuff, I give them
    the same, I receive them the same.

And now it seems to me the beautiful uncut hair
    of graves.   110

Tenderly will I use you curling grass,
It may be you transpire from the breasts of young
    men,
It may be if I had known them I would have loved
    them,

It may be you are from old people, or from
     offspring taken soon out of their mothers' laps,
And here you are the mothers' laps.   115

This grass is very dark to be from the white heads
     of old mothers,
Darker than the colorless beards of old men,
Dark to come from under the faint red roofs of
     mouths.

O I perceive after all so many uttering tongues,
And I perceive they do not come from the roofs of
     mouths for nothing.   120

I wish I could translate the hints about the dead
     young men and women,
And the hints about old men and mothers, and the
     offspring taken soon out of their laps.

What do you think has become of the young and
     old men?
And what do you think has become of the women
     and children?

They are alive and well somewhere,   125
The smallest sprout shows there is really no death,
And if ever there was it led forward life, and does
     not wait at the end to arrest it,
And ceas'd the moment life appear'd.

All goes onward and outward, nothing collapses,
And to die is different from what any one
     supposed, and luckier.   130

Section 5
Lines 80-82
    1. Who is the "other" Whitman refers to in line 80?

    2. How does Whitman's structure for these lines reinforce his point that the body and the soul are equals?

Answers
    1. The "other" in the poem refers to the body and the day-to-day life that centers around the body: eating, drinking, sleeping, working, playing, etc. The debate between body and soul has been a fixed convention in philosophy, religion, and literature since the medieval period. Generally the soul and the body were regarded as opposites and enemies, one good, one evil. But Whitman celebrates the joining of the two in a mystical union expressed in erotic imagery.

2. Whitman's repetition of key words ("Other," "must not abase," "I," "you") and inversion of sentence structure (Whitman inverts the phrase "I am the other" to "the other I am." In this way, "the other" appears at the beginning and end of the line.) show the contrast and balance of the body and soul.

Lines 83-86

1. Who is Whitman addressing in this stanza? The reader? The soul? Both?

2. How does the phrase "loose the stop from your throat" affect the way you read "the hum of your valvèd voice"? Give at least two connotations, that is, associations for "valvèd voice."

Answers

1. Whitman seems to be addressing the reader or a friend or a lover, but the possibility exists that he is at the same time addressing the soul. This "layering" works well since Whitman stresses that he and the reader share a common experience.

2. The word "stop" in this context conjures the image of an instrument with stops like an organ. "Valvèd" further adds to the image of an organ, a many-valved instrument. But "valvèd" also conjures the image of the heart. If we look back to "loose the stop from your throat," we get not only the image of the music of the voice about to pour out, but also the opening up of the heart.

Lines 87-90

1. In the first stanza, Whitman offers an affirmation; in the second stanza, Whitman issues an invitation. What does Whitman do in the third stanza?

Answer

1. In the third stanza, lines 87-90, Whitman recalls a memory of a time when no words were necessary, a time of perfect contentment. Whitman provides us with an illustration of the last line of the previous stanza; e.g., this is the kind of "lull" he likes.

Lines 91-98

1. Read line 91 aloud listening to the rhythm and the sound. How does the line reflect what it describes? (**Note:** The word "pass" in this line means "surpass.")

2. Look up the word "argument" in your dictionary. How many of its meanings does Whitman intend? Which do you think is the dominant meaning for this line?

3. Compare the diction Whitman uses in the previous stanza to the diction of lines 91-94. (**Hint:** List a few verbs and nouns from both.) How can you characterize the difference between the word choices?

4. Lines 92-98 all begin with the word "And." How does this repetition affect the speaker's tone?

5. Look at line 95. What does Whitman mean by "a kelson of the creation is love"?

6. How can Whitman talk about ants, stones and weeds after God, love, and brotherhood? Is he narrowing his vision or expanding on it?

Answers

1. The line begins swiftly with the accent on the first syllable then "spreads" through the use of the conjunctions and prepositions which connect the expansive abstract nouns "peace" and "knowledge," and through the openness of the alliteration of "all," "argument," and "earth."

2. The meaning of "argument" as a disagreement is the dominant one. But almost all of the other meanings are implied. For example, earth's "argument" or case may refer to what we learn from nature.

3. Some sample verbs and nouns from the previous stanza: "summer morning," "bosom-bone," "plunged," "reach'd," "tongue." Verbs and nouns from lines 91-94: "peace," "knowledge," "hand of God," "spirit of God," "spread," "arose." The words from the previous stanza are concrete; the words from the second stanza are abstract. The shift in diction signals a shift in the speaker's tone and stance from intimate to prophetic.

4. The repetition of the same word or phrase at the beginning of each line, in this case the word "And," is called anaphora. Whitman uses this repetition to recreate the tone and rhythm of an Old Testament prophet.

5. A "kelson" (also known as "keelson") is a nautical term for the timber or girder placed parallel with and bolted to the keel of the boat (the spine) for extra strength. Whitman is saying that love shores up or "girds" the creation.

6. Whitman does indeed go from the abstract and universal to the concrete and local. He points out that you can see these vaster meanings in everyday things, but that once you do, the things are still the same things you encountered before. What changes is the scope of your imagination or perception of everyday things and the depth of your appreciation.

Section 6
Lines 98-100

1. How do the first two lines of Section 6 pick up from Section 5?

2. Why does Whitman claim not to know what the grass is any more than the child does?

Answers

1. Section 6 picks up from the last words of Section 5: "heap'd stones, elder, mullein and poke-weed." Whitman begins with the seemingly mundane fact of "grass" and builds to his vision at the end of the section.

2. An adult's typical answer to a child's question "What is grass?" might be "grass is grass" or "grass is a plant" or "grass is what grows on the golf course." Whitman, like a child, finds these answers inadequate. Instead he lets his imagination explore the possibilities of meaning.

Lines 101-110

1. Whitman answers the child's question with four "guesses" in the form of

metaphors. List these metaphors and describe briefly how they answer the question "What is grass?"

2. In line 110, Whitman arrives at a fifth metaphor for "grass": "And now it seems to me the beautiful uncut hair of graves." Each of the previous metaphors has been prefaced by the words "I guess." What is the significance of Whitman's omitting "I guess" before this metaphor?

3. Read line 109 aloud. How does the alliteration of the line reflect its meaning. (**Note:** A "Kanuck" is a French Canadian. Whitman chose to use a "K" instead of a "C." A "Tuckahoe" is a colloquial term for a tidewater Virginian. And a "Cuff" is a black American.)

Answers

1. Whitman calls the grass metaphorically: 1) his disposition—implying that he is disposed to growing, to optimism, to sprouting up; 2) the Lord's monogrammed handkerchief—implying that the grass (and, indeed nature and our existence) is a reminder of God the Creator; 3) a child—implying that grass is the offspring of other grasses; 4) a hieroglyphic—implying that the grass is a symbol, sprouting as it does everywhere, of democracy and of equality.

2. The omission of "I guess" focuses our attention on this metaphor and gives it particular emphasis. Notice, too, that this line is set off by itself. This metaphoric definition of grass will be the dominant one for the rest of the section.

3. The alliterative hard "K" sounds of "Kanuck," "Tuckahoe," "Congressman," and "Cuff" make these different types of people equals. Whitman "gives them the same" recognition through giving them the same accent and sound. Notice also that the "K" sound has the crude, percussive sound of the body; it is the body which makes us equals.

Lines 111-118

1. How and why does Whitman link the grass to the four stages of human life?

Answer

1. The grass, "the uncut hair of graves," may come from the graves of "Offspring taken too soon out of their mothers' laps" or from "the breasts of young men" or from "old people" or from the "mothers' laps" themselves. Through these examples, Whitman recreates from the grass the entire cycle of life.

Lines 119-122

1. Why does Whitman describe the grass as "uttering tongues"?

2. What does "translate" mean in line 121?

Answers

1. The "uttering tongues" (resembling the grass itself) are the voices of the dead people, but this also alludes to the different "tongues" in which people speak, the different languages. The word "tongues" also connotes the mysterious language that some people use when in religious ecstasy. Whitman's perception of "uttering tongues" is his perception as a poet of the myriad voices he hears and puts into his poem.

2. Whitman, as the poet, wants to find a way to express the voices he hears. Much of Whitman's poetry is an attempt to "translate" the "hints" of "uttering tongues."

Lines 123–130

1. In the first two thirds of the section, Whitman describes the grass. How does his tone change at line 125?

2. How does "the smallest sprout show there is no death"?

3. In line 130, what do you make of Whitman's surprising word choice "luckier"?

Answers

1. At line 125, Whitman suddenly becomes didactic, that is, he makes statements as though they were accepted truth. Whitman's shift from the descriptive to the didactic is characteristic of his style. (Recall the shift in Section 5 from his storytelling to his prophetizing.)

2. Again Whitman points to the endless cycle of life. After we die, we return to dirt which eventually produces life.

3. Perhaps death is "luckier" than we imagine because it is, paradoxically, the first stage of new life—a kind of birth. Perhaps Whitman is also pointing to the accidental quality of death. We are never ready for it; it happens unexpectedly— like luck.

Further Question

1. Notice that Section 6 is made up of questions and answers beginning with the child's question "What is the grass?" followed by "Whose?" (handkerchief), followed by the paired questions of lines 124-25, "What do you think has become of the young and old men?/And what do you think has become of the women and children?" Why has Whitman chosen this structure for the section?

Answer

1. The question-and-answer structure works in more than one way to convey the meaning of the section. First, the question and answer format creates a tension in the poem. Secondly, it recreates for the reader the child's experience of exploring the world. Whitman does not want the reader to take his surroundings for granted. Like the child, the reader is encouraged to ask the simplest yet the most profound questions to get to an understanding of what it is to be alive.

Whitman, the poet, allows himself to examine the world with the same wondering innocence of a child examining the world for the first time.

Exercises and Assignments

1. Whitman's vision of a democratic society is obviously an ideal that has never been fully realized. What events of the last hundred years have been most damaging to this ideal? What events would Whitman have welcomed the most?

2. In "Song of Myself" Whitman was able to look on poverty, sorrow and degradation and still sing them as a larger affirmation of life. In the poem "As I Ebb'd with the Ocean of Life," he sticks with the viewpoint of the despairing person. Reread the poem. Then remember a time when you experienced depression or sorrow or confusion. How would you prefer to write about those times? From the inside or the outside? Choose one of your experiences and write about it either: 1. From the inside, in a mournful way, as Whitman does in "As I Ebb'd . . . " or 2. From the outside, in an affirmative way as Whitman does in "Song of Myself."

3. List the metaphoric comparisons you found in Section 26 of "Song of Myself." Write a brief paper explaining the significance of these metaphors.

4. In line 3 of "Out of the Cradle Endlessly Rocking," Whitman refers to "ninth-month midnight." "Nine-month" is the Quaker word for September. Give at least two reasons why Whitman chose "ninth-month" instead of "September."

5. Reread Section 5 of "When Lilacs Last in the Dooryard Bloom'd." How does the structure of this section imitate the movement of the train carrying Lincoln's coffin?

6. Read Section 23 of "Song of Myself" and then read "When I Heard the Learn'd Astronomer." Compare Whitman's views of science.

7. Whitman often spoke as an American magnified to heroic proportion, a personality representative of his America. Is there anyone occupying that role today? Whom do you consider a representative personality of America today? Whom does your chosen personality actually represent? (**Remember:** Few people in Whitman's time would have actually chosen him as their representative!)

8. Reread Sections 19 and 51 of "Song of Myself." Emerson once wrote, "A foolish consistency is the hobgoblin of little minds." Discuss these sections in light of this quote. How does Whitman feel about consistency?

9. Reread Section 2 of "Crossing Brooklyn Ferry." What is the resemblance (similitude) between the flood-tide and the ebb-tide and the people observing them?

10. In line 31 of "Out of the Cradle Endlessly Rocking," we see the word "translating." Look up "translate" in the dictionary. Which meaning is Whitman using? Explain.

11. In "Out of the Cradle Endlessly Rocking," to what is Whitman comparing a cradle that causes him to describe it as "endlessly rocking"?

12. In "When Lilacs Last in the Dooryard Bloom'd," Whitman presents an elegy on the death of Lincoln, a person whom he admired. Today, we have made Lincoln an

American folk hero. To what extent is this image like the one which Whitman presents of himself?

13. "When Lilacs Last in the Dooryard Bloom'd" is an elegy. Traditional elegies in poetry are pastoral in their treatment of death. Some of the characteristics of the pastoral elegy include:

- the making of the central figure into a rural character;
- the idea that the death of the figure is echoed by a sympathetic death of nature or a mourning by natural objects;
- a questioning of the justice of the death and its untimeliness;
- resolution in which there is a sympathetic rejuvenation of the natural objects.

Describe the features that appear in Whitman's poem. Could it be classified as a pastoral elegy?

14. In the film, Galway Kinnell points out that Whitman broke ground in using the "rude" Anglo-Saxon (Old English) word for the "elegant" Latin word. For example, notice Whitman's word choices in the following lines: "The blab of the pave" and "Rest the chuff of your hand on my hip." Go through Sections 20 and 33 (lines 822-846) and make a list of all the "rude" words. Check these words in your dictionary to see if they are Anglo-Saxon or Latin. Then make a list of words that you think Whitman would appreciate from recent slang and usage.

15. Whitman also broke ground by making the ordinary experiences and details of life and living into poetry. Find five examples of "unpoetic details" that Whitman has attempted to make poetic. How does Whitman transform these details into art? What sort of everyday "unpoetic" details could you use in a poem? Try writing a poem made up of these details.

Self Test (There is no Self Test for Whitman; see the Hart Crane unit Self Test.)

For Further Reading
Books by Walt Whitman

Leaves of Grass (a Norton Critical Edition). Blodgett, Harold W., and Bradley, Sculley, editors. New York: W.W. Norton; 1973.
Walt Whitman: Poetry and Prose. Kaplan, Justin, editor. New York: Library of America; 1982.

Books about Whitman

Allen, Gay Wilson. *A Reader's Guide to Walt Whitman.* New York: Farrar, Straus, and Giroux; 1970.
Jarrell, Randall. "Some Lines from Whitman." *Poetry and The Age.* New York: Ecco Press; 1980.
Kaplan, Justin. *Walt Whitman, A Life.* New York: Simon and Schuster; 1980.
Matthiessen, F.O. "Whitman." *American Renaissance.* New York: Oxford University Press; 1941.
Perlman, Jim; Folsom, Ed and Campion, Dan, editors. *Walt Whitman—The Measure of His Song.* Minneapolis: Holy Cow! Press; 1981.

Hart Crane (1899-1932)

Although Hart Crane published only two books in his lifetime, *White Buildings* (1926) and *The Bridge* (1930), he is regarded as one of the most important 20th-century American poets. His reputation rests primarily on his extraordinary craftsmanship and sweeping vision. In *The Bridge*, Crane set out, like Whitman, to write an American epic that unified past and present, East and West, myth and reality, in what he called a "mystical synthesis of America."

Crane, himself, had become something of a legendary figure. A reader of Rimbaud, Crane, perhaps following his injunction that "the poet should make himself a seer by the systematic disorientation of all the senses," viewed alcoholic and sexual excesses as a way to achieve a perception of the unity of all things. He believed his poetry should spring directly from ecstatic perception and recreate it for the reader. Eventually the behavior which produced ecstatic visions turned self-destructive, and Crane could no longer sustain his poetic vision.

Harold Hart Crane was born on July 21, 1899, in Garretsville, Ohio, a small town near the border of Pennsylvania. His father was a successful candy manufacturer (he invented the Life Saver) who wanted his only son and heir to become a businessman; his mother was a dominating woman who often made Crane her confidant concerning her problems in the marriage. Indeed, his parents' marriage was so strained that he spent most of his early childhood with his grandparents in Cleveland. In 1908, Crane's parents separated. A few months later they reconciled and lived unhappily together until their divorce in 1917. In the winter of 1916, Crane travelled with his mother to the Isle of Pines, south of Cuba, where his grandparents had a plantation. This journey gave him his first experience of the sea which was to become an important motif in his work.

Following his parents' divorce, Crane dropped out of high school. He managed to convince his parents to allow him to move to New York by telling them that he intended to study with tutors in preparation for enrollment in Columbia University. In fact, he had no real interest in attending college. He spent his time making literary contacts and trying to get his poems published. By the time he returned to Ohio, a year later, he had had some poems published and had become an associate editor of a small literary magazine, *The Pagan*. A few years of working at various jobs (among them an unsuccessful attempt to work for his father) convinced him to return to New York where he unknowingly moved into the room at 110 Columbia Heights, Brooklyn, from which Washington Roebling, the architect of the Brooklyn Bridge, had supervised its construction. In that room, Crane began to work on his epic poem *The Bridge*.

In 1924, Crane published his early attempt at a mystical vision of modern existence, "For The Marriage of Faustus and Helen," in *Secession*. He had begun this poem as a teenager in Cleveland. Further proof of his talent was the series of love poems called "Voyages" (*Little Review*, 1926), inspired by his relationship with a merchant marine, Emil Opffer. By the time *White Buildings* was published in 1926 to generally good reviews, Crane already had a reputation as a serious and gifted poet.

During this period, however, he had an unreconcilable argument with his mother and used an inheritance from his grandmother to spend some time abroad, mostly in France. Seven months later he returned to New York, and there finished *The Bridge* late in 1929. The publication of *The Bridge* (1930) was regarded as a major event in modern poetry, and it was extensively reviewed. Crane, himself, was not fully satisfied with the poem and was as aware of its faults as any of the critics. After the publication of the poem, he was not able to write. His drinking, always bad, became even worse and began to alienate his friends. He also found himself completely broke.

In 1931 he received a Guggenheim Fellowship, and friends urged him to go to Mexico. Following their advice, he made an attempt at an emotionally stable life and at a heterosexual relationship. But Crane felt he had lost his ability to write poetry, and while returning to New York on the *S.S. Orizaba*, he leaped overboard into the sea. He was 33.

The World of the Poems

The 1920s has been called the "Jazz Age," "the Machine Age," and the "Roaring '20s." Indeed it seemed that the American people underwent an extreme change of mood from the austerity of the war years to the hedonism of the 1920s. One example was the ratification of the Eighteenth Amendment (known as "Prohibition"), prohibiting the sale or transport of alcoholic beverages and the widespread defiance of this law. Illegal bars, called "speakeasies," sprang up in all of the major cities and the illegal sale of liquor, called "bootlegging," became big business. (In fact, the beginnings of organized crime can be traced to this period.)

Technological improvements and developments during the 1920s created a social revolution. First, the improvements in communication, such as rapid printing presses, typesetting devices, telephones, phonographs, radios, and silent motion pictures, had the effect of creating a more fragmented American culture. Second, the improvements in transportation made it easier to travel to remote parts of the country and made it seem smaller. People rode bicycles and trolleys. Automobiles and trucks were becoming more evident. Even airplanes, one of the most recent technological innovations, were occasionally spotted (to much excitement) in the skies. Third, electricity, generated by water power or coal burning plants, aided the mechanization of industry and made electrical lighting common in cities.

Other important developments included the Nineteenth Amendment allowing women the right to vote, and the popularization of jazz, a highly disciplined, yet improvisational form of music which created a sensation in New York City and other major cities in the country.

Hart Crane, writing during this period, had great faith in the technological progress of America—a faith that seems somewhat naive to us with our fears of nuclear holocaust and acid rains. Yet Crane was also sensitive to the alienation that technology could foster. Two of Crane's most important works, "For the Marriage of Faustus and Helen" and *The Bridge*, celebrate aspects of the machine age. As critic Alan Williamson says in his essay "Hart Crane": "He [Crane] saw a new vocabulary of spiritual heights and depths in the sensations of the machine age: the towers and bridges, the new sense of speed and space that had come with the airplane, the great violence of the factories and turbines, the beat of jazz."

As you watch the film, note the images of the 1920s that give you a sense of the excitement of the period. Later when you read the poems, you will see how these images inspired some of Crane's work.

Hart Crane: Ecstasy of the Imagination

In *Hart Crane: a Memoir*, critic and poet Malcolm Cowley describes Crane's search for the ecstatic moment from which he created his best poems:

> On Sunday afternoon, the third day of the party, Hart finally attained the state of exultation in which he was able to write, or put together, one of his more difficult poems . . . Hart went into his room, next to the big kitchen where we were telling stories, and for the next hour we could hear him pounding the typewriter while his phonograph . . . blared away at full volume. Sometimes the phonograph ran down, the pounding stopped, and Hart fell to declaiming what seemed to be lines of verse, although we couldn't hear the words through the closed door. At last the door opened. Hart came stamping out, his eyes blazing, with a dead cigar in one hand and two or three sheets of heavily corrected typescript in the other.
>
> "*Rread* that," he growled exultantly, like a jungle cat standing over its kill. "Isn't that the *grreatest* poem ever written?"

Crane, like the French Symbolists, used the imagination as an extension of reality. Through the imagination, he attained what he felt was an almost mystical vision of the unity of the entire world. To perceive this unity one had first to achieve a state of ecstasy where one could perceive, as Baudelaire did, a symbolic meaning in colors, sounds, smells. As a result, Crane's poetry takes place on "a heightened, often ecstatic plane, as if unable to tolerate the limitations of ordinary life."

Crane wants us to get beyond merely understanding the words. He wants us to experience the same exhilaration, the same ecstasy, the same vision of reality that he experienced in creating the poem. In his essay "General Aims and Theories," Crane explains his poetic intentions by contrasting what he calls "impressionist" poetry with his own "absolute" poetry. "Impressionist" poetry includes most of the work we are likely to come across in literary magazines. These poems rely on detailed description and, though they may contain subtleties, are fairly easy to understand after one reading. Crane's "absolute" poetry, however, is an attempt at registering a "truth." "Absolute" poetry conveys the "utmost spiritual consequences" of the poet's way of seeing the world; it conveys no less than an "apprehension of life."

What if you were asked "How do you feel?" at a moment when you were experiencing great joy. You would probably be at a loss for words because it's hard to analyze joy or happiness. These ecstatic moments are usually blurs of sensation.

Likewise, Crane's technical problem is how to find the language and form that express moments that cannot be expressed, moments that create a new reality. His answer is to treat language in a new way, or at least with a new emphasis. For example, instead of expecting words to stick to their dictionary definitions (their denotations), he allows them free range over their connotations, that is, all the meanings we associate with those words. Generally, when reading a poem, we consider the denotation of the words first, then the connotation. In Crane's work, we often need to find all the connotations of a word to understand it. The **Guided Reading** and exercises 3 and 4 in the **Exercises and Assignments** section will help you to further understand this aspect of Crane's poetry.

Another way in which he tries to convey those moments is through synesthesia, the perception or interpretation of one sense in terms of another. We often use synesthesia in our speech without even noticing it. Words like "sweet," "sour," "bitter" are all taste words, but we often apply them to how people sound or look: someone has a sweet face, a sour look, a bitter tone. (Similarly, think of some smell and sound words that we apply to things we like or dislike.) Crane's use of synesthesia is often more complex: "And Cortes, rode up, reining tautly in—/Firmly as coffee grips the taste—and away!" and ". . . but we have seen/The moon in lonely alleys make/A grail of laughter of an empty ash can." You will find more examples as you read.

Often to convey the complex reality of the imagination, Crane uses unusual modifiers such as: "chained bay waters," "circuit calm," "wine talons." Again, in reading these examples, you must allow yourself to explore various associations (and must have access to an unabridged dictionary). Crane saturated himself in language: words and phrases he overheard on the subway or on the streets, scientific words, Elizabethan words. He wanted to have them at his disposal when the ecstatic mood of creation was upon him. Many readers have commented that Crane's images are often so dense that even after they have read a poem a number of times, they cannot untie the knots. Aside from putting association and connotation first, Crane liked to imply ideas without actually stating them. For example, Crane uses the image "nimble blue plateaus" to describe the speed and altitude of an airplane. Crane later explained that the phrase "implies" the airplane by contrasting it with the "stationary elevated earth." When the going gets tough, remember that you can read Crane simply for the strange beauty of his compressed images.

Exercise: Crane talks in the film of spending his evenings "in music and in ecstasy." As we have discussed, Crane tried to express his ecstatic experiences and moments of expansive vision in his poems. People define ecstasy in many different ways. It may be a moment when you've achieved something very difficult—reached the top of a mountain or won a prize—a moment when the whole universe seems "right." Have you had any moments of ecstasy or sudden insight? Although expressing these experiences in words is difficult, trying it will help you understand what Crane is getting at in his poems. Take 30 minutes or so to record an experience of this kind.

Meet the Speakers

Derek Walcott is a Caribbean poet and playwright whose works include *The Star-Apple Kingdom, The Fortunate Traveller,* and *The Collected Poems.* His plays include the Obie-winning *Dream on Monkey Mountain* and *Pantomine.* Walcott was one of the first recipients of the prestigious MacArthur Fellowship. He currently teaches poetry and playwriting at Boston University.

Malcolm Cowley is an eminent critic who was also a close friend of Hart Crane. In important works such as *Exiles Return: A Literary Odyssey of the 1920s* and *A Second Flowering: Works and Days of the Lost Generation,* he provides rare close-up views of figures such as Ernest Hemingway, John Dos Passos, E. E. Cummings, F. Scott Fitzgerald, and William Faulkner.

Vivian Pemberton is an associate professor of English at Kent State University. Ms. Pemberton is currently editing a collection of Hart Crane's correspondence.

Richard Howard is a highly regarded poet who has also distinguished himself as a critic and translator. He has been honored by the French government for his translations of such writers as Claude Simon, Andre Breton, Alain Robbe-Grillet, Jean Genet, Andre

Gide, and Charles Baudelaire. Some of his major books of poetry include *Fellow Feelings*, *Two-Part Inventions*, and *Untitled Subjects*, for which he received a Pulitzer Prize.

Peggy Cowley was in the process of ending her marriage to Malcolm Cowley when she and Hart Crane began their love affair. Crane's affair with Ms. Cowley was one of the key events of the final year of Crane's life before his suicide in 1932.

Study Plan for This Unit

1. Complete the section **Before Watching the Film: Journal-Writing and Other Activities**.

2. Read the Crane poems, many of which are featured in the film. As we've mentioned previously, it's a good idea to read the poems or at least sections of the poems aloud. Remember: don't worry if you don't understand the poems completely. Crane's language is very dense—he uses compressed images, unusual juxtapositions of words, and allusions that are difficult to understand on first reading or even second reading. Crane packs a lot in. But you get a lot out of his work if you put the time and patience into opening up and understanding the poems.

Chaplinesque
Passage
For the Marriage of Faustus and Helen (Part I)
At Melville's Tomb
Voyages II
To Brooklyn Bridge (From *The Bridge*)
The Harbor Dawn (From *The Bridge*)
The River (From *The Bridge*)
Cutty Sark (From *The Bridge*)
O Carib Isle!
The Broken Tower

3. Watch the film.

4. Complete the section **After Watching the Film: Journal-Writing and Other Activities**.

5. Go through the **Guided Reading**.

6. Complete the **Exercises and Assignments** as specified by your instructor.

7. Take the **Self Test**.

Before Watching the Film: Journal-Writing and Other Activities

1. List anything you've read or seen recently in which the sea was an important symbol or image or setting. Then take note of the sea images in the film.

While Watching the Film

1. Jot down the images you see that make up the "Jazz Age."

2. Jot down any unusual or confusing images.

3. Watch the film clip of Charlie Chaplin very closely. In particular, watch his movements and gestures.

4. Note any vocabulary that isn't familiar to you.

After Viewing the Film: Journal-Writing and Other Activities

1. In the film, we see Crane's tower bedroom while we hear him say, "This place was the center and beginning of all I am and ever will be, the center of such pain as would tear me to pieces to tell you about." Crane's "pain" stemmed from his troubled childhood when he was torn between his parents. His tower room was an "elevating" and isolating place to which he could retreat to write. Did you have a place you used to escape to as a child or adolescent? Describe this place. Why did you go there? What were the things that bothered you then and caused you to seek refuge? Write in your journal about this place and time. Make this entry into a poem if you want to.

2. In the film you are bombarded with images of technology, nightclubs, traffic, trains, etc. These are images from "the Jazz Age"—the "Roaring '20s" of New York. Make a list of images that a filmmaker could use to convey the present day.

3. List all the images of the sea you remember from the film. In what ways was the sea important in Crane's work and life?

4. You can listen to the music of Crane's poems before you completely understand them. In the film, Derek Walcott, poet, points to line 4 of "Voyages II": "Her undinal vast belly moonward bends" as an example of how some of Crane's lines imitate the motion or shape of what he is talking about. Read the line aloud and then read aloud line 6. Then point out some of the features of the line that help to create the motion or shape: rhythm patterns, vowel patterns, the use of liquid consonants (l, r) as opposed to stop consonants (p, b, t, k, g).

Read through the rest of "Voyages II" to see if you can find other lines that contain similar shape and motion.

5. Read "The Harbor Dawn." Note how Crane uses sound to convey the setting and to give you a sense of mood and time. Crane conveys the scene mostly through what he imagines can be heard. Underline these sounds. Then try creating a list of sounds that convey a particular time, mood, or place. Describe a scene using sounds that suggest images.

6. Reread exercise 1 in the Whitman unit which asks you to compare Whitman's time to ours. Is Crane's America closer to Whitman's America or to ours? How?

Guided Reading

The following is the opening section of the book-length poem *The Bridge*. Read the entire section aloud before answering the questions.

Proem: To Brooklyn Bridge

How many dawns, chill from his rippling rest
The seagull's wings shall dip and pivot him,

Shedding white rings of tumult, building high
Over the chained bay waters Liberty—

Then, with inviolate curve, forsake our eyes   5
As apparitional as sails that cross
Some page of figures to be filed away;
—Till elevators drop us from our day . . .

I think of cinemas, panoramic sleights
With multitudes bent toward some flashing scene   10
Never disclosed, but hastened to again,
Foretold to other eyes on the same screen;

And Thee, across the harbor, silver-paced
As though the sun took step of thee, yet left
Some motion ever unspent in thy stride,—   15
Implicitly thy freedom staying thee!

Out of some subway scuttle, cell or loft
A bedlamite speeds to thy parapets,
Tilting there momently, shrill shirt ballooning,
A jest falls from the speechless caravan.   20

Down Wall, from girder into street noon leaks,
A rip-tooth of the sky's acetylene;
All afternoon the cloud-flown derricks turn . . .
Thy cables breathe the North Atlantic still.

And obscure as that heaven of the Jews,   25
Thy guerdon . . . Accolade thou dost bestow
Of anonymity time cannot raise:
Vibrant reprieve and pardon thou dost show.

O harp and altar, of the fury fused,
(How could mere toil align thy choiring strings!) 30
Terrific threshold of the prophet's pledge,
Prayer of pariah, and the lover's cry,—

Again the traffic lights that skim thy swift
Unfractioned idiom, immaculate sigh of stars,
Beading thy path—condense eternity: 35
And we have seen night lifted in thine arms.

Under thy shadow by the piers I waited;
Only in darkness is thy shadow clear.
The City's fiery parcels all undone,
Already snow submerges an iron year . . .   40

O Sleepless as the river under thee,
Vaulting the sea, the prairies' dreaming sod,
Unto us lowliest sometime sweep, descend
And of the curveship lend a myth to God.

Lines 1-4

1. Why does Crane describe the seagull's "rest" as "rippling"? What else do you usually associate with "rippling"?

2. Read the four lines aloud. How does Crane convey the sense of the seagull's ascending flight?

3. Note the use of "chained" and "Liberty" in line 4. What associations do these two words have?

Answers

1. When we read the line, we see the wind rippling the seagull's feathers, but we also see or sense the wind rippling the water below. Crane is a master of these "special effects." Without using simile or metaphor, he makes us think about and imagine these other images. Keep a lookout for more of these instances in the poem.

2. In the first line, the seagull is still at rest. At line 2, he takes off seeming to soar higher and higher between the pauses, until he is "building high" over the Statue of Liberty. The dash at the end of line 4 gives us the sensation of the seagull's gliding. You can almost watch the seagull take a dive between stanza 1 and 2 which begins with the abrupt "Then,."

3. "Chained bay waters" alludes to the Hudson and East rivers flowing together. "Liberty" in this line refers literally to the Statue of Liberty. Crane may be creating a paradoxical image here of Liberty in chains.

Lines 5-8

1. What is the seagull's movement in this stanza?

2. Where does Crane shift our point of view in this stanza?

3. How does the punctuation in line 8 imitate the meaning of the line?

4. Use the word "inviolate" in a sentence.

Answers

1. The seagull comes to another rest or glide on "Then," but with the brief pause supplied by the comma, the seagull picks up speed again and curves away and disappears.

2. Between lines 6 and 7, Crane shifts to an office worker's point of view. The office worker is distracted from his "page of figures to be filed away" by the scene outside his window.

3. The dash at the beginning of line 8 shifts us with the suddenness of an elevator dropping. Crane uses an ellipsis, the three dots which we use to glide over something

omitted, to give us the sensation of being ungrounded for a moment, the way we feel when an elevator drops suddenly. The ellipsis "drops" us suddenly from "our day."

Lines 9-12

1. Explain Crane's use of "sleights" in line 9.

2. Do you ever find yourself thinking that life is like a movie? If you do, describe what this feeling is like and when it's likely to occur. If you've never thought of life as a movie, try to explain why you think Crane is making this comparison. What does this comparison reveal about Crane's views about modern society?

Answers

1. "Sleights" in this line refers to the magician's "sleight of hand," that is, a trick. The movie appears real, but isn't.

2. Crane is saying that people caught up in modern society are dazzled by the images they see of reality and may be missing the truth. This image is like Plato's allegory of the Cave. In the allegory, Plato describes a cave in which people are chained before a screen placed in front of a fire. Behind the screen, people and objects are moving back and forth. The chained people, however, see only their shadows on the screen and therefore assume that what they're seeing is reality (not "shadow"). In Plato's view, only the people who leave the cave to discover the sun can be enlightened.

Lines 13-16

1. How and to what does Crane shift our attention in line 13?

2. Why does Crane refer to the Bridge as "Thee"?

3. We often call something "quick-paced" or "slow-paced." What effect does Crane achieve by calling the Bridge "silver-paced"?

4. Paraphrase line 14: "As though the sun took step of thee."

Answers

1. Crane shifts our attention to the Bridge by addressing it directly. It's as though we're watching a movie and the camera now swings to a panoramic shot of the Brooklyn Bridge.

2. The word "Thee" conveys Crane's reverent attitude toward the Bridge.

3. The word "silver-paced" captures at the same time the glint of the sun on the cables of the Bridge and the feeling of motion in the form of the Bridge. Again we have an example of Crane's ability to create special effects with words.

4. A possible paraphrase would go: "Although the sun passes over you, therefore leaving you behind, some measure of the sun's beauty is always seen in the Bridge." The Bridge is like a "stride" linking the two shores, but of course, is literally motionless.

Lines 17-20

1. Describe what scene is taking place in this stanza. Look up "bedlamite."

Answer

1. An insane person jumps off the Bridge.

Lines 21-24

1. What does "Wall" refer to in line 21? What is the pun on "Wall"?

2. Put line 21 in normal English word order.

3. How does Crane's word order for line 21 convey his meaning?

Answers

1. "Wall" refers to Wall Street, the financial district of New York City, which overlooks the Brooklyn Bridge. "Down Wall" is also a pun on the walls of the skyscrapers.

2. "Noon leaks down Wall from girder into street" is the normal word order.

3. In Crane's pattern, there is a sense of the noon light actually "leaking" down through the skyscrapers and tall buildings. Visually the line leaks down from the capitalized "Down Wall" (standing like two tall buildings) to "from" (still tall but not as tall as "Down Wall") to "girder into street noon leaks." Read the line aloud to get a sense of how the sentence also "leaks" down aurally.

Lines 25-29

1. Put "And obscure as that heaven of the Jews, Thy guerdon" in normal English word order. A "guerdon" is a reward.

2. Why is the "heaven of the Jews" considered "obscure"?

3. In line 27, how does Crane pun on the word "raise"?

4. What kind of character (or persona) does Crane give the Bridge by saying that it "bestows" "Accolades" and shows "reprieve" and "pardon"?

5. How many meanings of "accolade" apply here? Which are the dominant ones?

6. What is the tone of this stanza?

Answers

1. "Thy guerdon is as obscure as the Jews' heaven."

2. The Old Testament doesn't tell you much about heaven, but you know you want to go there. In the same way, the beauty of the Bridge leads you toward a spiritual goal without telling you much about it.

3. A homonym for "raise" is "raze," meaning to "tear down or demolish." In other words, "Time" cannot destroy the Bridge's accolade of "anonymity." The Bridge's obscure reward will not be better known in the future—it cannot be "raised" out of the water the way a sunken treasureship can be raised, nor can time destroy it.

4. Crane sees the Bridge as an omnipotent judge almost like God.

5. All of the meanings of "accolade" are present, but the dominant one seems to be "the ceremonial bestowal of knighthood."

6. Notice that Crane's level of diction, the kinds of words he chooses, is very formal. By this, he signals that he wants to present a grand subject in a grand tone.

Lines 29-32

1. What is Crane addressing in line 29?

2. Why does he call the Bridge a "harp and altar"?

3. What are the "choiring strings" in line 30?

4. What example has Crane already given us for how the Bridge is a threshold? Can you come up with other ways that the Bridge can be seen as a threshold?

Answers

1. In line 29, Crane addresses the Bridge using the rhetorical device of apostrophe. This is the device of speaking to an absent or dead person, or to an object or an abstraction, as though it were present, could hear and understand. It expresses an attitude more directly and vividly than if the object spoken to were merely spoken about.

2. The Bridge looks like a gothic cathedral from the front and a harp from the side. Crane celebrates the Bridge as an "altar" for the omnipotent spirit that he tries to build a bridge to in the poem. The psalms of this spirit play on the cables of the Bridge making it into a "harp." A harp is also a traditional symbol for song and poetry. Crane fuses sight and hearing and imagines the play of light on the cables as this spirit.

3. The "choiring strings" are the cables of the Bridge. In line 29, Crane refers to these cables as the "harp."

4. In stanza 5, the Bridge is a threshold to death for the suicide. In stanza 6, Crane points to the Bridge as a threshold to the sea and from the other direction to the land and the city. The Bridge may also be a threshold to our understanding of the spiritual in our secular, modern society.

Lines 33-36

1. Think of early evening. What is Crane describing in this stanza?

Answer

1. In this stanza, Crane describes the lights outlining the Bridge at night. These lights "beading" the Bridge become "eternal lights" to Crane's eyes. As night emerges, the true shape and meaning of the Bridge emerge.

Lines 37-40

1. Where is the speaker standing?

2. In line 39, what are the "fiery parcels"?

3. What is an "iron year"?

Answers

1. The speaker is standing beneath the Bridge.

2. The "City's fiery parcels" is a metaphor for the skyscrapers, the marquees, and the neon signs of the City. (Tourists used to visit New York just to see the advertising lights—something still new in those times.) "The fiery parcels undone" means that the lights have been turned off. "Parcels" connotes the materialist concerns of city dwellers.

3. An "iron year" implies that it was a hard year. But there are many other connotations.

Lines 41-44

1. Why does Crane describe the Bridge as "sleepless"?

2. What would be a synonym for "vaulting" here? Why didn't Crane use it?

3. Put lines 43-44 in normal English word order.

4. What is the "curveship"?

5. Why does God need a myth?

Answers

1. Crane emphasizes that the Bridge is omniscient like God who never sleeps. He also emphasizes the paradox of the Bridge which is motionless yet contains motion. "Sleepless" also refers to the speaker of the poem who now seems to be speaking in the deep of night.

2. Synonyms for "vaulting" are "cathedral-like" or "spanning." Again, Crane wants to emphasize the spiritual quality of the Bridge embodied in its upward motion and its energy.

3. O [Thou who are] sleepless as the river under thee, [and who are] vaulting the sea [and] the prairies' dreaming sod, sometime sweep [and] descend to us [who are] the lowliest, and lend a myth of the curveship to God.

4. The curve of the Bridge is its "curveship." This meaning carries a connotation of "lordship." The Bridge is also a "curved ship." And Crane also implies the meaning from physics that light follows a curve. Remember that earlier Crane celebrates the sunlight on the Bridge ("silver-paced, as though the sun took step of thee"), and the beauty of the light playing on the Bridge's cables which creates the "choiring strings." The light on the Bridge is a sign of the omniscient spirit Crane assigns to the Bridge.

5. "Lending a myth to God" is a way of reinvesting God with meaning in the modern world. As Alan Williamson says in his essay *Hart Crane*: "Crane prays to the Bridge to connect, in its 'sweep,' the 'lowliest' with the highest experience; and to generate a new, post-Christian religion—'lend a myth' to the wholly unknowable 'God.' "

Crane could at least claim a certain historical justification for using the Brooklyn Bridge in this way. The Bridge's designer, Washington Roebling, actually believed that he was creating a new kind of religious object for the machine age. The opening of the Bridge followed shortly after the completion of the transcontinental railroad, and was seen as a part of the same phenomenon: the technological linking together of the entire world which Whitman and Crane hoped would become a mystical linking to the spiritual realm.

Further Questions

1. How much time passes during the Proem? (A proem is a discourse or preamble.) Underline references to time.

2. Pick a stanza or two and describe the sequence of film shots you would use to film them. Describe what your point of view would be for each shot.

3. Why did Crane create so many shifting viewpoints in this section of the poem?

4. List the things to which the Bridge is compared and briefly explain each comparison.

Answers

1. As we read, the poem takes us through a single day in New York, from dawn to full morning to "street noon" to "all afternoon" to "traffic lights" to "darkness."

3. By covering the Bridge from all the angles (a foreshadowing of the exploration he undertakes in the rest of the poem), Crane fixes the Bridge as an object all by itself in space and time. The Bridge seems remote from the chaos of the City, aloof from our human worries, yet a constant and beautiful presence: a kind of threshold to a higher realm no matter which way you approach it.

4. The word "thee" is the first and most important comparison. Crane addresses the Bridge as if it were a spiritual being and then he personifies this Being in several ways. In stanza 4 he imagines it as someone striding over the water; in stanza 7, as a king or judge who praises, rewards, releases and forgives; in stanzas 8 and 9, as a spokesperson who speaks up for outcasts and lovers; and in stanza 9, as a modern madonna who cradles the whole scene in her overarching arms.

"Parapets" compares the Bridge to a castle or fortress. Since the Bridge is suspended over the river, it is more like a castle in the air.

"Caravan" compares the Bridge to a party of voyagers. Crane is perhaps thinking of the vehicles and pedestrians on the Bridge and trying to imagine an overriding unity of purpose or common goal to their separate errands.

The Bridge is compared to a "harp" because it looks like one from the side and because of the harp's associations with song and poetry and with heaven.

The Bridge is compared to an "altar" because from the front the bridge tower looks like the altar wall of a gothic cathedral and because Crane is using the Bridge to conduct his own sort of religious celebration.

"Thresholds" compares the archways of the Bridge to doorways looming into the future. Finally, "curveship" compares the curve of the Bridge's main horizontal cables to the arc of a spiritual journey from the present and things as they are to the future and things as they might be—or, perhaps even more mystically—from things as they seem to things as they are.

Exercises and Assignments

1. In *The Bridge* Crane chooses figures from folklore and history such as Christopher Columbus, Pocahontas, Rip Van Winkle, Walt Whitman and tramps to convey his vision of America. Make a list of figures from history and folklore that you would use in an epic poem about America. Explain your choices.

2. In the film, we see a film clip of Charlie Chaplin while we hear Crane's poem "Chaplinesque" being read. Crane admired Chaplin's comic technique and his ability to evoke feelings in his audience. Reread the poem and then consider the following questions and activities:

    a. What does the word "Chaplinesque" mean?

    b. Why does Crane use "we" throughout the poem?

    c. Crane tries to recreate Chaplin's movements and gestures in the language of the poem. Underline all the details in the poem that make you picture Chaplin.

    d. Then underline the places in the poem where the line imitates Chaplin's movement. **Note:** If you can, play back the film-clip sequence. Look closely at Chaplin's famous walk, and his gestures such as the cane twirling.

3. Read "At Melville's Tomb," one of Crane's most densely-packed poems. In a number of letters, Crane actually explained some of the images in this poem.

Here's a sample of how important it is to use whatever clues you can find to open up the poem. The following are lines 6-8 of "At Melville's Tomb":

> The calyx of death's bounty giving back
> A scattered chapter, livid hieroglyph,
> The portent wound in corridors of shells.

Note: A calyx is the outermost protective covering of a flower, consisting of a series of leaflike, usually green segments called sepals. Crane's explanation goes like this:

> "This calyx refers in a double ironic sense both to a cornucopia and the vortex made by a sinking vessel. As soon as the water has closed over a ship, this whirlpool sends up broken spars, wreckage, etc., which can be alluded to as *livid hieroglyphs*, making a *scattered chapter* so far as any complete record of the recent ship and crew is concerned. In fact, about as much definite knowledge might come from all this as anyone might gain from the roar of his own veins, which is easily heard (haven't you ever done it?) by holding a shell close to one's ear."

From reading Crane's explanation, we learn a lot about the way his mind and creative vision work. First, we realize how compressed his poetic expression is. After reading his explanation, you might have said to yourself, "you mean he meant all that"? Answer the following questions:

    a. What does Crane mean when he says you can learn as much about a ship from listening to the roar of your veins as you can by seeing the wreckage that bobs up after a shipwreck?

    b. What does the sound of the blood roaring in your veins tell you?

    c. Now reread the poem. How does Crane's comment change your reading of the poem?

    d. Crane's language is very dense. Often a single word contains multiple meanings and may be functioning both as a noun and as a verb. Look up the unfamiliar nouns and verbs in this poem. How many meanings and usages can you uncover?

    e. Melville's actual tomb, a stone with a scroll left blank, is at Woodlawn Cemetery in the Bronx. The wordlessness may be deliberate, may not be. Does this have any bearing on Crane's poem?

4. Read "Voyages II." Crane mentions in a letter about this poem that the word "adagios" "ushers in the whole world of music." Look up "adagio" in the dictionary. How does this word bring music into the poem? What does it add to your reading of the poem?

5. Read the poem "O Carib Isle!" Go back and underline all the words of motion in the first stanza. How else does Crane create movement in this stanza aside from using words of motion?

6. In the epic poem *The Bridge*, Crane often juxtaposed memories of scenes from his life with historical and other material. For example in the "[Rip] Van Winkle" section:

> So memory, that strikes a rhyme out of a box,
> Or splits a random smell of flowers through glass—
> Is it the whip stripped from the lilac tree
> One day in spring my father took to me,
> Or is it the Sabbatical, unconscious smile
> My mother almost brought me once from church
> And once only, as I recall—?
>
> It flickered through the snow screen, blindly
> It forsook her at the doorway, it was gone
> Before I had left the window. It
> Did not return with the kiss in the hall.

Try to recall images of your mother and father that have stayed with you from childhood. You may have images of a time when you felt angry with your parents or misunderstood by them. You may have images of a particularly joyous time. Jot down one or two images for each parent. Create a short poem or stanza using at least one of these images.

7. Read "The River." Crane creates a montage of billboard slogans to convey the speed of the train and the spirit of the time. Listen to TV commercials for about 15 minutes. Jot down any memorable phrases. Then write a collage poem from these TV commercial fragments. What do these fragments say about our times?

8. In the "Cape Hattaras" section of *The Bridge*, Crane addresses Walt Whitman: "Walt, tell me, Walt Whitman, if infinity/Be still the same as when you walked the beach/Near Paumanok—." Write Whitman's reply.

9. Read "My Grandmother's Love Letters." Now imagine you are leading one of your grandmothers (or grandfathers) "by the hand." What kinds of things about your life do you think she wouldn't understand? What kinds of things would she understand? Did she write love letters once?
Write a prose piece or poem in which you reveal some of the things your grandmother does and/or doesn't understand.

10. Read "The Broken Tower." Then make one list of the words connected to religion. Make a second list of words connected to music, and a third list of words connected to sky. What cross references do you see?

Self Test
Read the following poems and decide which one was written by Whitman and which one was written by Crane. Explain your choices.

I Saw in Louisiana a Live-Oak Growing

I saw in Louisiana a live-oak growing,
All alone stood it and the moss hung down from
    the branches,
Without any companion it grew there uttering joyous
    leaves of dark green,
And its look, rude, unbending, lusty, made me think
    of myself,
But I wonder'd how it could utter joyous leaves standing
    alone there without its friend near, for I knew I
    could not,
And I broke off a twig with a certain number of leaves
    upon it, and twined around it a little moss,
And brought it away, and I have placed it in sight in
    my room,
It is not needed to remind me as of my own dear friends,
(For I believe lately I think of little else than of them,)
  Yet it remains to me a curious token, it makes me think of
    manly love;

For all that, and though the live-oak glistens there in
    Louisiana solitary in a wide flat space,
Uttering joyous leaves all its life without a friend a
    lover near,
I know very well I could not.

Royal Palm

Green rustlings, more-than-regal charities
Drift coolly from that tower of whispered light.
Amid the noontide's blazed asperities
I watched the sun's most gracious anchorite

Climb up as by communings, year on year
Uneaten of the earth or aught earth holds,
And the grey trunk, that's elephantine, rear
Its frondings sighing in aetherial folds.

Forever fruitless, and beyond that yield
Of sweat the jungle presses with hot love
And tendril till our deathward breath is sealed—
It grazes the horizons, launched above

Mortality—ascending emerald-bright,
A fountain at salute, a crown in view—
Unshackled, casual of its azured height
As though it soared suchwise through heaven too.

Answers to Self Test

Answers to Self Tests begin on page 226.

For Further Reading

Books by Hart Crane

The Complete Poems and Selected Letters and Prose of Hart Crane. Weber, Brom, editor. New York:
Liveright; 1966.

The Letters of Hart Crane, 1916-1932. Weber, Brom, editor. Berkeley and Los Angeles:
University of California Press; 1965.

Books about Crane

Brown, Susan Jenkins. *Robber Rocks: Letters and Memories of Hart Crane, 1923-1932.*
Middletown, Ct.: Wesleyan University Press; 1969.

Cowley, Malcolm. "Hart Crane." *A Second Flowering: Works and Days of the Lost Generation.*
New York: Penguin; 1980.

Leibowitz, Herbert A. *Hart Crane: An Introduction to the Poetry.* New York and London: Columbia University Press; 1968.

Lewis, R.W.B. *The Poetry of Hart Crane: A Critical Study.* Princeton: Princeton University Press; 1987.

Trachtenberg, Alan. *Hart Crane: A Collection of Critical Essays.* Englewood Cliffs, NJ: Prentice-Hall; 1982.

Unterecker, John. *Voyager: A Life of Hart Crane.* New York: Farrar Straus and Giroux; 1969.

Williamson, Alan. "Hart Crane." *Voices & Visions: The Poet in America.* Vendler, Helen, editor. New York: Random House; 1987.

William Carlos Williams (1883-1963)

In 1907, when most of his fellow poets were exploring Europe, the 24-year-old William Carlos Williams was an intern at the Nursery and Children's Hospital in New York's Hell's Kitchen, a neighborhood best known for its dangerous criminals and drug addicts. There he "delivered some three hundred babies and faced every sort of complication that could be thought of." Williams was deeply impressed by the courageous young women who gave birth to healthy babies amidst squalor and degradation, and this experience—along with his scientific background and his appreciation of the "newness" of America—was to lead him in a very different direction from his contemporaries.

Williams was born in 1883 in Rutherford, New Jersey. His father had emigrated from England and his mother from Puerto Rico. He would spend nearly all of his adult life in Rutherford, in a house just a few miles from the one in which he grew up. At 14, Williams spent a year in Switzerland, followed by several years at the prestigious Horace Mann School in New York City, where he studied science. In 1902, he passed a special examination allowing him to enroll directly in the University of Pennsylvania Medical School. Here he met several poets who would be among the most influential of the day, including Hilda Doolittle (H. D.) and Ezra Pound. Pound was to remain a lifelong friend and advisor although Williams was as often to react against his advice as to take it.

As a poet, Williams was not an early success. His first volume, the privately printed *Poems* (1909), was a mannered imitation of Keats' sonnets, and his second book—*Tempers*, published in 1913 with Pound's help—was not more markedly original. Williams was already a married man with a private practice as a general practitioner and pediatrician in Rutherford. The poems that he then began to publish in Alfred Kreymborg's *Others* (where the works of Pound, Eliot, Amy Lowell, Marianne Moore and others also appeared) were different from anything he had done before, and by the time *Al Que Quiere* appeared in 1917, Williams had found his voice.

It was an original and truly American voice. For many other writers of Williams' day, America was a constraining force, Europe a place of liberation. Gertrude Stein summed up the pervading view with the statement: "You can't write in your parents' house." Williams' response was that you can't run away from your own life. It was not that he was anti-Europe: he had spent that formative year in Switzerland, a year as a doctor in Leipzig in 1909 (where he read German poets in the original), and in the 1920s he made several trips to Paris, where he met and made friends with such writers as Joyce, Hemingway, and Gertrude Stein and artists such as the sculptor Brancusi. But Williams was comfortable with the newness of America and with the technological advances that were changing everyday life: note the use of the car as an image in many of his poems, including: "The Young Housewife" and "To Elsie." He felt that American poetry should reflect the vitality of American speech and American life, not look backwards to the classics and to the literature of another country.

Williams' output is steady from 1917 on: *Kora in Hell* in 1920, *Sour Grapes* in 1921, *The Great American Novel* and *Spring and All* in 1923, followed by a new book every year or two afterwards, until his death in 1963. During much of this time Williams had a full-time medical practice and was liable to be called out to a patient at any hour of the day or night. Despite this prodigious output and awards from *Poetry* magazine and *The Dial*, Williams' reputation was slow in growing, and he did not really receive his due until the 1940s when he achieved widespread recognition with the publication of his American epic, *Paterson*. In later life, he received the Russell Loines Memorial Award, a National

Book Award, and a Bollingen Prize, and was appointed Poetry Consultant to the Library of Congress, a post he was prevented from taking because of irresponsible political charges that attacked his friendship with Ezra Pound and his own liberal activities in the 1930s. Today, Williams is recognized for the great contribution he made to helping create an indigenous American poetry, for his memorable poems, and for his lasting influence on younger American poets.

The World of the Poems

Like many of the other poets, Williams was born into an age when technological and scientific achievement caused changes in the way people perceived the world. The widespread availability of the car, the telephone, and later the radio, changed the very concept of distance and, consequently, of time. Williams was comfortable with the new technology and saw the possibilities of using it in his own work; he was one of the first poets to take advantage of the typewriter (a machine that only began to be mass-produced in 1879) to work and rework his poems visually. Williams' metaphor for the creation of a poem is borrowed from a technological age: "A poem is a machine made of words."

Williams read a great deal of poetry and corresponded with many poets. His work was affected both by what was going on in poetry and by his other interests and by aspects of his daily life as a suburban doctor.

Williams had wanted to be a painter in his early life, and he kept up with the developments in art, attending exhibitions, reading the influential art journals of the day—such as photographer and gallery owner Alfred Stieglitz's *Camera Work*—and meeting artists through his friendship with Stieglitz and other influential artists. The early 1900s saw a change in the concept of art and a great flowering of talent with the Cubist and Dadaist movements. For the first time, art was referring to itself as art—becoming self-conscious, not simply reflecting life but viewing art itself as a thing made. Paintings and sculpture were no longer "representations" of reality or depictions of scenes from the Bible or from classical antiquity. Instead, there were paintings in which eyes, ears and noses might exist on the same plane; everyday objects—such as the ceramic urinal in Duchamp's "Fountain"—were taken out of context, and transformed into art objects.

Williams had seen Duchamp's work, and he was familiar with the works of Picasso, Gris, Picabia, Braque, and Cezanne. He sought to do in his poems what these artists were doing with their paintings and sculpture, to lift "to the imagination those things that lie under the direct scrutiny of the senses, close to the nose." He used the theories that arose out of painting in his poetry—isolating words to transform them into art objects, and using "found objects" (letters, snatches of conversation) in his poems. He also set out to recreate the experience of viewing a painting in his later poems about the pictures of the 16th century Flemish painter Brueghel.

Scientific thought at this time was also changing the view of "reality." Einstein's and Heisenberg's theories mirrored the "simultaneity" of Cubist painting, in which time and space are no longer the fixed quantities that our sense had been trained to tell us they were. This sense of simultaneity can be seen in many Williams poems—including "Perpetuum Mobile" and "Young Love"—and he paid direct tribute to the world of nuclear science in his "St. Francis Einstein of the Daffodils" and by focusing on Madame Curie's discovery of radium in the third and fourth books of *Paterson*.

Williams' greatest influence was his medicine. He often said that poetry and medicine "amount for me to nearly the same thing." As a family doctor, Williams was present at the most intimate moments of people's lives. He treated people from all social classes, working in the rough working-class district called "Guinea Hill," where he saw the extreme misery of the poor during the Great Depression of the early thirties. He developed not only a great sense of compassion and empathy for his patients, but also realized how life was an ever present state of renewal, even amidst the direst poverty. Dr. Williams was too busy for sentimentality, but he came to feel a constant sense of wonder at life's exuberance, at its ability to blossom in the rubble. Williams wrote: "the saxifrage is my flower." The saxifrage is a flower that breaks through rock, finding a foothold for its blossoms in the most barren spaces. It is an appropriate emblem for Williams, who found beauty even in a shard of broken glass behind a hospital ("Between Walls").

William Carlos Williams: Poet of the Everyday

Williams' language often puzzles first-time readers of his poetry, for it does not have the elevated sound of, say, Keats or Wordsworth but seems closer to the kind of speech we hear every day. As the critic A. Walton Litz points out, Williams felt that the source of literature is ordinary speech and the poet must keep in direct contact with this source if his work is not to degenerate into dead stereotypes. In "January Morning," for instance, Williams writes:

> Well, you know how
> the young girls run giggling
> on Park Avenue after dark
> when they ought to be home in bed?
> Well,
> that's the way it is with me somehow.

(**Note**: Park Avenue was the street in Rutherford, not in New York.)

Although this excerpt can be read as two prose sentences, the lines are more than mere reporting of something someone might say. Notice the rhythmic quality of the language and how the line breaks isolate particular words. What Williams has done—in his own response to Pound's injunction to compose in the sequence of the musical phrase—is to capture the music of speech, to draw attention to the musicality of everyday language in much the same way as Duchamp draws attention to the artfulness of commercial objects.

Williams sought to build his poems solely from the material that was available to him in daily life, to avoid the abstract ideas, classical allusions, and extended metaphors from the past that comprise much of the technique of his contemporaries, Ezra Pound and T.S. Eliot. When Williams wrote "No ideas but in things," he was suggesting an alternative to cerebral intellectuality. He believed that the poet should stick to the material at hand and celebrate the mundane events surrounding him—crowds at a baseball game, a note pinned to the refrigerator, an old woman eating plums—for they have their own hidden beauty or truth. Williams celebrated the "life forces" in man and nature, and the themes that serve as the substructure for his longer poems are those of death and renewal (often symbolized by the spring) and of the sensual desires of men and women.

Williams recognized that there is no single "common" language, so we hear many different voices in his poems: old women, young housewives, workmen, newspaper reporters, educated and uneducated people, along with the voice of the doctor/poet himself. *Paterson*, in particular, uses a variety of voices to paint simultaneously a grand picture from many different perspectives.

While Williams uses commonplace phrases and subjects, his purpose is to make us look at words as if they are brand new, seen for the very first time. His surprising line breaks and the way he places words on the page make us look at them as words, as wonderful objects imbued with meaning. What Williams wanted to achieve is symbolized by the library fire in *Paterson*:

> An old bottle, mauled by the fire
> gets a new glaze, the glass warped
> to a new distinction, reclaiming the
> undefined.

Exercise: Read aloud the short poems "The Locust Tree in Flower," "Between Walls," and "The Red Wheelbarrow." Pay particular attention to the line breaks. How do they affect the way you read the poem? How does the form of poem on the page affect your reading of the poem?

Meet the Speakers

Marjorie Perloff, professor of English and Comparative Literature at Stanford University, has published several works on modern poetry. Her books range in subject from *Dance of the Intellect: Studies in the Pound Tradition* to *Frank O'Hara: Poet Among Painters*.

Hugh Kenner, Andrew W. Mellon Professor of the Humanities at Johns Hopkins University, is also a prolific critic and scholar. Kenner's keen interest in Williams can be seen in *Gnomon: Essays On Contemporary Literature* in which he assigns Williams an important place in the American literary tradition.

Allen Ginsberg first approached William Carlos Williams through a letter which Williams later used in his poem *Paterson*. Williams continued to be an influence on Ginsberg throughout his life and poetic career, from the days of the Beat Generation up to his projects at the Naropa Institute in Boulder, Colorado. Ginsberg's own books include: *Howl*, *Kaddish*, and *Mind Breaths*.

James Laughlin is the founder and director of New Directions, 98 ablishing house known for its support of experimental writers including William Carlos Williams. (For further information see **Meet the Speakers** in the chapter on Pound.)

Robert Coles was a personal friend of William Carlos Williams, and like him, is both a medical doctor and a writer. He has worked extensively with migrant workers in the South and studied race relations there. Among his many books is *Children of Crisis, Volumes 1-5*, in which he offers an analysis of racism from a psychoanalytic perspective.

Dr. William Eric Williams is the younger of William Carlos Williams' two sons. Like his father, he practices medicine as a pediatrician and family doctor in Rutherford, New Jersey.

Dickran Tashjian is the author of *William Carlos Williams and the American Scene, 1920-1940* in which he discusses the exchanges and interplay between Williams and the painters, sculptors, and photographers of the American avant-garde.

Study Plan for This Unit

1. Complete the section **Before Watching the Film: Journal-Writing and Other Activities**.

2. Read the following Williams poems, many of which are featured in the film. Read some of the shorter poems aloud. Pay particular attention to where Williams breaks the lines and creates new stanzas. Don't worry if you don't understand the poems on first reading. Relax and enjoy the music of them.

Queen Anne's Lace
Perpetuum Mobile: The City
The Young Housewife
Complaint
Danse Russe
Waiting
The Locust Tree in Flower
The Great Figure
Spring and All
Love Song
This Is Just to Say
Between Walls
To Elsie
Asphodel, That Greeny Flower
Young Love
The Delineaments of the Giants (Excerpts from *Paterson*)
The Red Wheelbarrow
A Sort of Song
The Wind Increases
At the Ball Game

3. Watch the program.

4. Complete the section **After Watching the Film: Journal-Writing and Other Activities**.

5. Go through the **Guided Reading**.

6. Complete the **Exercises and Assignments** as specified by your instructor.

7. Take the **Self Test**.

Before Watching the Film: Journal-Writing and Other Activities

1. Williams was greatly influenced by the modern painters of his day such as Gris, Braque, and Picasso. These were all painters who decided that the traditional forms were no longer important, that the purpose of art was to create more than what a camera sees. Read "The Great Figure" and then sketch, paint or create a collage which illustrates the poem. In the film, you will see a painting by Charles Demuth and an animated sequence based on this poem.

2. After reading through the list of poems, fill half a page of your journal with adjectives describing Williams' poems. Do any of these adjectives describe other poets you've read so far? Who? How are they different?

3. Write your response to the phrase, "No ideas but in things."

4. Write your response to the statement, "You can make a poem out of anything."

While Watching the Film

1. The poet Randall Jarrell once commented, "You've never heard a Williams poem until you've heard him read it." Several of the readings in the film are recordings of Williams reading his own work. Take notes on what you hear when Williams is reading.
   Note: The poem "Young Love," although read by the poet Allen Ginsberg, is by Williams. How does Ginsberg's style of reading contrast with Williams'?

2. While watching the film, jot down images of Williams as family man and doctor, and images that reveal his inner life as a poet. Make two lists.

After Watching the Film: Journal-Writing and Other Activities

1. Quickly write down your impressions of Williams as a person and as an artist. In a few days, come back to this entry and write comments on what you've written.

2. Read Williams' poem, "A Sort of Song." Then go back to the entries you made before watching the film and make comments. In particular, respond again to "No ideas but in things," and "You can make a poem out of anything."

3. In the film, it is mentioned that Williams' use of a typewriter affected the way he wrote poems. Specifically, it allowed him to see the form of the poem on the page and to treat the poem as an object of art. Try composing a poem using a typewriter or computer. Use the typography to create a visual effect on the page.

4. The following are brief excerpts from a journal Williams kept in 1908.

Birds observed, wild in & about R.fd.

May 9—The wrens changed houses and are now building in the house over door of shop.

May 10—Screech owl in edge of Kipp's woods. Chased me, darting at my head and making two clicking sounds each time. Once it made a sound between a neigh of a horse and squeak of a rat. 10 p.m.

Vegetation in yard, Observ. concern.

May 8—Mulberry tree not yet in full leaf. Certainly a dainty light tree. Reminds me of Bottcelli. Lilacs in full bloom.

May 9—Planted 6 eggplants.
" " "—small white birch tree which found in street uprooted.

For the next two days, record observations of birds and plants (even if you don't have a garden) in this journal. Write a poem based on these observations.

Guided Reading

"Spring and All" ("By the road to the contagious hospital") is a poem from Williams' *Spring and All* (1923) which many consider one of his best works. The book consists of poems interspersed with prose. None of the poems originally had titles. But when some of these poems were later collected, titles were added. Another famous poem from *Spring and All* is "The Red Wheelbarrow."

The poems in *Spring and All* stand on their own. However, it would be worthwhile looking up *Spring and All* and reexamining the poems in their original context. In fact, you may consider writing on the difference between reading a poem from *Spring and All* in and out of its original context. *Spring and All* is available in *Imaginations* and the recently-published *Collected Poems of William Carlos Williams, Volume One*, both from New Directions.

Read "Spring and All" aloud before answering the following questions. Remember that the answers to the questions are one person's interpretation.

Spring and All

By the road to the contagious hospital   1
under the surge of the blue
mottled clouds driven from the
northeast—a cold wind. Beyond, the
waste of broad muddy fields   5
brown with dried weeds, standing and fallen

patches of standing water
the scattering of tall trees

All along the road the reddish
purplish, forked, upstanding, twiggy   10
stuff of bushes and small trees
with dead, brown leaves under them
leafless vines—

Lifeless in appearance, sluggish
dazed spring approaches—   15

They enter the new world naked,
cold, uncertain of all
save that they enter. All about them
the cold, familiar wind—

Now the grass, tomorrow   20
the stiff curl of wildcarrot leaf
One by one objects are defined—
It quickens: clarity, outline of leaf

But now the stark dignity of
entrance—Still, the profound change   25
has come upon them: rooted, they
grip down and begin to awaken

Lines 1-6

1. What is a "contagious hospital" and what connotations does the term have that are picked up later in the poem?

2. Williams writes in cadenced verse which allows him to contract or expand his lines at will and to break them off at any point. Read the first stanza aloud, noting the line breaks. Which lines break at a grammatical (conventional) pause? Which do not? What effect does Williams achieve by these line breaks?

3. What season do you think the poem takes place in? Give evidence from the first stanza.

Answers

1. A "contagious hospital" is a hospital for contagious diseases. There is also a sense that the hospital is itself contagious. Hospitals convey an image of sterility, but they are also places of sickness and decay. Here, by the road to the hospital, a germ of life is beginning again. Hospitals are also places where people are born, and where people die. The hospital is a place where the life cycle can be witnessed, just as the natural cycle can be witnessed here by the side of the road.

2. Line 1 breaks at a conventional grammatical pause, the pause that occurs at the end of a dependent clause. The remaining lines are enjambed, that is, the line breaks without a pause created by punctuation or syntax. However, the line break at line 2 is not a smooth break. The awkwardness forces us to look closely at the word "blue" to decide if it is a noun ("out of the blue") or an adjective. Sometimes the poet uses awkward line breaks on purpose to force us to make these decisions. Sometimes the emphasis is purposely ambiguous. Lines 3 and 4 break choppily, but there is no ambiguity as to what the word "the" belongs to. In line 5, the break causes us to dwell for a moment on the "muddy fields."

Notice, however, that Williams does not stop the spill of lines with a period until line 18. By allowing the lines to more or less flow, he creates a rhythm for the "sluggish" approach of spring.

3. The poem seems to take place in the transitional season between winter and spring. Williams describes the clouds as surging and "driven from the northeast" by a "cold wind"—signs of winter. Yet, in the background, the fields are "muddy" usually a sign that the frozen ground is melting. Notice, too, that the word "spring" doesn't appear until the fourth stanza. The transition between winter and spring actually takes place during the course of the poem.

Lines 7-8

1. Why does Williams isolate these two lines to form a stanza? How does the visual impact of this stanza reinforce its content?

2. In line 7, what connotations does "standing water" have?

Answers

1. Like the intermittent puddles of water on the fields and the clumps of trees, the stanza itself creates a small "patch," a small break, a melting spot.

2. "Standing water" may be stagnant water or it may be pond water that spawns vegetation. In the previous line, "standing" describes the weeds that show just a bit more life than the "fallen" weeds. Later in line 10, the bushes and trees are "upstanding." The dual quality of the word "standing" perfectly suits Williams' observations in the poem that life (spring) comes out of death (winter).

Lines 9-13

1. What is the significance of the adjectives "reddish," "purplish" and "twiggy"?

2. How does Williams direct our eye in this stanza? What is the significance of this movement?

Answers

1. The indefiniteness, the fuzziness of the adjectives "reddish," "purplish," and "twiggy" convey the transitional quality of the season. The bushes and trees have not quite yet blossomed or been reborn.

2. We begin "along the road" eye-level with the bushes and trees. The line break at line 11 shifts us to a lower level, ground level where everything still looks dead. Williams points out that the awakening begins at the roots, deep in the ground, but the signs of life appear above ground. We are deceived into thinking that life takes place only above ground. He is training us to look more closely, to look beyond mere appearances.

Lines 14-15

1. To what is spring being compared in lines 14 and 15?

Answer

1. Williams compares spring to a drugged person, recalling the "contagious hospital" of line 1.

Lines 16-19

1. What or who does "They" refer to in line 16?

2. Williams repeats the words "cold" and "all" in this stanza. What effect do these repetitions create?

3. Why does Williams choose the word "familiar" to describe the wind?

Answers

1. "They" may refer to babies (we think of the hospital), or it may refer to the natural objects of the landscape: the vines, the bushes, the trees, the weeds, etc. Williams

102

creates ambiguity so that we may superimpose our human experience onto the natural world and vice versa.

2. The word "cold" emphasizes the inhospitable environment that the plants or babies are born into—whether that be the "cold wind" of early spring or the cold hospital room.

Say the word "all" aloud. The vowel sound forces you to open your mouth wide, like a baby's mouth shaping a scream and thus clearing its lungs to breathe. The word "all" looked at by itself implies the whole world.

3. Through the use of "familiar" Williams stresses that birth is part of a "familiar" cycle both in the natural world and in the human world. Williams reminds the reader that he knows the "cold wind." The use of "familiar" meaning "intimate" places emphasis on the vulnerability of the baby or plant.

Lines 20-23

1. How do lines 22 and 23 explain lines 20 and 21?

2. Read lines 22 and 23 aloud. How does the rhythm reinforce the sense of spring approaching?

3. What does "It" refer to?

4. Look up another meaning for "quicken" that enhances the poem.

Answers

1. Lines 20 and 21 provide the details of the emerging spring. "Now" we notice the grass (remember that in the first stanza the fields were still muddy), and the "wildcarrot leaf." Up to now the details have been fuzzy, "reddish/purplish. . .twiggy" bushes and trees. But as spring comes, identity is renewed. In lines 22 and 23, Williams instructs us in how to "read" the spring and the two previous lines (perhaps the entire poem) by looking beyond appearances and paying attention to detail. The details are homely, unlike many romantic poems about nature like Shelley's "Hail to thee blithe spirit!/Bird thou never wert."

2. The four heavy stresses (One by one objects are defined) and the repetition "One by one" forces us to consider each syllable carefully like each emerging leaf. Line 23 begins quickly with the stress on the second syllable just as spring is quickly beginning to emerge. But the colon stops us and asks us to look forward. Again Williams calls our attention to the new "clarity" in the landscape—the "outline of leaf," the necessity of taking in details.

3. "It" refers to the spring, or more generally life.

4. The dominant meaning for "quicken" is "to make alive; vitalize; speed up." Another meaning, however, is "to reach the stage of pregnancy when the fetus can be felt to move." Williams, a family doctor, must have been aware of this meaning. This meaning not only conveys an image of mother earth about to give birth, but also links the natural world again to the human world.

Lines 24-27

1. What connotations does the image "stark dignity" contain?

2. What are the two meanings of "Still" in line 25?

3. What is the "profound change" of line 25?

4. How does the phrase "grip down" convey birth?

Answers

1. "Stark" describes the landscape of the first and second stanzas. "Dignity" recalls the image of the hospital patient or even the newborn baby who enters the world "stark naked." We do not usually associate dignity with nakedness, but Williams implies here that true dignity comes from being who we are.

2. "Still" means both "silent, quiet" and "nevertheless." Notice that the adjective can either describe the "dignity of entrance" or the "profound change." "Still" meaning "nevertheless" implies that although the natural world looks dead, the spring is going to awaken.

3. "The profound change" is the transition from death to life. "Profound" meaning "deep" implies simultaneously that the change is important and that it happens deep down inside the earth or in the womb.

4. The physical image of gripping down is easy to see, but "grip down" is also a term from the delivery room. The doctor Williams probably instructed his patient to "grip down" before giving birth.

Further Questions

1. What is Williams' attitude toward birth and the natural cycle of life? Use evidence from the poem to support your conclusion. Begin by going through the poem and listing all the adjectives.

2. In the film, the footage for "To the contagious hospital" takes place in a hospital, including a sequence of a woman giving birth. Some viewers think that the sequence detracts from the poem. Others think that it adds something. Why do you think the filmmaker chose to treat the poem in this way?

Answers

1. Williams' poem about the coming of spring (usually associated with birth) seems on close reading to be a poem about death, or at least about a death struggle that culminates in life.

Some of the adjectives in the poem include: brown, dried, dead, leafless, lifeless, sluggish, cold, naked, and stark. Out of this dead landscape, Williams draws our attention not only to signs of life, but to signs of the struggle to obtain life. Williams, the doctor, had often witnessed patients and babies struggling to hold onto life. There is nothing romantic about this struggle in his view. For example: "They enter the new world naked,/cold, uncertain of all/save that they enter."

The renewal of life in spring is also an "awakening" of consciousness, of awareness. Throughout the poem, Williams instructs the reader to be aware of the details of life, and of the poem. Awareness or consciousness begins in "gripping down," making contact, just as the woman giving birth must stoically "grip down."

2. The filmmaker treats the poem as linking the birth of nature with human birth.

Exercises and Assignments

1. Record a dialogue between you and a friend or relative. Then transcribe it. Then read "The Last Words of My English Grandmother." Consider how Williams transforms spoken language into poetry. Now make your recorded dialogue into a poem.

2. Think back to the film's presentation of "Danse Russe" when we see the naked man's shadow dancing on the wall. Do you think the filmmaker chose an appropriate image to convey the meaning of this poem? Why or why not? What image would you choose to film the poem?

3. Williams' "This Is Just to Say" may have been a "found poem." Such poems are already existing texts, not originally meant as poems, which can be discovered in news articles, advertisements, menus, letters, graffiti, or just about anywhere else. The poet arranges the words to form a poem and may make a few word changes. Go find a poem and write a "found poem." Pay close attention to line breaks and stanzas.

4. Reread "To Elsie." What are the "pure products of America"?

5. Read "Asphodel, That Greeny Flower." What is the tone of the speaker in the poem? Give evidence from the poem to support your answer.

6. One of Williams' ambitions was to write poetry about American life in language based on the American idiom. Read "To a Poor Old Woman." How does Williams use American idiom to convey his subject?

7. From *Paterson* read "The Library Fire." Generally speaking this section of the poem describes the burning of a library. Ordinarily, an event of this kind would be regarded solely as a catastrophe. What is Williams' view of the library fire? Use evidence from the poem to support your conclusions.

8. Williams' poem, "Young Love," was originally part of *Spring and All* and followed a discussion of Juan Gris, a cubist painter. The cubists reduced forms to their basic geometry so that they were no longer imitations or representations of something real but existed on their own merit. In "Young Love," Williams adapts the cubist technique to poetry. He transforms a basic narrative about a failed love affair (or affairs) into a cubist collage. Find the juxtapositions in the poem. What impact do they have on you, the reader? What would be lost if Williams had chosen to simply remember the story in ordinary chronological order?

9. Read "The Widow's Lament in Springtime." This poem is a soliloquy, a form of monologue. Williams wrote the poem for a reader, but the widow, the speaker of the poem, seems unaware of an audience. Williams uses tense shifts and juxtapositions to recreate the flow of the woman's interior thoughts. Find these places in the poem. Then write an interior monologue or soliloquy, adopting a speaker whose persona differs from your own.

10. In the film, you heard a variety of people read "The Red Wheelbarrow." Find two or three people to read the poem aloud to you. What do you notice about the way they approach this poem? How did you read it? Do the different readings represent different interpretations?

11. How did Williams' training as a doctor help him to write "Queen Anne's Lace"? What are some of the details most people would have missed? Look up Queen Anne's lace in a flower book.

12. If you were writing a poem about your home town, what details and documents would you include?

13. In the film, the critic Hugh Kenner says, "For Williams, the poem sitting on the page is a visual object, and the way it sits on the page does not necessarily tell you anything about how to read it." Read and look at "The Wind Increases" and "At the Ball Game." How does the visual impact of each poem affect your interpretation? Does either of these poems work better visually than orally?

Self Test

Read the following poem "WCW" by A.R. Ammons.

WCW

I turned in
by the bayshore
and parked,
the crosswind
hitting me hard
side the head,
the bay scrappy
and working:
what a
way to read
Williams! till
a woman came
and turned
her red dog loose
to sniff
(and piss
on)
the dead horseshoe
crabs.

1. In what ways does this poem reflect the influence of Williams?

Answers to Self Test

Answers to Self Tests begin on page 226.

For Further Reading

Books by Williams Carlos Williams

Autobiography. New York: New Directions; 1967.

The Collected Poems of William Carlos Williams, Volume I: 1919-1939. Litz, A. Walton, and MacGowan, Christopher, editors. New York: New Directions; 1986.

The Doctor Stories. Coles, Robert, editor. New York: New Directions; 1984.

In the American Grain. New York: New Directions; 1956.

Paterson. New York: New Directions; 1963.

The Selected Letters of William Carlos Williams. Thirlwall, John C., editor. New York: New Directions; 1957.

Selected Poems. Tomlinson, Charles, editor. New York: New Directions; 1985.

Spring and All. Paris: Contact Publishing Company; 1923.

William Carlos Williams Reader. Rosenthal, M.L., editor. New York: New Directions; 1969.

Books about Williams

Breslin, James E. *William Carlos Williams: An American Artist*. Chicago: The University of Chicago Press; 1985.

Mariani, Paul. *William Carlos Williams: A New World Naked*. New York: McGraw Hill; 1981.

Weaver, Mike. *William Carlos Williams*. New York: Cambridge University Press; 1971.

Emily Dickinson (1830-1886)

Emily Dickinson was born on December 10, 1830 in Amherst, Massachusetts. Her father was Edward Dickinson, a prominent lawyer who served as a U.S. Congressman and as the treasurer of Amherst College. Edward Dickinson was a highly disciplined and imposing man. After her father died, Dickinson wrote, "His heart was pure and terrible and I think no other like it exists." Dickinson's mother, Emily Norcross Dickinson, was a meek woman who was prone to illness. She inspired Dickinson's love, but not her full respect. Dickinson once wrote, "Mother does not care for thought." The Dickinson family were all quite different and self-sufficient but, at the same time, very close. Dickinson's older brother, Austin, was witty, sensitive and ambitious, her younger sister, Vinnie, vivacious and sturdy. Vinnie once described the family: "[We] all lived like friendly and absolute monarchs, each in his own domain."

Dickinson, who was later to "select her . . . Society" so jealously, grew up in a crowded and lively home filled with friends, her father's law clerks and college associates and other civic connections. From 1840-1847 she attended Amherst Academy where she received an exceptionally rigorous education for a young woman of her day. After attending nearby Mount Holyoke Female Seminary for nearly a year, Dickinson returned home to Amherst due to homesickness and actual illness. Her earliest surviving poems, two valentines written around this time, already show her verbal artistry and intellectual precocity.

Dickinson's closest Amherst friend in the years after she left Mount Holyoke was Susan Gilbert, a bright and ambitious young woman with whom she could share her growing literary interests and philosophical speculations. Susan married Austin Dickinson in 1856, and the young couple set up housekeeping "across the hedges" at The Evergreens next door to the family homestead. Dickinson visited there frequently, enjoying the lively circle of friends Sue gathered about her, joining in games or improvising at the piano. She avoided the grander social events at which Sue presided, however, including visits of Ralph Waldo Emerson when he lectured in Amherst. Austin and Susan's three children brought Dickinson much pleasure, and the death of the youngest, Gilbert, proved one of the great sorrows of her later years.

From adolescence Dickinson exhibited shyness except in the company of a few close friends, and her tendency to reticence grew with the passing years until she restricted her social activity to an exceptionally lively correspondence with persons who were important to her. "My friends are my Estate . . ." she once wrote, and all through her life she was (as Vinnie later put it) "looking for the rewarding person." One such person was Ben Newton who read law in her father's office and was among the first to whom she revealed her poetic ambitions. Another was the Rev. Charles Wadsworth. The beginnings of their relationship are obscure, but she may have met him in 1855 on her trip to Washington and Philadelphia during her father's term in Congress. Wadsworth was an illustrious preacher in an age when the sermon was among the most popular art forms. He was her "closest earthly friend" and spiritual counselor and, in some accounts, an object of intense affection. Samuel Bowles is another close friend with whom some scholars think she may have been in love. He was a handsome, worldly man, editor of the *Springfield Republican*, a major newspaper of the day. All the Dickinsons counted on him to keep them in touch with the latest events, and he also brought them tales from his extensive travels.

Although she often sent them poems, she did not press these influential friends to help her publish. The literary man she did approach for advice was Thomas Wentworth Higginson, a well-known writer. Radical politically, he was an ardent abolitionist—a member of the "secret six" that plotted John Brown's raid on Harper's Ferry—and commanded a Negro regiment in the Civil War. He also championed women's rights and promoted female authors. But he was essentially a conservative about literature. When she wrote him in 1861 to ask if her verses "breathed," she was asking a man who was first concerned if they rhymed and scanned and were clear and consistent. Her unconventional rhyme and meter, her compression and ambiguity puzzled him. He praised the poems but with strong reservations and urged her to "delay to publish." Still, Dickinson valued him as a sincere and sophisticated person with whom she could discuss books and share her thoughts. She carefully cultivated their friendship and long continued the pretense of seeking his literary advice, though there is no known instance of her altering a poem at his suggestion.

A contemporary writer who did recognize Dickinson's genius was Higginson's friend Helen Hunt Jackson, a popular poet and novelist and early champion of the American Indian cause. She chided Dickinson for not publishing her poems and arranged for one ("Success is counted sweetest") to appear in *A Masque of Poets* (1878), an anthology in which all the poems were published anonymously. Dickinson must have smiled at the published guess that her poem had been written by Emerson.

In her lifetime, Dickinson published only 10 of the 1,775 poems that have survived. At the height of her creativity in the early 1860s she was writing several a week, sometimes several a day. This surge of poetic power seems to have been unleashed by a crisis in her life. It is unclear whether this crisis was a crisis of love, a religious crisis, one between her roles as woman and artist or a combination of these. Recently scholars have investigated her serious eye-trouble of the 1860s and wondered if the crisis was a fear of losing her vision, a loss that would have cut her off from nature and books, two of her greatest loves. But this avenue, too, has proved inconclusive.

Increasingly through the 1860s Dickinson restricted her movements and contacts. By 1870 she was not leaving the Dickinson grounds and would sometimes flee upstairs when visitors came to the house. However, she carried on an intense correspondence with close friends and generally would see them when they came to Amherst. She also kept up a rich literary dialogue with Higginson, Bowles, Jackson and others. Like Thoreau, who "traveled a good deal in Concord," Dickinson's inward, contemplative nature found all it needed close at hand.

The reclusive, restricted life hers became was certainly eccentric and may have been pathological. It can, however, also be seen as one intently centered on her writing, reading and thinking, and on her family and friends. Her life remains a challenging mystery, but one that is overshadowed by the even greater mystery of how great poetry gets created.

The World of the Poems

Emily Dickinson was born into an atmosphere of rigorous Congregationalist piety. The Dickinson family and the town of Amherst still prided themselves on their fidelity to the Puritan heritage of New England's founders. She was steeped in the Bible and Calvinist doctrine but often adapted the language of traditional religion to suit her own needs or to express ideas that those around her would have found blasphemous. In some ways, her poems hark back to the Puritanism of the previous century; in others they look forward to our own day with its uncertainty, self-awareness, and scientific perspective; often they do both at once.

The Connecticut River Valley where Dickinson lived had been the scene of great religious revivals, and the congregational Calvinism of her family was still a conversion religion in which a person had to undergo an emotional surrender to Christ before becoming a member of the church. Traditionally in this faith, man was seen as a degraded creature held down by original sin, who could only be saved by the grace of God, not by his own will. Those predestined for such salvation were called the Elect and the process Divine Election. These views were changing in the early 19th century. Will came to be more important than grace and in the revivals of Dickinson's girlhood it became almost a duty to experience conversion since it was *up to you* to merit God's grace.

Dickinson's relationship to this controversy is complex. Suffice it to say here that she never joined the church and couldn't accept the ideas of election and original sin, but *was* very concerned with salvation and spiritual rebirth. In poem after poem, she tested such terms as immortality, election, redemption, resurrection, and baptism by grace, sometimes trying to define or just to imagine them, sometimes questioning or extending them.

Like all Puritans, Dickinson and her Calvinist neighbors saw life as a "pilgrim's progress," a spiritual adventure in which everything was at stake. This is the key to her other great Puritan trait, introspection. As the biographer Richard Sewall says in the film, "She was in that great Puritan tradition of keeping diaries, of keeping the thumb on the spiritual pulse."

Historians still marvel at the almost clinical skill the early Puritan diarists needed to keep a scrupulous account of their dealings with God, and at the emotional intensity of their inner lives. This is one of the ways in which Dickinson comes closest to her Puritan forebears. In poem after poem, she looks deeply inward, thinking things through, grappling with feelings, and exploring states of the soul, all with an extraordinary combination of urgency and clear-sightedness.

People in the 1800s also had reason to keep a thumb on the *physical* pulse. Early deaths in childbirth or from tuberculosis, pneumonia and many infectious diseases were still terribly common. Dickinson's many poems on death may seem morbid to you until you realize how many loved ones she lost and recall that death was the hinge on which all of her spiritual questioning turned.

We have seen how vivid a drama the soul's journey through life made for the Puritans. Death was its final and decisive act, and still in Dickinson's time family and friends kept watch in the sickroom, wondering eagerly whether the person was "willing to die," which is to say, confident of eternal life. Dickinson used Calvinist ideas about death and the customs of her society as starting points for her own probes into this mystery.

Education in Dickinson's time was also largely religious, but Dickinson was lucky to attend two institutions which combined this with high standards, young, sympathetic teachers, and an unusual focus on science. Amherst Academy was connected with Amherst College, which was then run by a remarkable man, Dr. Edward Hitchcock, who was both a minister and a distinguished scientist. He saw no contradiction between the two, but read in nature analogies of spiritual truths and saw scientific observation as a way of more fully appreciating God's creation. As a result, Amherst had a curriculum rich in the sciences, and Dickinson studied botany, geology, and mental philosophy, among other subjects.

Nearby Mount Holyoke Female Seminary was founded by Hitchcock's pupil Mary Lyon, who was a devout evangelist and an accomplished chemist. Here Dickinson studied algebra, chemistry, and physiology and might have even studied astronomy. Girls then were often not educated beyond the three "R's," or if they were, it was only in religion and domestic economy and, for some, piano playing and singing. To gain such a grounding in science was rarer still.

Dickinson's science training helps to explain her precise use of terms such as marl, chrysolite, parallax, perihelion, corolla and calyx and the hundreds of exotic place names that occur in the poems. It also suggests a source for her skill in accurate observation, whether of plants and animals or the workings of her own mind. The greatest effect of her scientific studies, though, is in her experimental attitude to the great issues of life. This is also a good attitude for you to adopt as you consider her poems.

Emily Dickinson: Circumference and Compression

One of the best known things about Emily Dickinson is how she increasingly circumscribed her personal life, seeing fewer and fewer people and staying within the perimeter of the two Dickinson houses and their grounds. But the world you discover in her poems is anything but confining. It is rich in feeling, wide in its knowledge of nature and books and geography, and expansive in its vision. Explaining herself in an 1862 letter to Thomas Wentworth Higginson, Dickinson wrote, "My Business is Circumference—." Dickinson often used the word "circumference" metaphorically to explore the boundaries or outer limit of some "circle" of experience. Here we can only look at a few of these "circles," but as you read Dickinson, look for other ways in which she explores the edges and boundaries of things.

One circumference Dickinson investigated was death as the outer limit of life. In numerous poems, she tries to imagine crossing that barrier for insight into what lies on the other side. Dickinson longed for a true belief in immortality that would assuage her own fears and assure her of reunion with loved ones. Time and again she depicted death as the great "circumference," as a sealed door beyond which might lie the unbounded.

Similarly, Dickinson explored the circumference of her faith. Hers was "that religion/that doubts as fervently as it believes." She was too serious about religion to accept any faith she could not deeply feel and live by and too honest to say otherwise. She has been called "a great experimenter of the spirit."

In many of her poems, Dickinson drew a circumference around an abstract word in order to define it in her own way. Her definitions, however, are never dictionary definitions; often, they are metaphoric definitions which give the flavor of the thing being defined. Among these were: "'Hope' is the thing with feathers—," "'Nature' is what we see—," and "Much Madness is divinest Sense—."

"Vesuvius at Home"

Dickinson once wrote that she didn't need to go to Sicily or South America to see volcanoes, for she had her own "Vesuvius at Home." Many critics have speculated about the emotional and spiritual turbulence under the surface of her uneventful seeming life. Guesses are many and facts are few. What is clear is the great force that lies compressed under the surfaces of her language.

Compression is the hallmark of Dickinson's style. It is as noticeable in her letters as in the poems and even comes through in the bits of her conversation that various people recorded. Compression, however, is not just smallness but compactness. It comes from enclosing a great force or large expanse in a small container. Large themes and intense

111

experiences that other authors might have treated in an ode or cycle of sonnets, or a treatise or play, she would treat in a poem of maybe eight lines, and not very often more than 20.

For Dickinson, compression was primarily a paradoxical means of generating emotional force, spiritual expansion, and intellectual penetration. In trying to convey extreme emotions—feelings that press at the "circumference" of endurance and expressibility—Dickinson was able to suggest their uncontainability and explosive force precisely by confining them to such a small compass. Of course she also had to come up with apt comparisons and musical equivalents for the feeling, but much of the urgency and immediacy come from the pressure of this emotional energy against a constricting form.

Dickinson's preferred form for poetry was the hymn meter she knew from singing hymns as a girl. It is also called "common measure," "ballad meter" or "8's and 6's," and each name is instructive. It was a very common form at the time and was used for ballads as well as hymns and romantic lyrics. It alternates a line of iambic tetrameter (eight syllables) with one of iambic trimeter (six syllables), usually in quatrains rhymed abab. Some Dickinson poems fit to hymn tunes exactly. This one, for example, can be sung to the tune of "Oh God, Our Help in Ages Past":

> Experiment escorts us last—
> His pungent company
> Will not allow an Axiom
> An Opportunity

The hymn form is ironic here, though, because the poem's experimental attitude to life-after-death would have shocked Dickinson's hymn-singing neighbors.

Exercise: As you watch the film and read Dickinson, keep looking for the ways in which Dickinson explores the circumference of spiritual, emotional, and intellectual experience. You should also begin to consider where your own circumferences lie. Consider what boundaries you take for granted as a citizen, a student, a man, or a woman. What are the benefits and drawbacks to establishing certain boundaries?

Meet the Speakers

Richard Sewall is the author of *The Life of Emily Dickinson* for which he received a National Book Award. A tireless champion of Dickinson and a scrupulous scholar, he has done much to dispel mythic and erroneous views of her. He embarked on his 20-year project at the request of Millicent Todd Bingham, the daughter of Mabel Loomis Todd who was originally responsible for the publication of Dickinson's poems in the 1890s. In addition to the biography, Sewall has written *The Lyman Letters: New Light on Emily Dickinson and Her Family* and has edited *Emily Dickinson: A Collection of Critical Essays.*

Anthony Hecht is a Pulitzer Prize-winning poet and has been Poetry Consultant to the Library of Congress. Some of his most prominent works include: *The Hard Hours, Millions of Strange Shadows,* and *The Venetian Vespers.*

Adrienne Rich has become one of our most important poets and critics. She is also a respected figure in the broader feminist movement beyond literature. Her books of verse include: *The Will to Change: Poems, A Wild Patience Has Taken Me This Far,* and *The Fact of a Doorframe.* Her essay "Vesuvius at Home" was a ground-breaking study of Dickinson as a dedicated and self-conscious artist.

Joyce Carol Oates is a well-known writer in several genres. *Them*, *The Assassins*, *Do With Me What You Will*, and *Solstice* number among the more than 30 works of fiction, poetry, and social commentary she has published.

Study Plan for This Unit

1. Complete the section **Before Watching the Film: Journal-Writing and Other Activities.**

2. Read the Dickinson poems many of which are featured in the film. Try reading the poems aloud. This often helps you to hear the poems better. Read through all the poems at a moderate speed without stopping. Don't worry if you don't understand them completely.

"Faith" is a fine invention
Safe in their Alabaster Chambers—
Wild Nights-Wild Nights!
I felt a Funeral, in My Brain,
Of all the Sounds despatched abroad,
After great pain, a formal feeling comes—
Dare you see a Soul *at the White Heat?*
This was a Poet—It is That
I Died for Beauty—but was scarce
This World is not Conclusion.
I'm ceded—I've stopped being Theirs—
The Soul has Bandaged moments—
I cannot live with You—
My Life had stood—A Loaded Gun—
The Props assist the House
Tell all the Truth but tell it slant

3. Watch the film.

4. Complete the section **After Watching the Film: Journal-Writing and Other Activities.**

5. Go through the **Guided Reading**.

6. Complete the **Exercises and Assignments** as specified by your instructor.

7. Take the **Self Test**.

Before Watching the Film: Journal-Writing and Other Activities

1. Jot down any striking words or phrases from the poems you read.

2. Choose one of the following poems: "Wild Nights—Wild Nights!," "I felt a Funeral, in my Brain," "After great pain, a formal feeling comes—," "I'm ceded—I've stopped being Theirs—," "It was not Death, for I stood up." Consider the feelings the poem conveys. What kind of experience would create such feelings?

3. Read "Tell all the Truth but tell it slant—." Do you agree with the premise of this poem that it is better to get at the truth in a gradual, sideways fashion, for example, to

imply the truth without stating it or to convey it through a comparison? Or do you think it is better to state the truth flat out, directly? Consider the times when you've found it difficult to tell the truth. Then explain your answer.

4. Choose one of the following three passages from Dickinson's letters and re-express her opinion in your own words. Then say how you agree or disagree with it.

"My Friends are my estate. Forgive me then the avarice to hoard them. They tell me those [who] were poor early [in life] have different views of gold."

"A Letter always seems to me like immortality because it is the mind alone without corporeal Friend . . ."

"To shut our eyes is Travel. The Seasons understand this."

While Watching the Film

1. Jot down any striking words, phrases, or visual images that you encounter in the film.

2. In the dramatized scenes of Dickinson's home, notice the costumes and furnishings and the manners of the people. Notice the differing activities of men and women. Also pay close attention to the scenes of the surrounding countryside. What kind of country is it? What kind of house and town did she live in?

3. Listen for the various things that are said about Dickinson and religion both in her life and in her work.

After Watching the Film: Journal-Writing and Other Activities

1. Go back to your list of striking words and phrases and pick one you like. Then use it in a sentence to express something you want to say. Make the sentence *as short as you can* while still making your point.

2. Go back to the passage from Dickinson's letters that you wrote about before the film. Do you see anything more or different in it? Do you have any second thoughts about her opinion? If so, write them down.

3. Read "The Soul has Bandaged moments—." This poem describes a progression through three emotional states. Sketch out at least two different plots or brief stories in which a character goes through these states. You can use any kind of character or plot, or even a true story if it fits, but try to keep the emotions as close as you can to those of the poem.

Guided Reading

"The Soul selects her own Society—" is a good example of Dickinson's great compression, how much meaning and feeling she can pack into a few words. In the following **Guided Reading**, we look at the poem in some detail. However, you should remember that it is quite possible to enjoy and appreciate such a poem without analyzing it to such a degree.

In fact the purpose of Dickinson's compression is not to spin out a long train of thought after the poem, but to give you a true and intense experience of what she is writing about.

Read "The Soul selects her own Society—" aloud and then answer the following questions.

The Soul selects her own Society—   1
Then—shuts the Door—
To her divine Majority—
Present no more—   4

Unmoved—she notes the Chariots—pausing—
At her low Gate—
Unmoved—an Emperor be kneeling
Upon her Mat—   8

I've known her—from an ample nation—
Choose One—
Then—close the Valves of her attention—
Like Stone—   12

Lines 1-4

1. The first line states that the soul picks with whom she will associate. It can also be read with another meaning. What is this other meaning?

2. What does "Majority" mean in line 3? And what makes it "divine"?

3. When you read line 4 aloud you have to choose whether to pronounce the first word as a verb (pre-*sent*) meaning "to introduce" or as an adjective (*pres*-ent) meaning "being in some (understood or specified) place." Which way would you read it and why?

The next two words in line 4 pose a related question. Does "no more" mean "no additional ones" or "no longer"? You should consider all four possible combinations of these meanings before making your answer.

Answers

1. The soul chooses to keep herself company, to be alone and commune with herself.

2. In line 3, "Majority" has its usual meaning of the larger half of some group, especially the more than 50 percent of the votes that carries an election. The soul and her chosen society form a majority despite their small number because it is a "divine" majority. The soul is the "divine spark" that animates the body, the spiritual part of man. And as God can be said to form a "majority" in His domain (the universe) because His will overrules any number of human wills, so the soul, as the divine part of a person, can hold sway in her domain (the person's life) no matter how many others "vote" that she expand her "Society."

115

Another meaning of "majority" also comes into play and supports the first one. This is "majority" as the legal age at which one becomes a citizen or gains certain rights. So, there is also the idea here that the soul has come into her own and has a right to see, and not see, whom she will.

3. It is probably better to read "present" as a verb, but not because the grammar or meter rules out the other reading. Nor is it that the adjective fails to make sense with the rest of the poem. What gives the verb the edge is mainly that it *is* a verb and one with a clearly implied subject: *you*. To read the word as an adjective, you have to supply both subject and verb. Let's look at the various readings of line 4, "Present no more."

The verbal reading could be paraphrased:

> Present no additional [suitors or visitors beyond the soul's chosen one(s)] to her divine majority.

Or possibly:

> No longer present (formally introduce) [anyone] to her divine majority.

The adjectival reading could be paraphrased:

> [The other suitors or visitors—those not selected] are no longer present to her divine majority.

Or possibly:

> No other [suitors or visitors beyond the one(s) selected] are present to her divine majority.

Because you have to supply basic words and turn the word order about, the adjectival readings are a bit awkward. However, since Dickinson often uses ellipsis and inversion this extreme in other poems, such a reading cannot be ruled out. You should keep both in mind as you continue the **Guided Reading**.

Lines 5-8

1. The word "Unmoved" is prominently placed in the second stanza and is repeated. What attitude does it suggest on the part of the soul? If you see more than one possibility, note the others as well.

2. The soul in this poem seems to have a house. At least she has a door, a gate and a mat. Since the soul is being personified as a lady who is particular about her guests and suitors, the house could simply come with the lady. However, other Dickinson poems and other works of literature also use the figure of the house of the soul. What could this "house" be?

3. In line 6, why is the "gate" described as "low"?

4. Lines 7-8 are another of Dickinson's elliptical sentences in which the words left out are "understood." Write out these lines supplying the missing words. (There are several ways to do this.) What is especially unusual about the situation shown in these lines?

Answers

1. Some good answers are: indifferent, single-minded, obsessed, confirmed, resolved, faithful, severe, noble, haughty. Dickinson illustrates the soul's indifference to the material world, i.e. to the emperor and his trappings (the "chariots"), by making the two scenes by which the soul is "unmoved" similar in sound. The two halves of the second stanza do not have the same sentence structure, but they do have many parallel elements that are clinched by the slant rhyme ("gate/mat").

2. The eyes are often called "the windows of the soul." From here, it is a quick step to seeing the body as the soul's house and giving figurative meanings to the other features of a house, or to different kinds of housing.

In other Dickinson poems such as "Because I could not stop for Death—" and "What Inn is this" a tomb is seen as a house or lodging place. It may seem contradictory to imagine the soul in the grave rather than in heaven or hell, but in the Calvinist theology of Dickinson's heritage (as in others), the soul does not ascend to heaven until the Day of Judgement.

It is also common to speak of heaven as the "soul's true home." There are many hymns and spirituals that speak of going to heaven as "going home." Dickinson herself often refers to heaven in this way, including one poem and several letters in which she refers to Christ's saying that "In my Father's house there are many mansions."

3. If the soul's "house" is seen as the body, then the "gate" could be "low" because the physical realm of the body is lower than the spiritual realm of the soul. If the "gate" is seen more specifically as the eyes as in the phrase "windows of the soul," then they could be low because they are lowered in modesty or humility.

If the soul's "house" is seen as a tomb or mausoleum, the "gate" could be one in the fence around the plot, or an iron grate over the entrance. Then it would be "low" because these are often physically low.

If the house is rather seen as the soul's heavenly "mansion," the gate could be low because only the humble can enter there, as indicated by famous scripture passages such as "Blessed are the poor in spirit: For theirs is the Kingdom of heaven." And "Except ye be converted, and become as little children, ye shall not enter into the Kingdom of heaven."

4. Here are some examples of how the sentence would read with the "missing words" supplied: [She is] Unmoved [that] an Emperor [should] be kneeling upon her mat. Or: [She is] Unmoved [although] an Emperor [might] be kneeling upon her mat. Or: Unmoved [she notes] an Emperor [to] be kneeling upon her mat. (**Remember:** There are more possibilities.)

What is unusual is that an emperor should be kneeling to anyone. An emperor rules over a number of countries, some of which have their own kings, so even kings kneel to an emperor. Yet here the emperor is kneeling before a lady. It is interesting in this regard to look again at the word "low" in line six. If the gate is "low" because it belongs to the poor house of a person of humble station, then the emperor's homage is even more remarkable. It is a kind of Cinderella story in which a poor girl is courted by a prince. Only, here *she* refuses him.

Lines 9-12

1. Reread the third stanza aloud. Who or what is it that the soul has been known to choose? Again, if you see several possibilities, note them all.

2. Besides the valves of a plumbing system and the valves of a heart, valves can also refer to the shell halves of a marine creature such as a clam. Another meaning, current in the 19th century, was the two halves of a folding or double door. In line 11, what are "the valves of her attention"? What does each of these four meanings of valve add to the final image in the poem?

3. Reread the poem aloud once more, paying special attention to the rhythm and tone of the second and fourth lines of each stanza. How do these lines in the last stanza differ from the second and fourth lines in the first two? How does this add to their effect?

Answers

1. Readers have provided a surprising variety of answers to this question. Some can be gleaned just from the poem; others require the use of clues from other Dickinson poems or a knowledge of her times. Here we will stick pretty much to the poem.

The "One" the soul has been known to choose may be one true love; one best friend; Christ as her savior; herself, i.e., the unity (one-ness) and purity of being alone; or one human body to inhabit, i.e., to be the soul of a certain person in a particular place and time.

2. "The valves of her attention" could be her senses, especially her eyes and ears, especially as the links between the soul and the physical world.

The closed heart valves suggest her emotional unresponsiveness whether to alternative friends or suitors or to distractions from her spiritual goal. The closed valves of a plumbing system suggest the complexity of the human senses that take in the world in great detail and interact in many ways.

The closed valves of a shellfish suggest a particularly tight and stubborn closure, a surprising obstinacy in a humble creature. They also suggest the soul's rising out of an alien element (matter, the world) into her native one (heaven, the spirit) as the shell comes out of the ocean onto the beach.

The valves of a double door recall the door that gets shut in the first stanza. They also remind us of the doors of the tomb that is suggested at several points in the poem. This image is then strongly reinforced by the closing words, "Like Stone."

3. The second and fourth lines in the last stanza have only two syllables instead of four. They sound and look foreshortened. The tone is something like "That's that." or "That's it." or "So there." It is curt and final and doesn't invite an answer.

This line reinforces the firmness of the soul's resolve, the intensity of her focus on her chosen "One." This is especially true of "Like Stone" because of the silence following it. This line suggests that she is as good as dead to the others, and the abrupt ending closes the question. The silence at the end of the poem is like the soul's silence in answer to her other suitors.

Further Questions

1. Notice in the first stanza how the consonant sounds of "shuts" echo those of "selects." These two words have synonyms in the last stanza, "close" and "choose" and the same echoing of consonant sounds occurs there. Dickinson seems to be calling our attention to a special relationship between selecting and shutting out, between choosing and closing off. What is the relationship between them? In what ways does this relationship justify or explain the soul's exclusiveness?

2. Now that you have looked at the poem more closely, who or what do you think it is that the soul has been known to choose? Or do you think that Dickinson avoided selecting or choosing just one possibility so that she wouldn't have to shut out or close off the others? Support your answer with evidence from the poem.

Answer

1. Selecting or choosing one possibility always means shutting out or closing off some other one. This suggests that the soul's exclusiveness is something we all have to do to one extent or another. Still, one could say that she carries it to an extreme. It may be that she is not so much indifferent to the alternatives as she is obsessed with the "One" she has chosen. She cannot turn *to* the others without turning *from* her "One," and this she can't bear to do because her love is so great.

Exercises and Assignments

1. You will recall from the film and your reading that Dickinson had a complex relationship to the intense religious life going on around her. While her poems are full of biblical terms and meditations on Christian themes, they are also full of skepticism and unorthodox ideas. She could not count herself among the saved when religious revivals swept Amherst during her girlhood and later stopped attending church.

In light of this, read the poem "This World is not Conclusion." How would you interpret the last four lines of this poem? In particular, what is the tone of "Much Gesture" and "Strong Hallelujahs," and what are the "Narcotics"?

2. Read the poem "I'm ceded—I've stopped being Theirs—."

In a normal coronation the crown is not "chosen" but inherited by the rightful heir. For the speaker to "choose" a crown suggests that she is usurping a role that may not be hers or that some authority is denying to her. What implications does this have for the overall meaning of the poem?

3. In "I dwell in Possibility—" Dickinson contrasts the realm of "Possibility" with that of "Prose." What does this imply about her view of poetry?

4. Read "I felt a Funeral, in my Brain," and "It was not Death, for I stood up." Dickinson was concerned with the workings of her own mind, observing its radically shifting moods, its imaginative energy, and its impulse to push against the boundaries of what the world regards as sanity. The last experience is recorded in these poems. Most of us have had some experience that made us feel miserable. But if someone asked us to write about it, we'd probably be at a loss for what to write or say. It is part of the poet's remarkable art to find a way to communicate extreme emotion.

a. Choose one of the two poems and make a list of word choices and images that convey the mood of the poem.

b. Write your own poem about a nightmare or nightmarish experience. Try to convey your experience through images and suggestive word choices. (You may want to begin by simply writing about a dream or experience, using as many details as possible.)

5. Part of the challenge of reading Dickinson is to identify the different dramatic roles she enacts in her poems. The "I" in these poems is not always the poet, herself, speaking. Rather, she adopts different characters to speak through (Note: "characters" are often called "personas"). Read over the list of poems featured in the film. How many different personas (characters) does she use? What are they? Do you think some of these poems reflect the "real" Emily Dickinson? (Give a short list.)

6. Paradox is when two contradictory truths add up to a single truth. For example, we say a person is a "paradox" when we can't reconcile his contradictory behavior. You might say, "The guy (or girl) sent me roses, but he didn't call me for a date." You may look at it as a statement presented as truth although it seems to contradict itself. For example, "The more things change, the more things stay the same" (Alphonse Karr). Many poets use paradox because it reveals so much about life. Paradox can also be used to express ideas hard to get at directly, to jolt people out of a mental rut, or just for fun.

Awareness of paradox is often expressed by oxymoron, which can be translated from the Greek as "cleverly stupid." Oxymoron links, in one unit, words that seem to cancel each other out: "cold fire," "terrible beauty," "lucky disaster," "sweet sorrow" and "bittersweet."

Dickinson was particularly fond of using opposites in her poems and oxymorons to express the paradox of a subject or mood, and the ambiguity of existence. Here are some examples of the way Dickinson fused opposites in her language:

the Pain of joy
A Dome of Abyss
this smart Misery
To perish—of Delight
Confident Despair
A Haggard Comfort
A piercing Comfort
a bliss of sorrow
numb alarm
sordid excellence

Read through the featured poems and make a list of Dickinson's use of opposites and oxymorons. Then make up some of your own.

7. Read "After great pain, a formal feeling comes—" and then answer the following questions:

a. What is "formal" about the feeling that comes "After great pain"? Use adjectives from the poem itself to describe how this "feeling" is "formal."

b. Can you think of several different causes of pain that might lead to such profound numbness in their aftermath?

c. Do you think the speaker of the poem has "outlived" a painful experience like the kind she speaks of, or is she just discussing this secondhand? Support your choice with evidence found in the poem.

8. Read both versions of "Safe in their Alabaster Chambers—" and then answer the following questions:

a. In line 4, to what is the "Resurrection" compared by the use of the word "members"?

b. Read line 9 of the 1861 version aloud listening to the pitch of your voice. How does the sequence of vowel sounds in "Diadems—drop—" and "Doges—surrender—" imitate the actions being described?

c. How do the second stanzas differ in tone?

d. Which version of the second stanza do you prefer and why?

9. Choose two stanzas from "I heard a Fly buzz—when I died—" and repunctuate them with conventional punctuation. What is gained or lost?

10. Read "Because I could not stop for Death—." A common device in horror movies is to let the audience in on a dangerous situation before its potential victims know about it. You lean forward wanting to warn them. Dickinson uses a similar device in this poem but without some of the advantages of a movie.

The whole story is told from the "victim's" point of view; there is no actual "cut away" to a scene in which you see the situation from the outside. Yet Dickinson manages to have the speaker give away the situation without realizing it herself.

In what line does Dickinson accomplish this effect? How does it work? And how does it affect the way you take the speaker's story throughout the rest of the poem?

11. Read " 'Hope' is the thing with feathers—." Dickinson wrote many of these definition poems, that is, poems that begin with the logical pattern "X is Y." Look, for example, at "'Nature' is what we see—" and "Remorse—is Memory—awake—." Now make your own list of what hope "is." Then write your own definition poem. For example, your first line may begin: "Love is _____," or "Revenge is _____," "Success is _____," but don't feel confined to definitions of abstract words.

12. Reread "I'm ceded—I've stopped being Theirs—." For what role is the speaker being crowned? Wife or lover (the Queen of someone's heart), or as a self-sufficient woman or artist (the ruler of her own life or creativity)? Explain your choice, or why you think it could be more than one.

Self Test

1. The following poem, "The Last Scene," was written by William Winter, a contemporary of Dickinson, and appeared in *The Springfield Republican*, a newspaper she read:

> Here she lieth, white and chill;
> Put your hand upon her brow!
> For her heart is very still,
> And she does not know you now.

Ah the grave's a quiet bed!
She shall sleep a pleasant sleep,
And the tears that you may shed,
Will not wake her—therefore weep!

Weep—for you have wrought her woe;
Mourn—she mourned and died for you;
Ah, too late we come to know
What is false and what is true.

Now read Dickinson's "How many times these low feet staggered—":

How many times these low feet staggered—
Only the soldered mouth can tell—
Try—can you stir the awful rivet—
Try—can you lift the hasps of steel!

Stroke the cool forehead—hot so often—
Lift—if you care—the listless hair—
Handle the adamantine fingers
Never a thimble—more—shall wear—

Buzz the dull flies—on the chamber window—
Brave—shines the sun through the freckled pane—
Fearless—the cobweb swings from the ceiling—
Indolent Housewife—in Daisies—lain!

Now answer the following questions:

1. List the details each poet uses to make us aware of the contrast between the living person and the dead one. How do the two lists differ? Which poem dramatizes this contrast more effectively?

2. List the details in each poem that reveal something about the woman's life. Which poem better enables you to imagine the woman alive?

3. Both poets use imperative verbs: "put," "weep," and "mourn" in the first poem; "try," "stroke," "lift," and "handle" in the second. To whom are these commands addressed? How do they differ in the two poems?

4. What reaction is each poet asking from the reader? Which poem calls for the stronger reaction?

Answers to Self Test
Answers to Self Tests begin on page 226.

For Further Reading

Books by Dickinson

The Complete Poems of Emily Dickinson. Johnson, Thomas H., editor. Boston & Toronto: Little, Brown & Co.; 1960.

Emily Dickinson: Selected Letters. Johnson, Thomas H., editor. Cambridge: Belknap Press of Harvard University Press; 1971.

The Manuscript Books of Emily Dickinson: A Facsimile Edition. Franklin, Ralph W., editor. Cambridge: Belknap Press of Harvard University Press; 1981.

Books about Dickinson

Leyda, Jay. *The Years and Hours of Emily Dickinson.* New Haven: Yale University Press; 1960.

Rich, Adrienne. "Vesuvius at Home: The Power of Emily Dickinson." *On Lies, Secrets and Silence: Selected Prose, 1966-1978.* New York: W.W. Norton; 1979.

Sewall, Richard B., editor. *Emily Dickinson: A Collection of Critical Essays.* Englewood Cliffs, N.J.: Prentice-Hall; 1963.

Sewall, Richard B. *The Life of Emily Dickinson.* New York: Farrar, Straus and Giroux; 1974.

Wolff, Cynthia Griffin. *Emily Dickinson.* New York: Alfred A. Knopf; 1986.

Marianne Moore (1887-1972)

Known for her unusual subjects and distinctive poetic form, Marianne Moore was one of the most original poets of our time. Her poems, rich in quotations, scientific observations, and paradoxical meanings, take on a life of their own: to read a Moore poem is to enter a "new cosmos" held together under the invisible direction of the poet herself. Although her poems can bewilder a new reader with their difficulty, they earned their place in modern poetry alongside T.S. Eliot, Wallace Stevens and William Carlos Williams.

Marianne Moore was born in Kirkwood, Missouri, a suburb of St. Louis, on November 15, 1887, just ten months before the birth of T.S. Eliot in the same city; she was the youngest of two children. She never knew her father, John Milton Moore, for he had a nervous breakdown and was institutionalized when she was small. She was raised by her mother, Mary Moore and her grandfather, John Warner, a Presbyterian minister. After Warner's death in 1894, Mrs. Moore moved her family to Carlisle, Pennsylvania, an area which she believed could provide her children with a proper education. Perhaps because of the succession of personal losses that had fallen on the Moores, the three, mother, son, and daughter, formed a close bond that was never to break.

At Bryn Mawr College, from which she graduated in 1909, Moore was keenly interested in majoring in English but was discouraged by the faculty because of her low grades. This did not, however, dampen her enthusiasm: she began writing fiction and poetry, which she published in the undergraduate magazine. Though the response to her work was sometimes mixed (the Dean once commenting on a story of hers that "it was such a pity that a girl of her ability should be guilty of such affectations"), she "pressed on with increased zeal," sending her work to prestigious magazines such as the *Atlantic Monthly*.

Eventually, after a brief period teaching at Carlisle Commercial College, Moore convinced her mother to move with her to New York, where they would both spend the rest of their lives. It was at this time, 1916, that Moore's poetry had begun to attract serious attention with publications in *The Egoist* and *Poetry*. Through Alfred Kreymborg, editor of *Others*, Moore joined other writers such as William Carlos Williams, Amy Lowell, and Wallace Stevens. Ezra Pound, the leader of the new Imagist movement, praised her work for its "dance of the intelligence" and in 1935, T.S. Eliot wrote that "she is one of those few who have done the language some service in my lifetime."

As Moore was engaging the literary world with her verse, so too was she earning recognition for her prose; for four years she edited the famous *Dial* magazine, during which time she demonstrated her sharp eye, both as an editor and reviewer. She became especially interested in beginning writers, giving their books her careful attention. In 1934, she met Elizabeth Bishop (then a young writer), whose work Moore highly praised, and who became a lifelong friend.

Moore said that if anyone was to write a biography of her it would be a "rather tame affair." Though she called herself a "metropolitan recluse," she became, in her later years, a public figure, responding graciously to reporters and fans, answering up to fifty letters a day. Her enthusiasm for her public life brought with it a host of invitations: tea with boxer Muhammad Ali; an appearance on **The Tonight Show**; an honorary invitation to throw out the opening ball at Yankee Stadium. Her most unusual request came in 1955 when an executive at the Ford Motor Company asked her to help name their new car. This began a three-month correspondence where she was to suggest names such as "Mongoose Civique" and "Pluma Pliuma." Finally, Ford rejected them all in favor of their own idea: Edsel.

Marianne Moore loved animals and athletes, calling both "miracles of dexterity" and spent her life surrounded by those things which fascinated her. She took great pleasure in trips to the zoo, the circus, and the ballpark to watch the Dodgers play. It was her intense curiosity about the world around her and a "passion for language" that compelled her to write poem after poem. As she humbly explained, "I think each time I write it may be the last time; then something takes my fancy. . .I had no ambition to be a writer."

Marianne Moore had a long, rewarding writing career and received, in 1952, the National Book Award and the Pulitzer Prize for her *Collected Poems*. From the eight books of poetry published over a 50-year period, she collected these works into editions such as *Selected Poems* (1935), *A Marianne Moore Reader* (1961), and *The Complete Poems of Marianne Moore* (1967). She is also known for her collected essays and reviews and her translations of the *Selected Fables of La Fontaine* (1954). In 1986, *The Complete Prose of Marianne Moore*, edited by Patricia Willis, was published by Viking Penguin Inc. Moore died in New York on February 5, 1972; she was eighty-four.

The World of the Poems

Like William Carlos Williams, Marianne Moore was fascinated with machine technology. She wrote about clocks, engines, and steamrollers; she frequently referred to the "machine-like" qualities of her anteaters, elephants, pelicans and cats, admiring their precise engineering. While the scientific revolution was, for some critics, destroying the spirit of America, it became a springboard for Moore's insatiable curiosity. Having been "exhilarated" by her biology courses at Bryn Mawr, she grew to admire the detachment of scientists, their ability to observe things accurately, and their desire to communicate that information to an audience. As she once remarked, "Precision, economy of statement, logic employed to ends that are disinterested, drawing and identifying, liberate—at least have some bearing on—the imagination."

Along with her interest in science and technology, Moore was a connoisseur of art. She attended exhibitions and museums regularly and kept detailed notes of what she saw. This was not a mere hobby, but was a chance for Moore to become a painting's "imaginary possessor," transcending the boundaries of time and space. These art objects became the subjects for her poems, the result being that she often wrote about the relationship of art to life. Because art objects can themselves be representations of life, Moore was able to maintain the position of the detached yet interested observer that she so admired in the scientist.

Moore read an amazing range of material, from newspapers to travelogues, to science journals, to books on sports. She was an active reader and listener, judiciously recording the unusual sentence or passage into her journal. Similarly, she clipped newpaper articles, saved postcards, photographs, and letters, making editorial notes on the backs or in the margins. Moore was a habitual collector of the words and pictures that inspired her. Many of these things would spark her imagination and find themselves transformed in her poems.

One of the unique features of Moore's poetry is her abundant use of quotations. Poems like "Marriage" and "An Octopus" are composed almost entirely of quotations, Moore thus assuming responsibility for orchestrating them together into one complete piece. What is most interesting about her method is that she would take these borrowed phrases completely out of context, placing them in poems that have nothing to do with their original meaning. Unlike Eliot, who incorporated literary phrases of the past as a means towards deepening the roots of the poem, Moore recycled her quotations. (In a memoir of Marianne Moore, Elizabeth Bishop tells the story of how Moore and her mother would "make over" their clothes, transforming, for example, a pair of drawers into a slip. Perhaps Moore's tendency to quote comes from her strong practical nature.)

Another unusual habit of Moore's was her continual impulse to rewrite her poems long after their first appearance in magazines. This both perplexed and annoyed her audience who had become attached to an early version of a poem only to see it drastically altered in a subsequent collection. Whole sections would be omitted or added, syllabic verse would become free verse, quotation marks dropped or inserted, the phrasing changed. Poet Randall Jarrell argued that once in print, the poem is no longer only hers, it is everyone's and "we can protest just as we could if Donatello cut off David's leg."

Moore was writing in the spirit of her times, reinventing form and discovering new subjects, when one was applauded for doing so. With eloquent praise from two of the leading writers of her day, Ezra Pound and T.S. Eliot, Moore maintained "the courage of her peculiarities," writing poems that continue to surprise us today.

Marianne Moore: Constant Change

In an interview, when asked about what inspired her to write, Marianne Moore replied:

"Books, conversation, a remark, objects, circumstances sometimes make an indelible impression on one. . . For instance, you see a suit of armor. The moveability suggests a wearer—there is life under the mechanism; you are reminded of an armadillo, say, or a crayfish, and you recall the beauty of the ancient testudo, the shield laid on the shield of the Romans. Then perhaps the idea of conflict counteracts that of romance. Presently you see a live iguana and are startled by the paradox of its docility in connection with its horrific aspect. The idea of beauty outweighs the thought of painful self-protectiveness, and you have a developing theme."

Much of our thought follows this pattern: one thing leads to another, which leads to another, in a seemingly unrelated progression. Even our social interactions are comprised of one person saying something, which "reminds" the other person of something else. Marianne Moore was not unusual in taking these "mental excursions," at which she was a master. When something struck her, she followed a chain of startling images which led to a discovery about the original source, be it a suit of armor, or a comment made by her mother. The result was poetry that blazoned a bold and often surprising course.

Moore did not write directly about her own experience; instead she looked at the world of impersonal subjects for poetry. She liked animals and art objects, places and nature because they were beautiful and self-contained; she liked those things which functioned autonomously, calling them "models of exactness." Her impulse was to present a "thing" with the accuracy of the scientist, while still preserving its mysterious power to enchant. Allowing her mind to "free associate" (as demonstrated in the opening quotation), her poems became constructs of particulars, with detail sliding upon detail until the object became "lit with piercing glances into the life of things."

We read at the heels of her inventiveness and must always expect the unexpected. Her poems resemble collages, with fragments of quotations, images, ideas, descriptions (both poetic and "unpoetic") woven together to give her subject its distinctiveness. Even her syllabic stanzas (stanzas which follow a strict syllable count in each line; for example, a four-line stanza might have five syllables in the first line, three in the second, eight in the third and six in the fourth. This pattern would be repeated in each stanza of the poem.) with lines that jut out to the edge of the right margin, insist that the reader "watch" as well as read the lines as the poem unfolds. Dividing words at the end of the line, omitting transitions, and incorporating quotations are only some of the ways she demonstrated her inventiveness. She was one of the first poets to make use of the language of non-literary subjects (like business and science), thus earning the name "poet of the unpoetic."

In keeping with her contemporaries (Pound, Williams, and Stevens), Moore was seeking a new approach to form, one that was "less mannered," and more true to the rhythms of American speech. She believed that poems should create the effect of "flowing continuity" like conversations, one sentence falling into the next. In some other chapters, you have been asked to read poems aloud to appreciate them fully. With Moore's poetry, reading the poems aloud is less important. Unlike Whitman or Crane, whose poems were meant for the public to hear, Moore's poetry was written for the page. Her rhymes were so subtle, that you can often see them on the page before you can actually hear them.

Guided by the intensity of her vision, Moore's poems often transform the real to the imagined as a means towards discovering a truth. In her vigilant attempts to "see" what is before her in full light ("the love of doing hard things"), Moore moves between the actual and the imagined world, creating an inner tension between the two. In "The Pangolin," a poem which celebrates the connection between usefulness and beauty, she praises this "true" anteater for its "contracting nose and eye apertures/ impenetrably closable," while at the same time she is enchanted by how it steps "in the moonlight,/ on the moonlight peculiarly."

Just as Moore blurs the boundaries of perception, from the real to the imagined, so too does she create a world that is both abused and strengthened by change. When you read her poems, notice how many changes occur in a single poem: a sudden shift in tone, imagery, perspective, or anything else you observe. In addition, notice how frequently she dramatizes a situation which requires her subject to change, move, or react to an outside force. When we read "The Fish" we are struck by the damage inflicted in the sea. A mussel shell is "an/injured fan"; water "drives a wedge/of iron" through the cliff; barnacles "cannot hide" because of the "shafts of/the sun." But the cliff, which reveals "all/external/marks of abuse" becomes a "defiant edifice" against man's molestations and the wear of time.

According to Moore, danger is only a problem if we succumb to it. Danger is, in fact, not only a reality but a vital force in nature, for it gives rise to man's most admirable qualities: courage and determination. In poem after poem, we watch her subjects triumph over incoming threats: the mother bird in "Bird Witted" who is absorbed in feeding her young, is able, in an instant, to transform her maternal body into "bayonet beak" and "cruel wings" and wage "deadly combat" against a cat. Peter, a cat in another poem, is praised for his ability "to leap, to lengthen out, divide the air, to purloin, to pursue." For, as she says, "this is life;/to do less would be nothing but dishonesty."

Her own struggle was trying to define art (poetry) and its relation to life. Specifically, she was absorbed in the question of how poetry could best address life's constant changes, given the constraints of language and form. It is this struggle, to present a "true" picture of her subject, that makes for such complex and mystifying verse. Truth in life, as Moore sees it, is not a nice neat package, but rather a conspiracy of contradictions and paradoxes. (Notice, when you read her poems, how often she offers contradictory images and paradoxical meanings about one subject.) We, as readers, are invited into this changing world, asked to stay alert to the whirlwind of sensations spinning around us.

Exercise: Make a list of the dangers you perceive in your own life. These can be anything from the dangers of walking home late at night to the dangers of revealing private feelings to someone you care about. Write a poem which incorporates some of these dangers.

Meet the Speakers

Charles Tomlinson is an English poet with an international following. Among his books of verse are *The Way of the World, The Shaft*, and *Notes From New York*. In *Some Americans: A Personal Record,* he mentions such poets as Ezra Pound, Hart Crane, Wallace Stevens and Marianne Moore as chief influences on his work.

Clive Driver is the literary executor of the estate of Marianne Moore. He was formerly the Director of the Rosenbach Museum and Library in Philadelphia, and became a close friend of Moore during her last years. Driver is currently working on a biography of Moore.

Monroe Wheeler, formerly director of exhibitions and publications at The Museum of Modern Art in New York, originally met Marianne Moore in 1921. In 1923, he became her first American publisher, bringing out (in pamphlet form) her poem "Marriage." They continued to be close friends throughout her life.

Grace Shulman is a poet and critic. A close friend of Marianne Moore, she has recently published *Marianne Moore: the Poetry of Engagement*.

Richard Howard, a Pulitzer Prize-winning poet and critic, is also an accomplished translator of such French writers as Jean Genet, Andre Gide, and Charles Baudelaire. His own volumes of poetry include *Untitled Subjects, Fellow Fellings*, and *Two-Part Inventions*.

Patricia Willis is the curator of literature for the Rosenbach Museum and Library. She also edited *The Complete Prose of Marianne Moore*, a volume that reveals Moore's acumen as a critic of art and literature and as an observer of manners.

Kenneth Burke is a distinguished American literary critic and theorist whose poetry and short fiction are also widely admired. Among his major works are *The Philosophy of Literary Form: Studies in Symbolic Action, A Grammar of Motives* and *A Rhetoric of Motives*. He was a friend and champion of Moore and worked with her on *The Dial* magazine in the 1920s.

Study Plan for this Unit

1. Complete the section **Before Watching the Film: Journal-Writing and Other Activities**.

2. Read the Moore poems some of which are featured in the film.
A Grave
An Octopus
The Steeple-Jack
Marriage
The Mind Is an Enchanting Thing

The Fish
In the Days of Prismatic Color
Poetry
Critics and Connoisseurs
The Labors of Hercules
The Pangolin
In Distrust of Merits
Progress
Baseball and Writing

3. Watch the program.

4. Complete the section **After Watching the Film: Journal-Writing and Other Activities**.

5. Go through the **Guided Reading**.

6. Complete the **Exercises and Assignments** as specified by your instructor.

7. Take the **Self Test**.

Before Watching the Film: Journal-Writing and Other Activities

1. Find a hillside, rooftop, or upper floor of a building where you can observe the scene below. Write a panoramic description that reveals your point of view without ever stating where you are.

2. In your journal, write a paragraph explaining the following analogy: baseball is like writing.

3. Take fifteen minutes to observe an object that strikes you and without lifting your pen, "free associate" on paper. Let your mind drift farther and farther from the object, making note of each thought or image. (Moore, for example, when she saw a suit of armor, thought of an armadillo, which made her think of the ancient testudo; this led to the idea of conflict and romance.)

4. Read "The Pangolin." Go through and underline every scientific word or phrase. Then go through the poem again and circle every descriptive detail that involves some metaphoric comparison.

5. Moore, like Williams, is known for her use of "unpoetic details" in a poem. Find five examples of these details in the Moore poems you have read. Imagine her poems without these details; how would they be different?

6. Make a list of specialized words or phrases in one of your other fields of study (psychology, sociology, computer science, law), then write a poem which incorporates some of these words in a descriptive poem about a person, place or thing.

7. Pretend that General Motors has asked you to help name their new car. Invent at least four names that reveal the type of car you are trying to market; for example, the "Coupe de Ville" is a luxury car, the "Sting Ray" is a sports car.

While Watching the Film

1. Jot down any striking words, phrases, or visual images that you encounter in the film.

2. In the film, several people speak who knew Moore personally. Look for the similarities and differences in their views of her.

After Watching the Film: Journal-Writing and Other Activities

1. Having viewed the film, can you see how baseball, as a phenomenon, might appeal to a writer or artist?

2. How have the visual images of Mt. Rainier helped you to read and understand "An Octopus"?

3. Which visual presentation of a poem did you like best? Why?

Guided Reading

"The Steeple-Jack" is one of Moore's most celebrated poems for its juxtaposition of opposites and appreciation for incongruities. Before answering the questions, read the poem through once, and watch how your perception of the town changes as the poem unfolds. Let the speaker's words create images in your mind and try to notice the sudden shifts of perspective; don't worry if you can't understand the meaning implied in each line or phrase. The **Guided Reading** questions will help you to understand how the details reveal the poem's theme.

The Steeple-Jack

Dürer would have seen a reason for living   1
    in a town like this, with eight stranded whales
to look at; with the sweet sea air coming into
  your house
on a fine day, from water etched
    with waves as formal as the scales
on a fish.

One by one in two's and three's, the seagulls keep   7
    flying back and forth over the town clock,
or sailing around the lighthouse without moving
  their wings—
rising steadily with a slight
    quiver of the body—or flock
mewing where

a sea the purple of the peacock's neck is   13
    paled to greenish azure as Dürer changed
the pine green of the Tyrol to peacock blue and guinea
gray. You can see a twenty-five-
    pound lobster; and fishnets arranged
to dry. The

whirlwind fife-and-drum of the storm bends
    the salt   19

marsh grass, disturbs stars in the sky and the
star on the steeple; it is a privilege to see so
much confusion. Disguised by what
    might seem the opposite, the sea-
side flowers and

trees are favored by the fog so that you have   25
    the tropics at first hand: the trumpet vine,
fox-glove, giant snap-dragon, a salpiglossis that has
spots and stripes; morning-glories, gourds,
    or moon-vines trained on fishing-twine
at the back door;

cat-tails, flags, blueberries and spiderwort,   31
    striped grass, lichens, sunflowers, asters,
        daisies—
yellow and crab-claw ragged sailors with green
  bracts—toad-plant,
petunias, ferns; pink lilies, blue
    ones, tigers; poppies; black sweet-peas.
The climate

is not right for the banyan, frangipani, or   37
    jack-fruit trees; or for exotic serpent
life. Ring lizard and snake-skin for the foot,
  if you see fit;
but here they've cats, not cobras, to
    keep down the rats. The diffident
little newt

with white pin-dots on black horizontal spaced-   43
    out bands lives here; yet there is nothing that
ambition can buy or take away. The college student
named Ambrose sits on the hillside
    with his not-native books and hat
and sees boats

at sea progress white and rigid as if in   49
    a groove. Liking an elegance of which
the source is not bravado, he knows by heart
  the antique
sugar-bowl shaped summer-house of
    interlacing slats, and the pitch
of the church

spire, not true, from which a man in scarlet lets   55
    down a rope as a spider spins a thread;
he might be part of a novel, but on the sidewalk a
sign says C.J. Poole, Steeple-Jack,

in black and white; and one in red
and white says

Danger. The church portico has four fluted   61
    columns, each a single piece of stone, made
modester by white-wash. This would be a fit
    haven for
waifs, children, animals, prisoners,
    and presidents who have repaid
sin-driven

senators by not thinking about them. The   67
    place has a school-house, a post-office in a
store, fish-houses, hen-houses, a three-masted
    schooner on
the stocks. The hero, the student,
    the steeple-jack, each in his way,
is at home.

It could not be dangerous to be living   74
    in a town like this, of simple people,
who have a steeple-jack placing danger-signs
    by the church
while he is gilding the solid-
    pointed star, which on a steeple
stands for hope.

Lines 1-12

1. Who is Dürer? How might this first line influence your reading of the poem?

2. How does the word "etched" relate to Dürer?

3. What does Moore mean by "formal" in line 5?

4. In stanza one and two, how does Moore convey an appearance of order and calm in the town?

5. What, in stanza two, reveals a departure from order?

6. Where is the speaker located? How do you know?

Answers

1. Albrecht Dürer (1471-1528) was a German Renaissance artist known for his detailed etchings and paintings of the physical world. He is also known for his interest in seeing the extraordinary in the ordinary, the surreal in the real. He once made a difficult voyage to view beached whales (but he never saw them).

2. "Etched" reminds us of Dürer's etchings, which in turn reminds us that the point of view here is that of an artist, one who is interested in the "look" of things, i.e., their shape, color, and texture.

3. "Formal" refers to the preciseness of the waves, each one exactly like the next; though the speaker is observing external patterns of objects, she could also be suggesting

132

that the townspeople themselves are formal, following accepted rules and conventions.

4. Through her imagery, Moore brings "the sweet sea air" to your house, the waves are as ordered as "the scales on a fish," the gulls are flying in clear patterns over the clock and lighthouse as if to keep order in the town. Further, if you listen to line 7 you will hear the steady beat of the line (every other word receiving the accent) imitating the calmness of the gulls.

5. Order is threatened in the second half of the stanza when we see a "slight quiver of the body."

6. The speaker seems to move around. We feel included in the intimacy of her perspective ("the sweet sea air coming into your house"), while at the same time we follow her above the town (atop the steeple?) for a more panoramic view of whales, water and gulls. Then, suddenly, we are close enough to the flying gulls to see them "quiver."

Lines 13-18

1. Why does the exact color of the peacock's neck matter to the poet?

2. Contrast the writing in the first and second half of the stanza.

3. Gathering the images from the first three stanzas, where might this town be located? Does it seem real to you?

Answers

1. Again, the name of this color has the precision of a painter's pallet, which in turn intensifies what we are seeing. In addition, Moore is suggesting the revelation of something exotic in an ordinary scene.

2. The first half of the stanza is rich with poetic descriptions, words chosen for their sounds as well as their content. (Moore probably took delight in including "peacock blue" and "guinea gray.") The second half of the stanza contains no description; she is merely reporting the things she sees. It is as if the language, like the fish nets, has been taken out to dry.

3. This could be a New England town, one that is visited by tourists in the summer; however, with "eight stranded whales," water "etched" and "formal," a peacock purple sea, and a "twenty-five-pound lobster," the town becomes more spectacular, located somewhere in the poet's imagination. (Moore claimed that when she wrote this poem she was thinking about her own town, Brooklyn, and some New England towns she had visited.)

Lines 19-24

1. Suddenly, what was once serene and calm is now caught in a "whirlwind," with the speaker remarking that "it is a privilege to see so/ much confusion." Why might it be a "privilege" to be a witness to this?

2. How does Moore's arrangement of details and choice of line breaks reinforce what happens in the stanza?

3. Notice the leap from "salt/marsh grass" to "stars in the sky and the/star on the steeple." What kind of disruption is this?

4. How does Moore's use of "disguised" affect your concept of order in this town?

Answers

1. Order has been turned upside-down. But just by describing the storm as a "whirlwind fife-and-drum" she implies that the storm is a positive force. Moore is suggesting that the true order of the town is revealed in the chaos of the storm. "Confusion," then, is closer to the truth than order, for that is a far more accurate assessment of reality. Therefore, it is "a privilege" to be able to see the way she does, to see these glimmers of truth in what appears to be "confusion."

2. The details of the storm and the way in which Moore arranges them cause our eye to move around abruptly, from grass to stars to a church steeple. Also, the line breaks interrupt the phrasings, adding to the confusion. We have a storm that bends the salt; we have lines ending with the words "the," "so," "what" and "and." The result is a visual disruption as well as the one created by the storm.

3. Literally, the storm might have knocked off the star on the steeple; symbolically, the storm is disturbing the peaceful order in the town, even its systems of belief.

4. "Disguised" is a key word in the poem for it forces us to see the order in the first three stanzas as a misrepresentation of reality.

Lines 25-36

1. How is Moore's guide to the town unusual?

2. Moore took pleasure in the assonance and consonance of "moon-vines trained on fishing-twine"; are there other phrases in the poem that make use of assonance or consonance or alliteration?

3. How does "at the back door" relocate the poem?

4. In this stanza and the preceding one, list all the flowers that contain animals in their names. Notice how many of these animals we associate with danger.

Answers

1. These are not the words of an ordinary tour guide, but rather these are the words of one who has had a revelation about the town she is describing. The speaker is seeing it not just on one afternoon, but through time, night and day, wind and calm. She covers the sights with far more detail than an ordinary guide, transporting us, by way of naming the flowers, to more exotic places.

2. Phrases like "spots and stripes; morning-glories, gourds" and "sugar-bowl shaped summer-house."

3. From the tropics we return to the domestic scene established in the first stanza, as if back from a dream. We are no longer taking in the town from above: our perspective has returned to eye-level.

4. Fox-glove, snap-dragon, cat-tails, spiderwort, toad-plant, and tigers.

Lines 37-48

1. Contrast your present image of the town with your first impression.

2. What effect do the two maxims, in their altered state, have on the poem?

3. Why might Moore have chosen to say "not-native?" Replace it with a word that means the same thing.

4. How do you perceive the college student? What is his role in the poem?

Answers

1. It is no longer a simple, serene, resort town, but a place that is subject to sudden changes of weather, even danger, making the commonplace seem extraordinary.

2. Moore's use of maxims ("If the shoe fits, wear it," and "everything money can buy") deepens the sense of order that at first appears to pervade this town. She could be telling us more about these townspeople (who are noticeably absent up to this point) and the ways in which they live their lives. By twisting these maxims around, she is reinforcing the need to question these surfaces.

3. His "not-native" hat reveals that he is an outsider, someone who is removed from the scene. She could have said "foreign" which might have distinguished him as being from some other place, rather than pointing to his lack of connection with this town.

4. The college student is physically set apart: he watches the town from the hillside, appreciating the physical details of the landscape. Like Dürer, he objectifies the scene, paying attention to pattern, shape and color. Because he is detached yet so keenly interested, he is the one who notices the spire is "not true" in line 55. Moore identifies with this perspective, for not only does he notice the incongruities (boats progressing "as if in a groove," a crooked steeple), but he also values them.

Lines 49-54

1. What is the contradiction embedded in her image of the boats?

2. The phrase "knows by heart" is an expression whose meaning we take for granted. Seen in the formal context of this poem, we see it fresh. Explain the implications of the phrase.

3. Which meaning of "pitch" is the dominant one? Are there others that are significant?

Answers

1. Moore's boats are white and rigid, stuck like fixtures rather than moving objects. And yet they "progress," even though we do not see their movement.

2. Literally, it means to have memorized something. Here it implies that the student has studied this scene so carefully, because he has lived there and is now returning, that it has become part of him. He not only knows every detail of the scene but has great feeling for it.

3. Literally, "pitch" is the highest point of a structure. The "pitch of the church" also implies a church's religious "pitch" or speech intended to attract converts.

Lines 55-60

1. What is meant by "not true" in line 55?

2. What do the various details about C.J. Poole (and the fact that the poem is named after him) suggest about him as a symbolic figure?

3. C.J. Poole actually was a steeple-jack in Brooklyn, where Moore lived. Can you see why she favored using his name in this poem?

Answers

1. Literally "not true" means that the steeple is not at a straight 90 degree angle. Symbolically, if we think back to the speaker's revelation that "it is a privilege to see so/much confusion," we can infer that she is also being ironic. The storm, which by lifting the guise of order from the town revealed its truth, has also knocked the steeple askew, thereby correcting it.

2. The steeple-jack wears scarlet, "might be part of a novel," and "lets/down a rope as a spider spins a thread." This is the most attention any character has received in the poem. The speaker's excitement over the storm leads us to believe that she admires the steeple-jack's willingness to attempt something dangerous. Once again we have a "confusion" of order: although he appears to be repairing the steeple, he wears red (the color of the devil) and spins a thread (catching the church in its web?).

3. She may have enjoyed the pun in "C" (sea) and "Poole" (pool).

Lines 61-67

1. What is ironic about placing danger signs by a church?

2. What is the effect of the sudden shift between the end of stanza 10 and the beginning of stanza 11?

3. What might waifs, children, animals, prisoners, and presidents have in common?

Answers

1. It is ironic that a church, normally associated with safety and salvation is suddenly seen as a dangerous place.

2. Moore shifts from the heavily loaded word "danger" to the objective reporting of "the church portico has four fluted/ columns." She ignores the implications of putting danger signs around a church, and focuses instead on the outside of the building. The effect is a heightened sense of the town's incongruities: not only are there danger signs around a church, but the apocalyptic warning is juxtaposed against the ordinary-looking church portico. (Here again, we are reminded of Dürer who painted apocalyptic visions in ordinary settings.)

3. They are all on the outside of society.

Lines 68-74

1. What is gained by the repetition of "houses"?

2. What else in the poem is contained, yet not at home?

Answers

1. The repetition of "houses" suggests two meanings: on first reading we see them as homes for these animals. But the irony here is that all these houses are not homes but temporary containers; the children are in school, the post-office is in a store, the fish and hens are confined the same way the schooner is "on the stocks." The repetition helps to sharpen the contrast of the hero, the student, the steeple-jack who are all at "home."

2. The "eight stranded whales" and the "twenty-five-pound lobster." (Though not specified, it appears that this unusually large lobster is in a cage or trap somewhere, out for display, since the image that comes directly after is fish nets.)

Lines 75-80

1. What is the effect of beginning the last stanza with a line that is similar to the first line in the poem?

2. What is the tone of the first two lines? Is it ironic? Support your answer.

3. What are the various definitions of "gilding"? Which definition might be important to the poem?

4. What is the relationship of hope to danger in the end of the poem?

Answers

1. Though it may seem we have made a complete circle by repeating, in essence, the first line of the poem, we know we are not at the same place that we began. Our concept of order has been challenged throughout the poem with the unveiling of contradictory images.

2. Although this seems like a "simple" community with its church and school, student and steeple-jack, the fully revealed scene becomes far more complex. Appearances aren't always what they seem; the people may take refuge in false beliefs, hide behind oversimplified maxims, rely on the illusion of their "ordered" world. Gathering all her images of danger, from the storm to the steeple-jack climbing a steeple, we know that it is indeed dangerous to be living here. Yet danger is what "gives us a reason" to live in a place like this. Danger and confusion triumph over safety and order because they are far truer to life's realities.

3. Gilding means to cover with a thin layer of gold; to give a deceptively improved appearance; to adorn unnecessarily. Though Moore admires the steeple-jack's gesture, she has thrown doubt on whether man can actually repair the damage.

4. The ending is ambiguous. Hope and danger are equally woven into the ending of the poem, just as they are both vital parts of the community. And just as the speaker is seemingly undisturbed by a town that places danger signs around its church, so too is she celebrating the genuineness of all the town's contradictions. A place where ordinary people confront the dangers of their lives, while still holding out the star of hope, is for Moore a heaven on earth.

Further Questions

1. In "The Steeple-Jack," Moore uses syllabic verse (verse which follows a strict syllabic stanza pattern) which has become the hallmark of her poetry. Unlike metered poetry, syllabic verse is unaccented, giving the poems a "matter of fact" tone which Moore liked. Go through and count the syllables for each line of one stanza (each stanza should be about the same); what is the form? What effect does it have on the poem?

2. Count the number of times Moore uses the word "sea" or "see." Is this deliberate? Why?

3. In 1955, Moore revised this poem by omitting all the lines after "it is a privilege to

see so much confusion," up until "a steeple-jack in red." How would the poem have changed?

Answers

1. In 13 stanzas of 6 lines each, the syllabic pattern is 11, 10, 14, 8, 8, 3. We can't hear the syllabic pattern the same way we can hear the strong beats of metric verse. In that way, none of the words carries more weight than others, lines flow into one another without pause. The syllabic form becomes more a visual presentation than an aural one, giving poems a distinctive "look" on the page.

2. Moore repeats the words 11 times, drawing our attention to the fact that this poem is a visual portrait, something seen. But just as she asserts her ability to see, she also is doubting whether we can really see the way things are. Her sight is transformed to insight as she sees through the deceptive simplicity into the hazards and dangers of living.

3. She eliminated what could be for her extraneous detail ("liking an elegance of which the source is not bravado") and writes instead a "modester" version, one that is leaner, more directed towards its meaning. This edited version lacks the pleasure of her floral observations, the celebration of words, the discovery of the exotic in the ordinary.

Exercises and Assignments

1. Closely observe a live animal (cat, dog, bird, pigeon, cockroach, etc.) or a picture of one. Take notes on its physical appearance and the way it behaves, making sure to note particulars. Then, write a paragraph or a poem which both describes the animal and captures the essence of it. Reveal your fascination without the use of abstract words like beautiful or fascinating.

2. Write a short Marianne Moore imitation incorporating quotations, some real and some imaginary. These can be selected from conversations, books, magazines, signs, pamphlets, anything you choose. Also, try to use two new words that you find in the dictionary.

3. How do Moore's poems contradict what you believed to be true about poetry? What kinds of departures does she make? Consider her subjects, form, diction, revisions, notes, and anything else that strikes you as unusual.

4. After rereading "The Steeple-Jack," write a description of a real or imaginary place. (This could be a town, a train station, a backyard, a bedroom, etc.) Either in the form of a poem or a paragraph, begin with the lines "Moore would have seen a reason," and end with "It is a privilege to see so much confusion." Try to subtly reveal confusion through your use of opposites and contradictions.

5. In "Poetry," Moore presents her now famous definition that poems are "imaginary gardens with real toads in them." Why did she choose toads rather than daisies or rabbits? Based on your reading of Moore's poetry, what did she mean by this phrase?

6. Write down four questions you would like to ask Moore about her poetry. Answer them.

7. "Marriage" has been hailed by various writers as "an anthology of transit," "a rapidly moving train," and "a masterpiece of sudden departures." Based on your reading

of the poem, which definition seems the most accurate? Why? If none of these descriptions seem accurate to you, make up your own, then support your choice.

8. Read "I May, I Might, I Must." Moore creates a tension between what she says and how she says it. After paraphrasing the poem, explain how the form (its rhyme and meter) affects the poem's meaning.

9. Read "The Mind Is An Enchanting Thing" and answer the following questions:

a. In the title, the mind is an "enchanting" thing, whereas in the first line she calls it an "enchanted" thing. What is the difference between a mind that is enchanting and enchanted?

b. List all the senses referred to in the poem. What is she saying about the relationship between the mind and the senses?

c. This poem is constructed with syllabic stanza patterns of 6, 5, 4, 6, 7, 9. In addition to the syllabics, the stanzas form a distinctive design on the page. Discuss the way in which the visual appearance of the poem affects the content.

10. In "A Grave" and "An Octopus" Moore creates analogies for the sea and a state park as if they were animate objects. After reading each poem, write three paragraphs in which you explain the analogy for both of these subjects.

11. Read "The Fish" and answer the following questions:

a. How does Moore depict the sea in the poem "The Fish"? Support your answer with lines and images from the poem.

b. Who, if either, wins the battle between the sea and the cliff? Explain your answer.

12. In many of Moore's poems, the title is part of the first line. If you were to ask her why she did this, how might she answer you? As a reader, what do you feel is achieved by this technique?

13. Select two of Moore's poems which make use of descriptive detail. After reading these poems, find at least three categories of description. For example, she often transforms her nouns into adjectives to describe an object. The swan (in "Critics and Connoisseurs") has "flamingo colored, maple leaf-like feet." You could call this category "Adjectival Nouns."

14. Read "Critics and Connoisseurs." In this poem, Moore recalls observing a swan and an ant as a means towards making accusations about both critics and connoisseurs. What is her feeling about these two groups of people? Look up the definitions for critic and connoisseur before answering the question.

15. In the long version of "Poetry," Moore argues that the "usefulness" of things gives them their importance.

a. Keeping this in mind, what about the pangolin (in "The Pangolin") does Moore find to admire?

b. Does she find any of these traits in Man? (Refer to the last 3 stanzas of "The Pangolin.")

16. Compare and contrast the long and short version of "Poetry." What is the effect of omitting all but the first three lines of the poem?

17. In "The Labors of Hercules," contrast the undesirable behavior with that which is desirable.

Self Test

Read the poems "Snail" and the later version called "To A Snail." Compare and contrast the two. Consider the following questions: How has the structure changed? Has the meaning changed? If so, how? Which version do you think is better? Why?

Snail

If "compression is the first grace of
   style," you have it. The absence of feet and your occipital
      horn
     Are perfectly in keeping with the philosopher's
     Definition. Contractility is not a virtue but
        modesty is
       A virtue, and that you instance both aesthetic
         and "real" virtue
       Is so true
As that virtue "is." It is not the
   Acquisition of any one thing that is able to adorn—
     It is the incidental quality that acquire
       As a concomitant of things that are hid, and that is
        present only in
       In conjunction with things that are infinitely
         more worth while than style
       Is worthwhile.

To A Snail

If "compression is the first grace of style,"
you have it. Contractility is a virtue
as modesty is a virtue.
It is not the acquisition of any one thing
that is able to adorn,
or the incidental quality that occurs
as a concomitant of something well said,
that we value in style,
but the principle that is hid:
in the absence of feet, "a method of conclusions";
"a knowledge of principles,"
in the curious phenomenon of your occipital horn.

Answers to Self Test

Answers to Self Tests begin on page 226.

For Further Reading

Books by Marianne Moore

Collected Poems. New York: Macmillan; 1952.

Complete Poems. New York: Viking; 1981.

A Marianne Moore Reader. New York: Viking; 1961.

The Complete Prose of Marianne Moore. Willis, Patricia, editor. New York: Viking; 1987.

Books about Moore

Auden, W.H. "Marianne Moore." *The Dyer's Hand, and Other Essays.* New York: Random House; 1962.

Bishop, Elizabeth. "A Memoir of Marianne Moore." *The Collected Prose.* New York: Farrar, Straus and Giroux; 1984.

Costello, Bonnie. *Marianne Moore, Imaginary Possessions.* Cambridge: Harvard University Press; 1981.

Hall, Donald. "Marianne Moore." *Writers at Work: The Paris Review Interviews, Second Series.* New York: Ecco Press; 1980.

Jarrell, Randall. "Her Shield and the Humble Animal." *Poetry and the Age.* New York: Ecco Press; 1980.

Tomlinson, Charles, editor. *Marianne Moore: A Collection of Critical Essays.* Englewood Cliffs, NJ: Prentice-Hall; 1970.

T.S. Eliot (1888-1965)

Thomas Stearns Eliot was probably the most famous and influential American poet of this century. He not only created a new poetic style, but he changed the way people view poetry. The beauty of his poetic language and imagery was immediately apparent to his readers, and the ideas expressed in his criticism and exemplified in the poetry helped to create a new approach to poetry in general, one that was sympathetic to his aims and which allowed a deeper understanding and appreciation of his work. In this way, Eliot essentially created his own audience. Although his critical influence—which dominated literary criticism for 30 years—has waned in recent decades (and his critical essays on other writers are now often looked at for the insight they give into Eliot himself), T.S. Eliot's poetry continues to be rediscovered and read with new delight by each successive generation.

Eliot was born in 1888 in St. Louis, Missouri, where his father was a successful manufacturer. His grandfather, William Greenleaf Eliot, started a Unitarian mission in St. Louis and became the founder and first president of Washington University. Eliot attended Smith Academy in St. Louis, and later went east to Milton Academy. He also spent many of his summers in New England, at the family's summer house in Gloucester, Massachusetts. An older brother taught him to sail, and 30 years later Eliot immortalized one of his favorite sailing areas on Cape Ann in "The Dry Salvages," the third poem in his *Four Quartets*. In 1906, Eliot entered Harvard, where he studied languages, literature and philosophy. While at Harvard, he read Arthur Symons' *The Symbolist Movement in Literature* which introduced him to Jules Laforgue and other important French Symbolists. In the three years after this time, Eliot wrote some of his most famous early poems including "The Love Song of J. Alfred Prufrock," "Preludes," and "Rhapsody on a Windy Night." Eliot received his M.A. in philosophy in 1910 and then spent a year in Paris, studying at the Sorbonne and attending lectures by the noted philosopher Henri Bergson. Paris was the focal point for new movements in art and literature, as well as being suffused with a sense of the past. Eliot's stay there helped him in formulating his idea that the past lives on and is part of the present. This idea is exemplified in his poems by his direct borrowing of lines, words, and phrases from great poetic works of the past.

From 1911-1914, Eliot studied Oriental Philosophy and Sanskrit at Harvard and was a teaching assistant in the philosophy department. In 1914 he received a Harvard Travelling Fellowship. He first journeyed to Marburg in Germany, but had to leave urgently for England when war was declared. In London he was introduced to Ezra Pound and through him met a number of other influential writers, including novelist Ford Madox Ford and, later, Wyndham Lewis, editor of the prominent literary/art magazine *Blast*. Pound immediately recognized Eliot's genius and sent "The Love Song of J. Alfred Prufrock" to Harriet Monroe, editor of *Poetry*, telling her that Eliot had "trained himself and modernized himself on his own." Pound now assumed considerable influence in Eliot's life: he overcame Monroe's reluctance to publish the poem, and he prevailed on Eliot to stay in London and devote himself to writing poetry. "Prufrock" appeared in *Poetry* magazine in June 1915, the same month that Eliot married Vivien Haigh-Wood, the daughter of a British painter.

Eliot's unannounced marriage and his decision not to return to academic life in the United States created a rift with his family in St. Louis. He made a brief and unsuccessful visit to patch things over and then returned to England, with his father no longer willing to lend him any financial support. Although he had successfully completed and submitted his thesis, he now chose not to return to Harvard and defend it orally, which would have been the final step towards his degree. His decision to return without financial resources to a country at war shows how determined he was to continue his aim, together with Ezra Pound, of creating a new poetry. He supported himself and his wife for a while by teaching high school, and in 1918 went to work as a clerk at Lloyds Bank. He helped supplement his limited salary by editing *The Egoist*, an important literary journal. *Prufrock and Other Observations* had appeared in 1917, followed by *Poems* and a collection of important critical essays, *The Sacred Wood*, in 1920; Eliot was beginning to have a marked impact on the literary world.

In 1920, T.S. Eliot began intensive work on a long poem that had been on his mind for some time. This poem later became *The Waste Land*. In 1921 he obtained leave from the bank due to a physical and nervous breakdown and went to the English coast to recuperate, moving on to a sanatorium in Lausanne, Switzerland. There he completed the poem, which he later showed to Pound, who suggested many important cuts and rearrangements. Eliot published *The Waste Land* in the October 1922 issue of *The Criterion*, the magazine he was now editing. *The Waste Land* burst upon the world of poetry "with the effect of an atomic bomb," as William Carlos Williams later described it. The masterful depiction of fragmentation in the modern world caught the imagination of his generation, and Eliot's reputation was now secure. His financial situation improved as well, and in 1925 he left the bank to become a director at the publishing house of Faber & Gwyer (later Faber & Faber). Emotionally and spiritually he was near despair, however; his wife had developed a nervous illness which became drastically worse over the years. Eliot's "The Hollow Men" (1925) indicates how bleak his outlook was at this time and how deep his spiritual anguish.

Eliot began to move towards resolving his questions of existence by embracing an all-encompassing faith. In 1927 he was confirmed in the Anglican church and, in the same year, he became a British subject. He now described himself as "a royalist in politics, a classicist in the arts, and Anglo-Catholic in religion." His work reflected his embracing the Anglican faith: first in the "Ariel Poems" (1927-30) and later in *Ash Wednesday* (1930) and the poems that made up *Four Quartets* (1935-42). After finishing "Little Gidding," the last of the four related poems, Eliot devoted himself for his remaining 20 years to writing plays and critical essays. He was awarded the Nobel Prize in 1948. At Eliot's request, his ashes were interred in the small English village of East Coker, the town made famous by his poem of the same name and the place from which Eliot's ancestor had set out for America 300 years earlier.

The World of the Poems

Eliot's developing years as a poet coincided with a period of great social and cultural ferment, as late Victorianism gave way to the 20th century. The repressive moral authority of the Victorian era—which nevertheless had its comforting certainties and stable social order—was under siege on all fronts. Philosophy, art, and literature had begun to undercut the very idea of reality as it was perceived in the 19th century; science and technology were advancing at an unprecedented rate; in music, Stravinsky heralded a revolution in technique and conception with his "Rite of Spring," which actually set off a riot when first performed. Women, too, were beginning to change their roles—demanding the vote, in addition to recognition as the sexual and intellectual equals of men.

In Europe the clash of 19th and 20th centuries had its terrible culmination in the

143

First World War. The war was essentially the result of a last-ditch effort by Europe's rulers to consolidate their empires. Far from being over quickly as everyone involved expected, the war dragged on for four years and decimated an entire generation. The war was fought using 19th-century tactics best suited to bayonet charges and hand-to-hand combat by foot soldiers. The weaponry, however, was of the 20th century and for the first time included aerial bombing, poison gas, and the widespread use of machine guns. Millions of young men died in the trenches, killed by an enemy they never saw, fighting for a few hundred yards of mud of benefit to no one. Death was haphazard, meaningless, and absurd. One could die from an unseen bomb while eating breakfast rations, from diarrhea caused by dysentery, from an infected scratch, or trapped in barbed wire like an animal in a snare. Under these circumstances, people began to question whether life itself had any meaning. The social fabric, too, began to unravel as people reacted to the folly of a governing order that had brought about this pointless mass destruction.

T.S. Eliot was not personally involved in the fighting, but, living in England during the war years, he was surrounded by its evidence. Among the dead were his close friends Jean Verdenal (to whom *Prufrock and Other Observations* is dedicated) and Karl Culpin, a companion from Oxford. T.E. Hulme, a young philosopher whom Eliot never met but whose philosophy greatly influenced him, also died in the trenches. "I think we are in rats' alley/Where the dead men lost their bones," Eliot writes in *The Waste Land*, using the soldiers' term for the area where bodies lay out of reach and unburied. The spectral figures of returning soldiers who had been gassed or wounded haunted the streets of London, making Eliot's borrowing of Dante's description of the "living dead" a contemporary social commentary.

The years following the war were also times of great social change, with the rise of the labor movement and social reform in Britain. Mass culture was on the rise and the cultural and political dominance of the aristocracy was on the decline. Eliot was a true divided figure of his age; he was both at the forefront of the literary rebellion and in favor of a return to a traditional, class-oriented ruling order.

T.S. Eliot: Fragmentation and Allusion

The innovations that give such power to Eliot's poetry are also the things that pose the greatest difficulties upon first reading. One example is his use of fragmentary lines and disconnected dialogue, in contrast with the formal linking structure of traditional verse. Many of Eliot's lines seem designed to jar the ear rather than connect one idea to another. When the poem is looked at *as a whole*, however, it can be seen that the breaks from one idea to another or one voice to another are only drastic and violent in their immediate context, not in terms of the overall unity. Ideas or voices are continuously picked up again throughout the longer poems (such as *The Waste Land*), making them more like the playing of motifs in a symphony. Each repetition lends new poignancy to the motif and the lack of clearly marked connections allows a greater compression of imagery, as well as causing the reader to play a more active role in deciphering and understanding the poem. Eliot's technique here is similar both to that of an extended musical composition and to the use of "collage" by Cubist painters (and, later, the photomontage of filmmakers or photographers) where disparate elements are combined to create a unified whole. *The Waste Land* is also a journey through the landscape of the mind, imitating the way the mind is able to combine seemingly unconnected thoughts in a "stream of consciousness" (a technique used with great success by the novelist James Joyce in the same period). Finally, the use of fragmentary images in the poem highlights the poem's subject: the fragmentation of modern life.

Another difficulty to be faced on first reading Eliot's poems is that he is clearly borrowing lines and phrases from other work. Eliot borrows from others but does not imitate them: he uses the allusions to create new associations, as well as for ironic effect. The effect on the reader of recognizing (or looking up) the source of an allusion results in a deepening of understanding and association. When the pub scene in "A Game of Chess" (*The Waste Land*) closes with the words, "good night, sweet ladies, good night, good night," we recognize them as the words spoken by the tragic heroine Ophelia in *Hamlet*, who was driven mad by love. The association compounds when we remember that Ophelia drowned herself while garlanded with flowers. The interplay of associations compounds the tragedy of Lil (in "A Game of Chess") who looks "so antique/(And her only thirty-one)," a sad fate but an unheroic one.

Eliot often uses his associative borrowings for humorous, mocking, or ironic effect to point out the tawdriness of the present compared with the heroic past. The 17th-century poet Andrew Marvell's magnificent lines "But at my back I always hear/Time's winged chariot hurrying near" become in *The Waste Land* the ridiculous "But at my back from time to time I hear/ the sound of horns and motors (. . .)." Time's urgency is shown to be still present in the waste land of the modern world, but, like everything else, it is trivialized.

Tradition was more than a useful technical tool for Eliot. He saw it as the essence of culture, something a poet must absorb into himself until the past becomes part of the present and all literature "has a simultaneous existence and composes a simultaneous order." This idea is part of Eliot's theory of "impersonality": the poet is seen as the vehicle for the poem, which is the amalgam of the poet's inner life, experience, and the tradition of which he is a part. The poet is merely the conduit or catalyst by which the poem is created.

Eliot did not, however, feel that it was necessary for the reader to perceive every allusion in order to appreciate a poem. Another important idea of Eliot's was that of the "auditory imagination," that great poetry is perceived and appreciated unconsciously before it is made available to the conscious mind. Eliot's ear for the memorable phrase was so acute that we are, in fact, often moved by the language of his poems long before we can track down their multiplicity of meaning.

Another important concept that Eliot uses and has explained in his critical writing is that of the "objective correlative." Simply put, this means that the inner experiences of the poetic narrator are given an outward manifestation by what he describes, that the external world duplicates or mirrors the internal one. In "Preludes," for example, the loneliness and despair of the narrator is expressed by "A lonely cab-horse steams and stamps."

Exercise: When you have read Eliot's poems and have explored some of his uses of allusion, you may wish to explore how you and your friends allude to experiences you hold in common. Someone telling a story may say, "So I told him, 'Frankly, my dear, I don't give a damn,' " and the chances are we will instantly recognize the allusion to the movie *Gone With The Wind*. Or someone struggling with a difficult homework problem may say mournfully, "If I only had a brain," and we will immediately think of *The Wizard of Oz*. Think back to some of the memorable phrases from these and other movies or favorite childhood TV shows; how many references do your friends recognize? Are you able to slip some of these phrases into conversation without their being noticed? Or do people immediately say, "Aha, that's from . . . "?

Meet the Speakers

Frank Kermode is a noted English scholar and critic. Formerly a professor at London and Cambridge Universities, he was recently at Columbia University. Editor of *Selected Prose of T.S. Eliot*, he has also written on John Donne, William Shakespeare, Wallace Stevens and D.H. Lawrence.

William Alfred is a professor of English at Harvard University and a successful playwright. His highly acclaimed plays include *Hogan's Goat*, *Cry for Us All*, and *Curse of an Aching Heart*.

Peter Ackroyd is an English writer whose work has been praised in England and the United States. His *T.S. Eliot: A Life* is the most ambitious biography of Eliot to date.

Joseph Chiari was a personal friend of Eliot and has written *T.S. Eliot: A Memoir* and *T.S. Eliot: Poet and Dramatist*, among other works.

Quentin Bell, the nephew of Virginia Woolf, balances careers as a painter, sculptor, potter, writer, and critic. He is the author of *Virginia Woolf: A Biography* and *Bloomsbury*, in which he describes the British cultural circle of which his parents were prominent members.

Stephen Spender is an English poet and critic. As a young man he was part of a group of young poets that included W.H. Auden and C. Day Lewis. Spender has published many books, including *Collected Poems: 1928-1985*, *The Destructive Element*, and *T.S. Eliot*.

Grover Smith is professor of English at Duke University. He has published two books on T.S. Eliot, *The Waste Land* in the Unwin Critical Library and *T.S. Eliot's Poetry and Plays* from the University of Chicago Press.

Study Plan for This Unit

1. Complete the section **Before Watching the Film: Journal-Writing and Other Activities**.

2. Read the Eliot poems many of which are featured in the film. Read the poems or part of the poems aloud, paying attention to Eliot's vivid imagery and rhythmic language.

The Love Song of J. Alfred Prufrock
Preludes
Rhapsody on a Windy Night
The Waste Land
from Four Quartets: Burnt Norton and Little Gidding

3. Watch the film.

4. Complete the section **After Watching the Film: Journal-Writing and Other Activities.**

5. Go through the **Guided Reading**.

6. Complete the **Exercises and Assignments** as specified by your instructor.

7. Take the **Self Test**.

Before Watching the Film: Journal-Writing and Other Activities

1. Write a free-associative, interior monologue describing some activity, such as walking into the living room to call a friend, driving to the cinema, etc.

While Watching the Film

1. Eliot was influenced by both jazz and classical music (note the titles: "Preludes" and *Four Quartets*). Listen carefully to the music in the film. Write down your impressions of how this music relates to the poems you have read. What music would you have chosen if you were the filmmaker?

2. Jot down images of the sea and of rivers as they occur in the film. Eliot describes the river as "a strong, brown god."

After Watching the Film: Journal-Writing and Other Activities

1. Eliot's title "Burnt Norton" is the name of a house Eliot once visited. Write a brief poem describing a house belonging to a friend or casual acquaintance (or any historic home you may have visited). Imagine the activities that may have taken place there, the kinds of people who once lived there.

2. The earliest version of *The Waste Land* was titled "He Do the Police in Different Voices" (from Dickens' *Our Mutual Friend*), and we can hear many different voices in the final version of the poem. Write a poem describing a single event, using the different voices of varying characters (an old man, a recent immigrant, a lawyer, a waitress in a coffee shop, etc.).

3. Create your own photo-montage. You may wish to look up examples of this technique in an art book.

Guided Reading

Note: Given the length and the layers of meaning in this poem, there will undoubtedly be points of interpretation that are not covered in the **Guided Reading**. This is just a guide, and should not be taken as the final word on the poem.

The Love Song of J. Alfred Prufrock

> *S'io credessi che mia riposta fosse*
> *a persona che mai tornasse al mondo,*
> *questa fiamma staria senza più scosse.*
> *Ma per ciò che giammai di questo fondo*
> *non tornò vivo alcun, s'i'odo il vero,*
> *senza tema d'infamia ti rispondo.* *

Let us go then, you and I,
When the evening is spread out against the sky
Like a patient etherised upon a table;
Let us go, through certain half-deserted streets,
The muttering retreats   5

* If I believed my answer might be heard by anyone who could return to the world, this flame would leap no more. But since no one ever returned alive from these depths as far as I know, then I answer without fear of infamy. (Dante, *Inferno: Canto, XXVII*, lines 61-66.)

Of restless nights in one-night cheap hotels
And sawdust restaurants with oyster-shells:
Streets that follow like a tedious argument
Of insidious intent
To lead you to an overwhelming question . . .   10
Oh, do not ask, 'What is it?'
Let us go and make our visit.

In the room the women come and go
Talking of Michelangelo.

The yellow fog that rubs its back upon the
    window-panes,   15
The yellow smoke that rubs its muzzle on the
    window-panes,
Licked its tongue into the corners of the evening,
Lingered upon the pools that stand in drains,
Let fall upon its back the soot that falls
    from chimneys,
Slipped by the terrace, made a sudden leap,   20
And seeing that it was a soft October night,
Curled once about the house, and fell asleep.

And indeed there will be time
For the yellow smoke that slides along the
    street
Rubbing its back upon the window-panes;   25
There will be time, there will be time
To prepare a face to meet the faces that you
    meet;
There will be time to murder and create,
And time for all the works and days of hands
That lift and drop a question on your plate;   30
Time for you and time for me,
And time yet for a hundred indecisions,
And for a hundred visions and revisions,
Before the taking of a toast and tea.

In the room the women come and go   35
Talking of Michelangelo.

And indeed there will be time
To wonder, 'Do I dare?' and, 'Do I dare?'
Time to turn back and descend the stair,
With a bald spot in the middle of my hair—   40
(They will say: 'How his hair is growing thin!')
My morning coat, my collar mounting firmly
    to the chin,
My necktie rich and modest, but asserted by a

simple pin—
(They will say: 'But how his arms and legs are
    thin!')
Do I dare   45
Disturb the universe?
In a minute there is time
For decisions and revisions which a minute
    will reverse.

For I have known them all already, known them
    all—
Have known the evenings, mornings,
    afternoons,   50
I have measured out my life with coffee spoons;
I know the voices dying with a dying fall
Beneath the music from a farther room.
        So how should I presume?

And I have known the eyes already, known them
    all—   55
The eyes that fix you in a formulated phrase,
And when I am formulated, sprawling on a pin,
When I am pinned and wriggling on the wall,
Then how should I begin
To spit out all the butt-ends of my days and ways? 60
        And how should I presume?

And I have known the arms already, known them
    all—
Arms that are braceleted and white and bare
(But in the lamplight, downed with light brown
    hair!)
Is it perfume from a dress   65
That makes me so digress?
Arms that lie along a table, or wrap about a
    shawl.
        And should I then presume?
        And how should I begin?

                    . . . . .

Shall I say, I have gone at dusk through narrow
    streets   70
And watched the smoke that rises from the
    pipes
Of lonely men in shirt-sleeves, leaning out of
    windows? . . .

I should have been a pair of ragged claws
Scuttling across the floors of silent seas.

And the afternoon, the evening, sleeps so
    peacefully! 75
Smoothed by long fingers,
Asleep . . . tired . . . or it malingers,
Stretched on the floor, here beside you and me.
Should I, after tea and cakes and ices,
Have the strength to force the moment to its
    crisis? 80
But though I have wept and fasted, wept and
    prayed,
Though I have seen my head (grown slightly
    bald) brought in upon a platter,
I am no prophet—and here's no great matter;
I have seen the moment of my greatness flicker,
And I have seen the eternal Footman hold my
    coat, and snicker, 85
And in short, I was afraid.

And would it have been worth it, after all,
After the cups, the marmalade, the tea,
Among the porcelain, among some talk of you
    and me,
Would it have been worth while, 90
To have bitten off the matter with a smile,
To have squeezed the universe into a ball
To roll it towards some overwhelming question,
To say: 'I am Lazarus, come from the dead,
Come back to tell you all, I shall tell you all'— 95
If one, settling a pillow by her head,
    Should say: 'That is not what I meant at all.
    That is not it, at all.'

And would it have been worth it, after all,
Would it have been worth while, 100
After the sunsets and the dooryards and the
    sprinkled streets,
After the novels, after the teacups, after the
    skirts that trail along the floor—
And this, and so much more?—
It is impossible to say just what I mean!
But as if a magic lantern threw the nerves in
    patterns on a screen: 105
Would it have been worth while
If one, settling a pillow or throwing off a shawl,
And turning toward the window, should say:
    'That is not it at all,
    That is not what I meant, at all.' 110

No! I am not Prince Hamlet, nor was meant to
    be;
Am an attendant lord, one that will do
To swell a progress, start a scene or two,
Advise the prince; no doubt, an easy tool,
Deferential, glad to be of use,   115
Politic, cautious, and meticulous;
Full of high sentence, but a bit obtuse;
At times, indeed, almost ridiculous—
Almost, at times, the Fool.

I grow old . . . I grow old . . .   120
I shall wear the bottoms of my trousers rolled.

Shall I part my hair behind? Do I dare to eat a
    peach?
I shall wear white flannel trousers, and walk
    upon the beach.
I have heard the mermaids singing, each to
    each.

I do not think that they will sing to me.   125

I have seen them riding seaward on the waves
Combing the white hair of the waves blown
    back
When the wind blows the water white and
    black.

We have lingered in the chambers of the sea
By sea-girls wreathed with seaweed red and brown 130
Till human voices wake us, and we drown.

Title and Epigraph

    1. What kind of person does the name J. Alfred Prufrock call to mind?

    2. How does the tone of the epigraph contrast with the title?

Answers

    1. The name suggests a person who is genteel, fussy, perhaps a little affected.

    2. The light, humorous tone of the title (Eliot's word was "levity") contrasts with the serious situation of a spirit trapped in hell who is considering whether to tell his story. The speaker of those lines was a contemporary of Dante whom the poet had placed in hell despite a good reputation on earth. Look for similar contrasts in tone—from ironic to serious—throughout the poem.

Lines 1-10

1. Who is the speaker and who is being addressed?

2. How does the simile in line 3 change your expectation of how the poem will go?

3. What kind of neighborhood is described in lines 4-10? How does this neighborhood correspond with Prufrock's psychological state?

4. What is the "tedious argument of insidious intent" and what is the "overwhelming question" to which it leads?

Answers

1. Prufrock is the speaker and he seems to be inviting the reader along on a journey. It is also possible that he is talking to another side of himself. Keep a lookout for further mention of the "you" in the poem.

2. This simile may be meant to suggest the pale band of light that appears after the sun has gone down, possibly implying that time is running out for Prufrock. Ether is used to render a patient unconscious before a painful operation, and Prufrock would like to anesthetize himself to the pain of revealing his passion. In any case, the simile entirely deflates the romantic expectation created by the first two lines.

3. Eliot is describing the cheap side of town where lonely men may spend a night with a prostitute in a run-down hotel or cheer themselves with food and alcohol in a cheap restaurant/bar. It is tawdry and a bit sordid.

4. The "argument" is, at least in part, with his physical desires; it is tedious because it keeps recurring and its intent is insidious because Prufrock is both drawn to this side of himself and repulsed by it. The "overwhelming question" may be, on the one hand, something Prufrock wants to ask someone; on a larger scale, though, it is the question of human purpose: how are we to live our lives?

Lines 13-14

1. Who was Michelangelo and why does Eliot make him the subject of the women's conversation?

2. How do we know that the women are not speaking with deep seriousness about Michelangelo?

Answers

1. Michelangelo was an artist of immense power whose greatness makes parlor talk seem still more trivial by contrast. His best known works include the ceiling paintings of the Sistine Chapel and the Pieta. He is also famous for his heroic sculptures such as his David. No one would mistake Prufrock for the model for one of these sculptures.

2. We know the women are speaking superficially because of the comic rhyme, "come and go . . . Michelangelo."

Lines 15-22

1. What is the fog being compared with? What is the reason for this comparison?

2. Why is the word "window-panes" repeated?

Answers

1. The fog is compared to a cat, a sensual animal.

2. The window-panes suggest someone on the outside looking in. This is the way Prufrock feels at the time and at the social gatherings he attends.

Lines 22-34

1. What does the repetition of the word "time" suggest about Prufrock's life?

2. What is suggested by the phrase "time to prepare a face to meet the faces that you meet"?

3. What tone is created by the alliteration and phrasing of "taking of a toast and tea"? What is the irony in "that lift and drop a question on your plate"?

Answers

1. The repetition of the word "time" suggests the lonely, dark hours and minutes Prufrock has ahead of him. Though afraid of growing old and dying, Prufrock also feels he has too much time, because for him time is repetitious and empty.

2. Eliot implies here that Prufrock and others adopt social masks to protect their vulnerability.

3. The alliterative "taking of a toast and tea" mocks Prufrock's genteel prissiness. "That lift and drop a question on your plate" also evokes tea-time and highlights the humorous irony of seeking the answer to the dilemma of existence at a tea party.

Lines 37-47

1. How is interior monologue used in this section?

2. Explain how Prufrock's description of his clothing reveals his personality.

Answers

1. Interior monologue is used to show the various shifts in perspective as Prufrock continues his internal dialogue, then imagines how others see him, then explains how he sees himself, finally returning to the question of whether to assert a place for himself in the universe. Note how the different sections of the poem connect by association: "visit" (line 12) leading to mention of "the room" in which it will take place; "toast and tea" (line 34) again calling forth the scene in this room (lines 36-37).

2. He is proud of his conservative, somewhat prissy dress. The strong adjectives for his clothing—"my collar mounting firmly," "my necktie rich and modest, but asserted . . . "—contrast humorously with his weakness of purpose.

Lines 49-61

1. What is Prufrock's tone in this section?

2. Explain the phrase "measured out my life with coffee spoons."

3. How will Prufrock's question "disturb the universe"?

4. What metaphor appears in lines 55-60?

5. What is suggested by the word "butt-ends"?

6. What is suggested by Prufrock's use of the word "presume"? Is this word appropriate to his quest?

Answers

1. Prufrock has clearly attended many social gatherings and knows the superficiality and tediousness of these gatherings as well as the loneliness they inspire in him. His tone is one of weariness, of being a knowledgeable outsider.

2. Coffee spoons are tiny and rather elegant, and are used to measure out small amounts of sugar. Prufrock feels he has taken life in small doses, and this phrase again reminds us of the genteel confines of his existence.

3. Trying to break through the shell of convention and say something genuine and heartfelt to a woman could disturb Prufrock's social universe, turning him into a figure of fun or pity. The real issue for him is whether to presume to live life to its fullest, to take a definite stand that could lead to fulfillment or disaster.

4. Prufrock compares himself with an insect pinned and wriggling against the wall, an apt metaphor for someone who feels he has been pigeon-holed as a stodgy bachelor.

5. "Butt-ends" are the discarded ends of cigarettes and could imply that Prufrock's life is almost extinguished. He is left with only the butt-ends of memories.

6. The word "presume" suggests a polite taking of liberties (as in the phrase: "May I presume to call you by your first name?"). Its politeness contrasts humorously with the seriousness of Prufrock's quest and with the grandeur of such phrases as "dying with a dying fall."

Lines 61-74

1. What is Prufrock's reaction to "arms that are downed with light brown hair"?

2. What do lines 70-72 reveal about his state of mind? And why in lines 73-74 should he have been "a pair of ragged claws"?

Answers

1. For a moment Prufrock lets himself go. The memory of a sensuous woman almost overcomes his deep feeling of boredom.

2. Prufrock wonders what will happen if he reveals the depths of his loneliness to someone—most likely a woman. Then he compares himself with a crab, a creature that is all instinct and not likely to torture itself mentally. Note that the crab is described almost as if it doesn't have a body. This may indicate that Prufrock fears a woman would just pity him, or perhaps that he cannot help seeing himself from the outside, or that he feels guilty about his fantasy of real contact.

Lines 75-110

1. Examine the metaphor in lines 75-78. Why does Eliot use the word "malingers"?

2. Throughout the poem, Eliot contrasts the grandeur of the past and of the language of the past with Prufrock's "mock heroic" tea-time quest. What ironic juxtapositions of past and present occur in these stanzas? Look up the stories of Lazarus and John the Baptist.

3. How does the rhyme scheme reinforce the irony?

4. Read lines 81-86 without the parenthetical qualifiers: "grown slightly bald," "and here's no great matter," and "and snicker." Then read the lines again with the qualifiers. What effect does Eliot achieve by including the qualifiers?

5. Who is "the eternal Footman" and why does he inspire fear?

Answers

1. This time it is the evening itself being compared to a cat. Prufrock would like to rest peacefully and be "smoothed by long fingers." At the same time, as a sensual and unthinking animal, the cat is seen by him as something menacing.

2. A powerful, soul-searching biblical imagery—"wept and fasted," "I am Lazarus come back from the dead"—is contrasted with the superficial atmosphere of polite social gatherings: "tea and cakes and ices" . . . "the cups, the marmalade, the tea." John the Baptist was the prophet who baptized Christ. A story about him that is used widely in literature and the arts is that he spurned King Herod's wife, who then had him beheaded and his head brought in on a platter. Prufrock refers to John the Baptist in the lines "I have seen my head (grown slightly bald) brought in upon a platter,/I am no prophet" The irony of the juxtaposition is both that Prufrock would not so appeal to a woman that she would want him killed for rejecting her, nor is he of the prophet's heroic stature. In the Bible, Lazarus was brought back to life by Christ. Prufrock imagines performing the miracle of bringing himself back to life to "tell you all" about his subterranean existence.

3. The rhymes often mix the momentous with the inconsequential: "ices" and "crisis"; "head brought in upon a platter" and "here's no great matter." Note that this is a pattern throughout the poem.

4. The qualifiers undercut the apparent seriousness of the passage.

5. "The eternal Footman" suggests death (who in folktales would stand at the foot of a sick person's bed) or possibly St. Peter. Prufrock is afraid that, at the final reckoning, his life will be judged as having been ridiculous, just as he is afraid that a woman would not take him seriously.

Lines 111-122

1. Why is Prufrock "not Prince Hamlet"?

2. What is the tone of lines 120-121? What reason would someone have to wear the bottoms of his trousers rolled?

Answers

1. While Hamlet is famous for his vacillations and digressions (like Prufrock), Hamlet is always at center stage. Prufrock, on the other hand, likens himself to a minor character who would not really be noticed. Perhaps Eliot is be being ironic here, intending us to see that there are more likenesses between Hamlet and Prufrock than we at first realized.

2. The tone is one of lamenting but is humorously maudlin. One reason for rolling up the bottoms of one's trousers would be to wade in the sea, another is that as people enter old age their bones tend to shrink and their clothes seem too large.

Lines 121-125
1. What is Prufrock's attitude to his own lovesong at this point in the poem? Does he think that he could be accepted?

2. Why are mermaids introduced in this section?

Answers
1. Prufrock has clearly given up hope and wonders if he is capable of any sensuous act, even one as simple as eating a peach.

2. The mermaids sing of a world of vitality and erotic promise that Prufrock cannot enter.

Lines 125-131
1. What is Prufrock's mood in these lines? What does the imagery imply about the outcome of his quest?

2. What is suggested by the final line of the poem? What is its tone?

Answers
1. Prufrock's mood is dreamy and resigned. The imagery suggests the he has allowed himself a last moment of revery as to what sensual love could be. "The white hair of the waves" recalls an earlier sensual moment: the arms "downed with light brown hair." The word "lingered" is at once sensuous but also suggests that Prufrock has waited too long.

2. The line implies, along with other things, that we can only feel alive in fantasy or in the prisonlike isolation of our inner selves. In the outer life of relationships and ambitions to which "human voices wake us," we "drown." Another way of viewing this line is that "we drown" not in the sea, but in the stifling voices of the drawing room. In either case, Prufrock arrives at the realization that the breakthrough he dreamed of is impossible.

Further Questions
1. Give examples of the sea imagery found in the poem. What is the effect of this imagery?

2. Make a note of the shift in tenses in the last seven stanzas and throughout the poem. What does this shift in tense tell us about Prufrock's approach to asking his question? How does this structure reinforce the poem as a whole?

3. Having worked through the whole poem, what might you find ironic about the title?

Answers

1. Images of the sea occur throughout the poem, beginning with the oyster-shells in the restaurants, possibly including the lonely men who smoke pipes and lean out of windows (suggesting sailors on leave), then the "pair of ragged claws," followed by "I shall wear flannel trousers and walk upon the beach," and culminating with the image of mermaids, waves, and chambers of the sea. There is the sense that Prufrock himself is some kind of sea-dweller who wishes he could come on land and tell his story. The sea is also seen as a place to immerse oneself and escape the "human voices."

2. The changes in tense suggest that Prufrock's internal questioning is not restricted to the present occasion, but that he has considered making his proposal in the past and will do so again in the future. They also imitate Prufrock's pattern of thinking, giving us a sense of an internal argument moving back and forth in time.

3. The love song is being sung by Prufrock to himself (and to the reader), but it is unlikely to ever be heard by a woman. He doesn't expect to rise up like Lazarus and tell his tale. Rather he is like the man in Hell in the epigraph who doesn't believe anybody could escape to tell his story. Eliot's poem is "the love song" that Prufrock never sang—at least aloud.

Exercises and Assignments

1. In what way is the moon an "objective correlative" in "Rhapsody on a Windy Night"? What other examples of objective correlatives can you find in this poem?

2. What are "preludes"? (**Note:** This word has more than one meaning.) How do the four sections in the poem "Preludes" act as preludes? What is the attitude to modern urban life in this poem? Use examples from the poem to support your answer.

3. In *The Waste Land*, how does Eliot make use of the following lines from Shakespeare's *The Tempest* (Act I, scene 2)? Look these lines up in their context.

> Full fathom five thy father lies;
> Of his bones are coral made;
> Those are pearls that were his eyes:
> Nothing of him that doth fade
> But doth suffer a sea-change
> Into something rich and strange.
> Sea-nymphs hourly ring his knell:
>   Ding-dong.
> Hark! now I hear them,—Ding-dong, bell.

4. Eliot's imagery is hauntingly physical and often borders on a feeling of disgust for physical sensation: "A rat crept softly through the vegetation/ Dragging its slimy belly on the bank," "the young man carbuncular." Make note of some of the other instances of this kind of imagery, and then write a few paragraphs exploring how this tallies with the historic events of Eliot's formative years and with his depiction of alienation from the modern world.

5. How does Eliot contrast water and aridity in his poems? What is the purpose of this contrast?

6. Detail some of Eliot's uses of irony, both humorous and serious. How does the irony deepen or change your impression of a particular poem?

7. Explore Eliot's combining of specific details of landscape with abstract ideas in any one of the *Four Quartets*.

8. Eliot has been described as writing about the individual out of tune with his time. Choose one of his poems and explore this idea with specific reference to that poem.

9. *Four Quartets* has a symmetrical structure of five sections each; choose a section from one of the poems and compare/contrast it with the same section from another of the *Quartets*. What similarities can you find?

10. Many of Eliot's poems have as their central theme the nature of time. Choose one of the poems and make a note of all the references to time. How would you summarize Eliot's treatment of time in this poem?

11. Explain, with reference to the poem, the lines from "Little Gidding": "[. . .] the end of all our exploring/Will be to arrive where we started/And know the place for the first time."

Self Test

T.S. Eliot alludes to the following poem by the 17th-century poet and satirist Andrew Marvell in several poems, and particularly in "The Love Song of J. Alfred Prufrock" and *The Waste Land*. Read the Marvell poem carefully. You will probably want to read it several times in order to get used to the 17th-century diction. You will find it easier to follow the narrator's argument if you see it as proceeding in three stages corresponding with the poem's division into three sections. Then write a few paragraphs answering the following questions. What lines from Prufrock refer to "To His Coy Mistress"? What similar concerns do the two poems share? Are both poems ironic or are we intended to take them at face value? Do the two poems take the same attitude to romantic love? Why did Eliot make so many references to Marvell's poem and how does it relate to Eliot's major interests as a poet? (You may find it useful to think about the themes of Eliot's *Four Quartets* when responding to the last question.)

To His Coy Mistress

Had we but world enough, and time,
This coyness, lady, were no crime.
We would sit down, and think which way
To walk and pass our long love's day.
Thou by the Indian Ganges' side
Should'st Rubies find; I by the tide
Of Humber would complain. I would
Love you ten years before the Flood;
And you should if you please, refuse
Till the conversion of the Jews.
My vegetable love should grow
Vaster than empires, and more slow.
An hundred years should go to praise
Thine eyes, and on thy forehead gaze.

Two hundred to adore each breast;
But thirty thousand to the rest;
An age at least to every part,
And the last age should show your heart.
For lady, you deserve this state,
Nor would I love at lower rate.
   But at my back I always hear
Time's winged chariot hurrying near;
And yonder all before us lie
Deserts of vast eternity.
Thy beauty shall no more be found,
Nor, in thy marble vault, shall sound
My echoing song. Then worms shall try
That long preserv'd virginity,
And your quaint honour turn to dust,
And into ashes all my lust.
The grave's a fine and private place,
But none, I think, do there embrace.
   Now therefore, while the youthful hue
Sits on thy skin like morning dew,
And while thy willing soul transpires
At every pore with instant fires,
Now let us sport us while we may;
And now, like amorous birds of prey,
Rather at once our time devour,
Than languish in his slow-chapt power.
Let us roll all our strength and all
Our sweetness up into one ball,
And tear our pleasures with rough strife
Through the iron gates of life.
Thus, though we cannot make our sun
Stand still, yet we will make him run.

Answers to Self Test

Answers to Self Tests begin on page 226.

For Further Reading
Books by T.S. Eliot

Collected Poems, 1901-1962. New York: Harcourt Brace Jovanovich; 1963.

Selected Essays of T.S. Eliot. New York: Harcourt Brace Jovanovich; 1950.

The Waste Land: Facsimile and Transcript. Eliot, Valerie, editor. New York: Harcourt Brace Jovanovich; 1974.

Books About Eliot

Ackroyd, Peter. *T.S. Eliot: A Biography*. New York: Simon and Schuster; 1984.

Kenner, Hugh. *The Invisible Poet: T.S. Eliot*. New York: Harcourt Brace Jovanovich; 1959.

Kenner, Hugh, editor. *T.S. Eliot: A Collection of Critical Essays*. Englewood Cliffs, N.J.: Prentice-Hall; 1962.

Tate, Allen, editor. *T.S. Eliot: The Man and His Work*. New York: Delacorte Press; 1966.

Wallace Stevens (1879-1955)

Wallace Stevens was a deeply private man who liked to contemplate the world from within his own isolation. Although he was one of the major poets of his era, he spent most of his life working as an insurance executive in Hartford, Connecticut, and kept himself physically apart from the poetic mainstream. Holly Stevens, his daughter, has detailed how Stevens largely kept himself isolated at home as well, spending much of his time in his study reading, writing poetry, or listening to classical music. Stevens has been accused of withdrawing from the world; in fact, he separated himself from it in order to perceive it better from the perspective of his imagination.

Wallace Stevens was born in 1879 in the small industrial town of Reading, Pennsylvania. His father, who came from generations of Pennsylvania farmers, was a prominent lawyer and businessman who instilled in Wallace and his two brothers the virtues of hard work and making money. His mother was a self-taught schoolteacher who sang hymns in church on Sundays and read nightly from the Bible to her three sons. Stevens was to remark later that he had acquired reason from his father and imagination from his mother.

Stevens received a strong grounding in languages and literature at Reading's best schools, and in 1897 he went on to become a special student at Harvard. At this time, Harvard was in the midst of a revolution in philosophy, led by the philosopher-poet George Santayana and the noted psychologist and philosopher William James, concerning man's belief in an ordered universe. This debate, and in particular James' philosophical explorations into man's need to believe in a higher order while testing this belief experimentally, remained central to Stevens' poetry and thinking throughout his life. Stevens also wrote poetry while at Harvard and one of his sonnets so impressed Santayana that he wrote a sonnet of his own in response. Stevens edited Harvard's literary journal, *The Advocate*, at times writing (under a variety of pseudonyms) most of the stories and poems that filled the magazine.

In 1900, Stevens left Harvard without getting a degree and moved to New York City, where he worked for a time as a newspaper reporter. He was disturbed by the abject poverty and misery he encountered through his work, and he often found himself "bathed in tears" by the pathos surrounding him. With some prodding from his father, Stevens decided to become what he called in his journal "a bustling, money-making lawyer" and enrolled in New York Law School. He passed the bar exam in 1904 and went to work for various companies—primarily in insurance law—which gave him the opportunity to travel widely in the United States. In 1916, he went to work for the Hartford Accident and Indemnity Company, remaining in their employ for the rest of his life. His dedication to insurance work has often been remarked upon, especially as Stevens was later to turn down a prestigious teaching appointment at Harvard which might have led to his early retirement from the Hartford company. One clear influence was his father, who frequently exhorted him to "paddle your own canoe" and to "make a place for yourself upon the front bench," and Stevens was undoubtedly affected by his father's nervous breakdown following bankruptcy in 1901. Also, it should not be surprising that a poet who was willing to take such enormous risks in his imaginative life should have sought to create a stable daily life.

After Harvard, Stevens continued to write poems, which he would have privately bound and would send to his future wife, Elsie Kachel, on her birthdays. He published only a few of these poems in such literary magazines as *The Trend*, Harriet Monroe's

Poetry, and Arthur Kreymborg's *Others*. Nevertheless, he began to acquire a small but influential circle of admiring readers. Stevens' first volume of poems, *Harmonium,* appeared in 1923, when he was 44. Although it is generally recognized today as containing some of his finest poems, *Harmonium* received little favorable critical attention and sold poorly. Stevens did not publish another volume of poetry for nearly 12 years—although it is not known whether this was because of disappointment at his first book's reception or because he was securing his position at the insurance company. When *Harmonium* was reissued in 1931, it began to attract more attention.

In 1934, Stevens was made vice president of the insurance company and the following year he published his second volume, *Ideas of Order*. Two more books followed in quick succession: *Owl's Clover* (1936) and *The Man with the Blue Guitar* (1937). Wallace Stevens' reputation was firmly established by the new works and by the growing recognition of his achievement in *Harmonium*. He continued to publish at a steady rate and his later works include *The Auroras of Autumn* and a book of essays, *The Necessary Angel*. Stevens was awarded the Bollingen Prize in 1949. His *Collected Poems* was published in 1954, one year before his death, and it received both the National Book Award and the Pulitzer Prize. His remarkably innovative language and his willingness to write meditative poems in a modern style have influenced a diverse range of present-day poets, including James Merrill, John Ashbery, and Mark Strand.

The World of the Poems

Wallace Stevens was a meditative, philosophic poet who was deeply affected by his reading and daily life, although he was at the same time keenly aware of the larger world around him. Many of his apparently private meditations were prompted by external events, most notably the two World Wars and the Great Depression of the 1930s. Stevens was criticized for not focusing more on social and political issues—most notably during the 1930s—but, like many meditative thinkers, Stevens felt that man's relationship with God and nature is of immediate and pressing importance. To understand the influences on Stevens as a poet, we need to examine not so much the history of his period as the details of his daily life—his work, nature, music, art, and reading—which provided the raw material for the ultimate source of his poetry, his imagination.

Stevens' professional training was as a lawyer and the philosophy behind the practice of law influenced the style of his poems. When writing a brief, a lawyer has to examine a question from all sides and make its contradictions apparent. In the title of the poem "Chaos in Motion and Not in Motion," we can see how Stevens placed contradictions side by side. His poems search for answers but do not provide them; rather, Stevens sets out to frame the questions correctly.

Another major influence was nature. On Sundays, for most of his life, Stevens would go on long walks in the countryside, often covering as much as 30 or 40 miles. His poems have some of the rhythmic quality of a long walk, and Stevens used images from these country walks in even his most philosophical poems. One such poem, "The Man on the Dump," probably stemmed from the sight of a local dump he and his daughter, Holly, would pass on their walks. A man had built a house on the edge of the dump, and Holly Stevens recalls: "We spent hours imagining things about him, and making up stories."

It is significant that Stevens' long walks usually took place on Sundays. Religion was a major part of his early upbringing, and even in his young manhood in New York City he frequently read from the Bible and from books about the lives of the saints. Sunday always remained a special day for him, and nature was in many ways a solace or substitute for the organized religion in which he no longer felt he could believe.

For Stevens, the seasons of nature corresponded with aspects of the human spirit, and he would often contrast the summery landscape of Florida (where he made seasonal visits with business acquaintances) with the autumnal landscape of New England. Florida's lushness formed a special symbol of radiance, of the vibrancy of life and the richness of possibility, in Stevens' poetic imagery. The New England winter—when Stevens could not take walks and did not write poetry—required a change in outlook for the observer: "One must have a mind of winter/To regard the frost and the boughs/Of the pine-trees crusted with snow."

Stevens loved fine objects and would order things from all over the world. The oriental rugs and the tea chests from the Far East allowed him to create for himself the exotic places of their origin. He was strongly influenced by painting, and he collected artworks through a dealer and ordered art catalogues from France. Stevens corresponded with people all over the world, including a young Cuban poet and a Korean scholar. He never visited Europe or the Far East—leaving America only once to go to Cuba—but, with the help of the letters and objects sent to him, he was able to recreate these places in his imagination.

Wallace Stevens: The Power of the Imagination

As the critic Helen Vendler has pointed out, Wallace Stevens had three interrelated projects in his poetry. These were 1) to demonstrate the transforming power of the imagination, 2) to make a response to what he called "the disappearance of the gods," and 3) to break away from England's domination of the poetic tradition and come up with a poetry specific to the American landscape and language.

In his poetry, Stevens did not seek to create a likeness of the world but instead explored how the mind perceives the world and how this perception changes according to mood, season, and other factors. Acted on by the imagination, the world is like a "sea surface full of clouds," constantly shifting, changing color, changing shape. Stevens did not deny the existence of the "real world"—he would not have argued, for example, that if a tree falls in a forest and no one hears it, it does not make a sound. However, if there is someone there to hear it, the sound of the falling tree will be transformed by the hearer and will resonate in his memory. It will become more than it was, for it will still exist in the mind of the listener long after all its audible vibrations have disappeared. Thus when Stevens writes that "the ear" is "superior . . . to a crow's voice," he is suggesting that the imaginative mind can transform the harsh sound of the crow into something beautiful . . . perhaps through allowing this sound to call forth memories of a particular time or place, such as a day spent walking in a New England forest.

Stevens saw the imagination as the ultimate human virtue. In "Disillusionment of Ten O'Clock," he notes with humorous irony that people lacking imagination "are not going/To dream of baboons and periwinkles." In another poem, "The Idea of Order at Key West," he shows how the dusk in Florida and the ocean itself are enhanced and defined by the mind of the artist, whose voice "made the sky acutest at its vanishing." The imagination does not simply rearrange details of the world, it re-creates the world.

In his poetry, Stevens did more than state the abstract idea that the imagination transforms reality; he set out to chart the actions of the imagination on particular scenes and images, using individual examples to demonstrate the general principle and to show that the imaginative perception is constantly changing. As he titled one of his poems, "Not Ideas about the Thing but the Thing Itself," it's not the abstract thought that counts, but the specific occurrence.

Stevens' second project was to examine how we respond to the question of our own existence once we begin to doubt the doctrines of orthodox religious faith. Stevens felt that man possesses a "blessed rage for order," that we need to understand and order our world . . . even if we constantly readjust this understanding. Stevens created various names for this replacement for religious faith—including "an idea of order" and "a supreme fiction"—but he always insisted that it was something we wrote "notes toward," rather than a fixed doctrine. Again, Stevens' purpose was to record the process of thought and show ideas as they came into being. Even when he writes: "We say God and the imagination are one," there is the qualifying clause "we say" to suggest that this is just one way of looking at things.

Stevens' third project, to create a new poetic language, has left a lasting influence on modern poetry through the extraordinary beauty and originality of this language. His use of words has been described as "extravagant" and "outrageous." Stevens demonstrated that, like Humpty Dumpty in *Alice in Wonderland*, a poet can make words mean whatever he chooses them to mean. Stevens freed the modern poet from the constraints of a formal, classical diction and from its opposite, a poetry that imitates everyday speech. "No one speaks the way Wallace Stevens writes," the poet Mark Strand remarked in a recent interview.

Stevens' purpose was to push language to its limits and thus describe the things that are felt or sensed but cannot be put into words. We have all experienced the difficulty of trying to describe the taste of something to another person; we know what an orange tastes like, but how can we describe it? When it comes to describing an emotion or subconscious perception, this difficulty magnifies. Stevens saw that the only way to express the inexpressible was to break through the barriers of ordinary language by divorcing words from their usual contexts. "The outlandish was another day/Of the week, queerer than Sunday," he wrote in "The Auroras of Autumn," and we can appreciate these lines without fully understanding what they mean.

Wallace Stevens used a large number of poetic techniques to push his language to the limits. These include metaphor (birds described as "flying wedges"), alliteration ("convolvulus and coral"), onomatopoeia ("Chieftain Iffucan of Azcan in caftan/Of tan with henna hackles, halt!" used to depict the blustering of a bantam rooster), and synecdoche ("No turban walks across the lessened floors.").

Exercise: Choose one of the Stevens poems featured in this unit. How many of the poetic techniques mentioned above are you able to identify?

Meet the Speakers

Mark Strand is a poet whose books include *Darker, The Late Hour,* and *The Story of Our Lives.* Wallace Stevens' work has been a source of inspiration for Strand, whose own poems evoke the guilt, anxiety and absurdity of postwar man.

James Merrill is one of the neo-metaphysical poets who began writing after World War II. He has written many books of verse, including: *Water Street, Braving the Elements,* and *The Changing Light at Sandover.* Merrill is a member of The National Institute of Arts and Letters and received the National Book Award in 1967.

Harold Bloom has become one of our foremost contemporary literary critics. In *Poetry and Repression: Revisionism from Blake to Stevens* and *Wallace Stevens: the Poems of Our Climate,* he champions Stevens as one of the greatest poets of our time.

A. Walton Litz is a scholar, a professor of English literature at Princeton University, and the author of *Wallace Stevens, the Poetry of Earth* and *Introspective Voyager: the Poetic Development of Wallace Stevens.* He has also written on Ezra Pound, T.S. Eliot, and William Carlos Williams.

Helen Vendler is Kenan Professor of English literature at Harvard University, the poetry critic for *The New Yorker*, and the senior consultant for the **Voices & Visions** series. Her *Wallace Stevens: Words Chosen Out of Desire* and *On Extended Wings: Wallace Stevens' Longer Poems* have established her as a leading proponent of his work.

Joan Richardson is the author of *Wallace Stevens, A Biography: The Early Years, 1879-1923,* the first volume of a two-volume biography. She is also a professor of English at LaGuardia College in New York.

Study Plan for This Unit

1. Complete the section **Before Watching the Film: Journal-Writing and Other Activities.**

2. Read the Stevens poems which are featured in the film. As mentioned before, it is a good idea to read the poems or sections of the poems aloud. Also try re-reading several of the poems or sections from them. Stevens' language is ornate and unusual, so don't worry if you do not understand a poem the first time you read it. It should grow more comprehensible with additional, careful reading.

Chaos in Motion and Not in Motion
O Florida, Venereal Soil
The Snow Man
The Rock (Section I)
Peter Quince at the Clavier
Men Made Out of Words
Part IV of the second section, "It Must Change,"
    in Notes Toward a Supreme Fiction
Sunday Morning
The Idea of Order at Key West
The Auroras of Autumn
Final Soliloquy of the Interior Paramour
The Planet on the Table

3. Watch the film.

4. Complete the section **After Watching the Film: Journal-Writing and Other Activities.**

5. Go through the **Guided Reading**.

6. Complete the **Exercises and Assignments** as specified by your instructor.

7. Take the **Self Test**.

Before Watching the Film: Journal-Writing and Other Activities

1. Often in a poem, Stevens assigns special meanings to colors. For example, green for vitality, blue and red for the possibilities of the imagination, white for death and sterility. As you read, jot down the unusual uses of colors in the Stevens poems. Write some sentences or a poem of your own in which you use color to represent an idea or feeling.

2. After a trip to the supermarket or a walk around your neighborhood, write a brief description of the things you saw. Then write a brief description of a completely imaginary landscape, perhaps that of a country where you've never been but have always wanted to go. Compare these descriptions. Which is the more vivid? What kinds of details caught your attention?

While Watching the Film

1. Stevens was concerned with the seasons—both those of nature and the "human seasons"—and he was particularly interested in the moments when seasons change. Make note of the changing seasons as they occur in the film.

2. Every reader of poetry gives his or her own special emphasis to the rhythms and sounds of the poem. Listen carefully to poet James Merrill's reading of "O Florida, Venereal Soil" or "The Snow Man." How does his reading help you interpret the poem?

3. List the images of different landscapes featured in the film.

4. Stevens was influenced by painting. Note the paintings featured in the film and any painterly techniques used by the filmmakers.

After Watching the Film: Journal-Writing and Other Activities

1. Mark Strand remarked that Wallace Stevens is a poet about whom one is constantly changing one's mind. Read one of the poems featured in this unit and write down whatever impressions of it come to mind. Pick it up another day, or several hours later, re-read it and again write down all your impressions (but without looking at what you wrote the first time). Then compare your impressions. Did you understand the poem differently on the second reading? How so?

2. In "Men Made Out of Words," Stevens writes: "Life consists of propositions about life." Jot down some of your own "propositions about life," the things that you believe to be true about your life or life in general—although you may not be able to prove them.

3. If you were directing this film, what images would you have chosen to convey Stevens' feelings about his favorite landscapes?

Guided Reading

(**Note:** Because of its length, we are able to include only three of the eight stanzas of this poem. It should be noted that Stevens saw the final stanza as a form of "answer" to the first stanza. Stevens had the final stanza appear as the second stanza in an abridged version of the poem printed in *Poetry* magazine. Read the entire poem in your anthology before answering the questions in the **Guided Reading**.)

Sunday Morning

I

Complacencies of the peignoir, and late
Coffee and oranges in a sunny chair,
And the green freedom of a cockatoo
Upon a rug mingle to dissipate
The holy hush of ancient sacrifice.   5
She dreams a little, and she feels the dark
Encroachment of that old catastrophe,
As a calm darkens among water-lights.
The pungent oranges and bright, green wings
Seem things in some procession of the dead,   10
Winding across wide water, without sound.
The day is like wide water, without sound,
Stilled for the passing of her dreaming feet
Over the seas, to silent Palestine,
Dominion of the blood and sepulchre.   15

II

Why should she give her bounty to the dead?
What is divinity if it can come
Only in silent shadows and in dreams?
Shall she not find in comforts of the sun,
In pungent fruit and bright, green wings, or else   20
In any balm or beauty of the earth,
Things to be cherished like the thought of heaven?
Divinity must live within herself:
Passions of rain, or moods in falling snow;
Grievings in loneliness, or unsubdued   25
Elations when the forest blooms; gusty
Emotions on wet roads on autumn nights;
All pleasures and all pains, remembering
The bough of summer and the winter branch.
These are the measures destined for her soul.   30

VIII

She hears, upon that water without sound,
A voice that cries, "The tomb in Palestine
Is not the porch of spirits lingering.
It is the grave of Jesus, where he lay."
We live in an old chaos of the sun,   110
Or old dependency of day and night,
Or island solitude, unsponsored, free,

167

Of that wide water, inescapable.
Deer walk upon our mountains, and the quail
Whistle about us their spontaneous cries;   115
Sweet berries ripen in the wilderness;
And, in the isolation of the sky,
At evening, casual flocks of pigeons make
Ambiguous undulations as they sink,
Downward to darkness, on extended wings.   120

Title
1. What does the title tell you about the poem?

Answer
1. Sunday is the first day, a weekly reminder of the resurrection in Christian society, and Sunday morning is the time when religious Christians would normally be in church. Note that the word "Sunday" can be divided into Sun-day, or day of the sun, and that sun-worshipping is a motif throughout the poem.

Stanza I

Lines 1-2
1. What are "complacencies" and a "peignoir" and what do these words tell us about the woman in the poem?

2. What sense do you get about the setting of the poem?

Answers
1. Complacency is a feeling of satisfaction or comfort. "Complacencies of the peignoir" suggests that the peignoir is the essence of comfortableness. A peignoir is a woman's loose-fitting dressing gown, so we know the woman in the poem has not yet gotten dressed for the outdoors (perhaps to go to church).

2. The "coffee and oranges in a sunny chair" suggest a breakfast room on a sunny morning.

Lines 3-5
1. What purpose does the cockatoo serve?

2. What does the phrase "mingle to dissipate" suggest to you?

3. What is "the holy hush of ancient sacrifice"?

Answers
1. A cockatoo is a colorful, crested bird from Australia. Here, it represents a sense of the spontaneous and the exotic. For Stevens, the color green is often symbolic of the earth's bounty and lushness.

2. The words "mingle" and "dissipate" are essentially opposites. "Mingle" means to

bring together or combine. "Dissipate" means to scatter or drive away; it also means to vanish or disappear, as would happen to the soul if there is no afterlife. The choice of words suggests that the woman is not leading a dissipated life (as a strictly orthodox person might believe), but is seeking alternative sources of belief.

3. This phrase could have several implications: "holy hush" could refer to the silence of a cathedral or to the quiet of suburban streets on a Sunday, when people are attending religious services. "Ancient sacrifice" could refer to the crucifixion of Christ and its recapitulation during Mass, or it could refer to the human or animal sacrifices that formed part of more primitive religions.

Lines 6-10
1. What is suggested by the phrase "the dark encroachment of that old catastrophe"?

2. What images are contrasted in lines 9-11?

3. Where would a "procession of the dead" be found?

Answers
1. Death is often symbolized by darkness, and it encroaches in that it is not welcome. "That old catastrophe" could refer to man's ancient fear of a death that is final and absolute, to the Great Flood (when rain darkened the skies), or to the death of Christ. The "encroachment of that old catastrophe" also refers to memories of the day's religious origin. There are other possible associations as well.

2. The strong, vibrant image of pungent oranges and bright, green wings contrasts strongly with the subsequent images of death.

3. Stevens is imagining the history of religion as a pageant of beliefs. These beliefs can only live in a present-day believer—otherwise, they are a procession of dead beliefs. There is also a suggestion of despair in the woman's viewing the fruit and the bird as things associated with a procession of the dead.

Lines 11-12
1. What is suggested by "wide water, without sound"?

2. What poetic techniques does Stevens use in these lines?

Answers
1. "Wide water, without sound" calls to mind a world where there is no surface life, human or animal—in other words, eternity. The "wide water, without sound" also suggests the expanse of time.

2. Stevens uses repetition, consonance, and assonance. Say "wide water, without sound" aloud; notice how you have to stretch your lips wide and how the words have a liquid sound to them.

Lines 12-15
1. How would you characterize the woman's state of mind in lines 5-15?

2. Why is Palestine silent?

3. What is suggested by "dominion of the blood and sepulchre"?

Answers

1. She is sinking into revery and becoming less aware of her surroundings. Note the repetition of the words "dream" and "without sound." Her mind is beginning to take her far away.

2. This could indicate the silent contemplation of revery, and it could foreshadow a loss of faith in which Palestine no longer calls forth associations of the Holy Land or a place of resurrection.

3. One definition of "dominion" is a sphere of influence, a realm, or a country that is a protectorate of another country (as Palestine was to Britain at the time of the poem). To "have dominion over" means to rule or exercise control over a place or person. The word stems from the Latin dominus, which is a synonym for God. Stevens frequently uses this word to indicate an ordering principle. A "sepulchre" is a burial vault. The phrase itself could suggest that Palestine rules over death and sacrifice, not over life and the pleasures of being alive.

Stanza II

Lines 16-22

1. How is religious orthodoxy characterized in lines 16-18?

2. What is contrasted with religious belief?

3. What grammatical form do these lines take and why?

Answers

1. Religious orthodoxy is presented as something that only yields its rewards once you are dead. The speaker is wondering what imperative would make the woman give up the "bounty" of a physical existence for an afterlife that may not exist.

2. The physical sensations of the earth are contrasted with a heaven that is just a thought or dream.

3. The ideas are presented in the form of questions, thus showing that an answer has not yet been found. There is a further suggestion that life is an unanswered question.

Lines 23-30

1. What alternatives to a religious orthodoxy are offered in these lines?

2. Are the things that make up this new "divinity" all positive values?

3. Why are we advised to remember the "bough of summer and the winter branch"?

4. Explain the phrase "measures destined for her soul."

Answers

1. We are told that divinity must live within the woman herself; i.e., that it is still up to her to find her own belief and her reasons for living, and that these need to come from within rather than from an outside authority. Note the use of the word "must." Stevens is not telling us that the woman has found her answer.

2. The things that make up life include "passions of rain" and "grievings in loneliness," as well as "unsubdued elations." Stevens is indicating that we need to accept pain as well as pleasure as part of the wonder of physical existence.

3. Bough and branch are synonyms (although the word "bough" does connote leafiness, while a branch could be bare). The living summer bough will become the dead winter branch, and vice versa, in nature's endless cycle of renewal. Stevens is pointing to the necessity for death as a counterpoint to life and the permanence of the seasonal pattern.

4. Stevens' use of the word "destined" implies that once the woman begins to doubt her faith she no longer has a choice, she has to use the "measures" provided by the physical world. No religious experience or belief would have meaning for her unless she could relate it to her personal experience. This is the only way she can take the "measure" of the possibility of achieving spiritual insight. Measures may also suggest musical measures or steps she takes toward dealing with life. Stevens is again presenting us with a paradox by describing the abandonment of belief using such religiously charged words as "destined" and "soul."

Stanza VIII

Lines 106-109

1. How do these lines recall the first stanza of the poem?

2. Find the paradox in lines 106-109. What's the significance of this paradox?

3. How would you interpret the phrase "not the porch of spirits lingering"? Before answering this question, be sure to look up the word "porch" in your dictionary.

Answers

1. The words "water without sound" and "Palestine" first appeared in Stanza I, indicating that this final stanza is a response to the first one.

2. The woman is hearing a voice cry upon water "without sound." This suggests that the woman has found an answer where there was none before. It could also imply that the answer does not really exist.

3. That "the tomb in Palestine is not the porch of spirits lingering" implies that this is not the place from which salvation will come. Note that besides being a place one might wait after knocking at the door, the porch, historically, is an entrance to a church or temple. If the spirits were lingering on the porch, this would suggest that they are waiting to be admitted either into eternity or back into the world (i.e., that there is an existence after death). Religious belief has also been waiting "on the porch" to be readmitted into the woman's life.

Lines 110-113

1. How do the phrases "old chaos of the sun" and "old dependency of day and night" conflict with or support each other?

2. What is "unsponsored, free"? What is "inescapable" in lines 112-113?

Answers

1. Stevens is suggesting that the world beneath the sun is chaotic and disorderly; at the same time, we depend on the sun to provide us with the constants, day and night, by which we regulate our lives. In a scientific sense, the clause "We live in an old chaos of the sun" is accurate, too. Astronomers have suggested that the earth is a piece of the sun that has broken off and cooled down; the sun itself is chaotic as it is made up of constantly exploding gases.

2. The adjectives describe several different nouns and pronouns: "We," "solitude," and "water." For example, in our "island solitude" we live "unsponsored" by God and "free" of dead beliefs. However, we cannot both live this "unsponsored, free" life and escape from it. Look for ways these adjectives pertain to "wide water" and "We."

Lines 114-120

1. How does the poem treat the world of nature now that religious faith has been abandoned?

2. Why are the flocks of pigeons "casual"? What is Stevens saying about chance and randomness in these lines?

3. Why are the undulations "ambiguous"? What would happen if they were not ambiguous?

4. How does the structure of lines 117-120 enhance their content?

5. What image do you get from the line "downward to darkness, on extended wings"?

6. "Elegant variation" means to use different words to say the same thing. Stevens uses elegant variation to reinforce his ideas without repeating them exactly. Look back over this whole section, and note any examples of this technique.

Answers

1. Nature is presented as an earthly paradise where deer walk upon the mountains and quail whistle. More than that, these are *our* mountains and the quail whistle *about us*, rather than some landscape of the afterlife. The narrator of the poem is saying that by accepting death we will finally be able to appreciate the physical beauty of the world.

2. The word "casual" aptly describes the way flocks of pigeons are of no fixed size and seem to lack a formal order. It also suggests that no divine hand placed them there and there is nothing preordained about their appearance.

3. The word "ambiguous" implies that the answer to the question of religious faith provided in this section is, like any answer, not absolute. Also, in earlier religions, the sight of birds flying was often taken as an augury, a sign of what would happen in the future. For us, today, the pigeons' undulations seem to suggest a pattern, yet we cannot

decipher it. Have you ever watched birds flying back and forth at sunset? There seems to be some order to their activity, as if they are "skywriting," and this would suggest they are trying to tell us something if only we were able to interpret it.

4. There are frequent pauses in these lines—after "And," "sky," "make," "sink" and "darkness"—suggesting the tentative, back-and-forth wheeling motion of the birds. The final phrase, "on extended wings," trails off in emphasis like the birds fluttering down into darkness.

5. Stevens is calling to mind an image of angels about to descend into the underworld. This image also suggests the brave leap into the unknown that the woman has made by deciding to abandon a faith that no longer has meaning for her.

6. "Tomb" and "grave"; "unsponsored," "spontaneous," and "casual"; "solitude" and "isolation" are similar to each other in meaning, although not exactly synonymous.

Further Questions
1. What meter, if any, is the poem written in?

2. Who is the narrator of the poem? What sort of voice does this narrator have?

3. How is the woman described in the poem?

Answers
1. The poem is written in a loose unrhymed iambic pentameter. Each section is made up of 15 lines, suggesting a loose sonnet form.

2. The poem is narrated in the third person by an omniscient voice, which we assume is the poet's. The diction is elevated and impersonal. Although the woman featured in the poem is the source of the ideas and feelings, her own voice is heard only twice: in Stanza IV and Stanza V.

3. There is no actual description of the woman, which makes her appear to be a detached spirit or pure mind. In the first stanza, she is defined by her clothing and the objects surrounding her: the peignoir tells us that she is comfortably dressed, the oranges and coffee (which are described as if they, not the woman, are in a sunny chair . . . almost as if Stevens is describing a still life painting) tell us that she is enjoying a late, Continental breakfast. Throughout the rest of the poem, she is defined only by thoughts which may be hers or the unknown narrator's.

Exercises and Assignments
1. In "O Florida, Venereal Soil," Stevens is addressing a beloved place and asking it to yield up its riches to "the lover." Write a poem in which you address a place you care about and ask it to show you the things you love about it.

2. In the film, we are shown images of a hurricane in the tropics to accompany the poem "Chaos in Motion and Not in Motion." This poem may also be thought of as a description of a "mental hurricane" when a person becomes disoriented and loses his sense of order and self. Write a few paragraphs exploring this idea with reference to the poem. Explain the paradox in the title.

3. In "The Snow Man," Stevens writes that "one must have a mind of winter" to appreciate and understand the things that winter represents. Explain this idea, with reference to the poem. What would happen if you looked at winter with "a mind of summer" or looked at the summery landscape of Florida with a mind of winter?

4. In the Eliot unit, we discussed the important part allusion plays in modern poetry. It is a good idea to read Stevens' poems in an annotated anthology so that you can identify allusions that may otherwise not be apparent to you. You will also find it useful to examine more closely some of these allusions, using the reference books in your local library. A dictionary or an encyclopedia is a good place to start, and your librarian should be able to point you to more specific reference sourcebooks. (Some useful reference books found in most public libraries include *The Reader's Encyclopedia*, *The Reader's Encyclopedia to Shakespeare*, *Granger's Index to Poetry*, and various concordances to the Bible, dictionaries of phrase and fable, and classical encyclopedias.)

Read "Peter Quince at the Clavier," then look up the references to Peter Quince in Shakespeare's *A Midsummer Night's Dream* and to the story of Susanna and the Elders in the *Apocrypha*. Write a brief paper explaining how these allusions help you to understand the poem. (Imagine that you are writing to explain to another student why he/she would find it useful to look up references.)

5. The female figure in "The Idea of Order at Key West" is described as "the single artificer of the world/In which she sang." (An artificer is a skilled worker.) Assuming that the woman represents the imagination, describe how she recreates the world of Key West. **Note:** Stevens probably wrote, or at least completed, this poem in Hartford, Connecticut. How does this information tie in with his idea of the imagination as creator in "Ideas of Order," the title of the group of poems in which this poem was published?

6. We can probably assume that the imagination is the "interior paramour" of "Final Soliloquy of the Interior Paramour." Stevens suggests that it is the imagination that lights our way in our passage through life. Explore, in a few paragraphs, how Stevens uses light in this poem.

7. Compare the first section of "The Rock" with "The Planet on the Table." In both poems, Stevens is looking back at his life and his achievement as a poet. Do both poems take the same attitude? Are they both equally optimistic or pessimistic? What is the "planet on a table"?

8. Paul Klee is known to have been Stevens' favorite painter. Look up a Paul Klee painting in an art book in your local library and spend some time looking over it carefully. What aspects of Klee do you feel appealed most to Stevens? In what ways are Stevens' poems similar to Klee's paintings?

9. Auroras are patterns of light that constantly change, shifting colors and position. The dawn is known as Aurora, and the film uses images from the "northern lights" or Aurora Borealis, the most spectacular of the auroras we are likely to see. For Stevens, the way we perceive the world is constantly changing and thus changes the world we perceive. Explore the changes of perception in "The Auroras of Autumn." Write a brief poem that describes how your own perception of an event, season, or place changed with the passage of time.

10. Trace the shifts in tone and attitude in the speaker throughout the entire poem, "Sunday Morning."

11. In "The Rock," Stevens looks back on life at his 70th birthday. Write a brief poem in which you look back at the events that have made you who you are. Alternately, imagine yourself to be 70 years old and write a brief poem as if you were looking back at your life from this age.

Self Test

Wallace Stevens was strongly influenced by the Romantic, meditative poets of the early 19th century—such as Wordsworth and, especially, Keats—and the contemplative character of Stevens' own work often has more in common with these poetic predecessors than with his contemporaries. Many of Stevens' poems can be seen as modern "answers" to Keats—where Keats writes "Ode to . . ." Stevens often writes "Anecdote of . . . ." (Compare "Ode on a Grecian Urn" and "Anecdote of the Jar.") Read the following Keats poem, "To Autumn," and write a few paragraphs in which you explore the similarity of themes and style between this poem and Stevens' "The Auroras of Autumn" and "Sunday Morning."

To Autumn

1

Season of mists and mellow fruitfulness;
Close bosom-friend of the maturing sun;
Conspiring with him how to load and bless
With fruit the vines that round the thatch-eaves run;
To bend with apples the moss'd cottage-trees,
And fill all fruit with ripeness to the core;
To swell the gourd, and plump the hazel shells
With a sweet kernel; to set budding more,
And still more, later flowers for the bees,
Until they think warm days will never cease,
For Summer has o'er-brimm'd their clammy cells.

2

Who hath not seen thee oft amid thy store?
Sometimes whoever seeks abroad may find
Thee sitting careless on a granary floor,
Thy hair soft-lifted by the winnowing wind;
Or on a half-reaped furrow sound asleep,
Drowsed with the fume of poppies, while thy hook
Spares the next swath and all its twined flowers:
And sometimes like a gleaner thou dost keep
Steady thy laden head across a brook;
Or by a cider-press, with patient look,
Thou watchest the last oozings hours by hours.

3

Where are the songs of Spring? Aye, where are they?
Think not of them, thou hast thy music too,—
While barred clouds bloom the soft-dying day,
And touch the stubble-plains with rosy hue;
Then in a wailful choir the small gnats mourn
Among the river sallows, borne aloft
Or sinking as the light wind lives or dies;
And full-grown lambs loud bleat from hilly bourn;
Hedge-crickets sing; and now with treble soft
The redbreast whistles from a garden-croft;
And gathering swallows twitter in the skies.

Answers to Self Test
Answers to Self Tests begin on page 226.

For Further Reading
Books by Wallace Stevens

Collected Poems. New York: Vintage Books; 1982.

The Letters of Wallace Stevens. Stevens, Holly, editor. New York: Alfred A. Knopf; 1981.

Opus Posthumous. Morse, Samuel French, editor. New York: Vintage Books; 1982.

The Palm at the End of the Mind: Selected Poems and a Play. Stevens, Holly, editor. New York: Alfred A. Knopf; 1981.

Books about Stevens

Bates, Milton J. *Wallace Stevens, A Mythology of Self.* Berkeley: University of California Press; 1986.

Brazeau, Peter. *Parts of a World: Wallace Stevens Remembered.* Berkeley: North Point Press, 1985.

Kermode, Frank. *Wallace Stevens.* New York: Grove Press; 1961.

Vendler, Helen. *On Extended Wings: Wallace Stevens' Longer Poems.* Cambridge: Harvard University Press; 1969.

Elizabeth Bishop (1911-1979)

During her lifetime, Elizabeth Bishop was one of the most honored of American poets, having received, among other awards, the Pulitzer Prize, a Guggenheim Fellowship, the Academy of American Poets Fellowship, and the National Book Award. Since her death, particularly with the publication of *The Complete Poems* (1983) and *The Collected Prose* (1984), Bishop's work has been praised even more warmly. Her poems were always admired for the purity and precision of her descriptions, and now readers have come to see how, even in her early poems, the outer facts and attention to external detail combine to give shape to and reveal an internal emotional realm. The poet Robert Lowell once remarked, "There's a beautiful formal completeness to all of Elizabeth Bishop's poetry. I don't think anyone alive has a better eye than she has: The eye that sees things and the mind behind the eye that remembers."

Born on February 8, 1911, in Worcester, Massachusetts, Bishop spent most of her early childhood living with either her maternal grandparents in Great Village, Nova Scotia, or her paternal grandparents in Worcester. Her father died when she was eight months old, and when Bishop was four years old her mother was placed permanently in a mental institution. Although her mother did not die until 1934, Bishop never saw her again. Two of Bishop's prose pieces, "In the Village" and "The Country Mouse," detail this early period of her life—her relative happiness in Nova Scotia and her unhappiness in Worcester with her stern paternal grandparents—and foreshadow the themes of loss and dislocation in her poems.

Ill as a child with eczema and asthma, Bishop received little formal schooling until she went to boarding school at Walnut Hill in Natick, Massachusetts, from 1927-30. In 1930, she entered Vassar College, where she began publishing poetry and prose in "little" magazines. In 1934, she graduated from Vassar with a B.A. in English Literature. In the same year, she met the poet Marianne Moore, who was then 47. Their meeting and friendship are detailed in "Efforts of Affection: A Memoir of Marianne Moore," included in Bishop's *Collected Prose*.

Bishop and Moore shared a passion for, among other things, the circus and the poems of Gerard Manley Hopkins. Moore's settled life (she shared an apartment with her mother in Brooklyn and rarely travelled) could hardly have contrasted more with Bishop's rootless one, but the two poets with their parallel yet distinct interests in visual art and close observation became lifelong friends.

During the 1930s, Bishop lived for a time in New York City, then travelled to France, England, North Africa, and Spain, as well as Key West, Ireland, and Italy. It was while she was living in Paris that she became familiar with the French literary and artistic movement called Surrealism (see **The World of the Poems** for an explanation of Surrealism).

In 1939, Bishop settled in Key West, where she would live for most of the next nine years. Of that period Bishop said, "The light and blaze of colors made a good impression on me, and I loved the swimming." The effect of the Floridian landscape on Bishop's writing can be seen in poems such as "Florida," "Jeronimo's House," and "Little Exercise."

Bishop's first book of poetry, *North and South*—praised for its restraint, calm, subtlety, and proportion—was published in 1946, the same year she met the poet Robert Lowell, who became a close friend. You can see their mutual influence on each other's work if you read Bishop's poem "The Armadillo" and Lowell's poem "Skunk Hour."

On a journey to South America in 1951, a violent allergic reaction to the fruit of the cashew forced Bishop to halt her journey in Rio de Janeiro. When she recovered, she decided to stay in Brazil, where she remained, living with her friend Lota de Macedo Soares, for almost 20 years. Brazilian landscape and literature had a powerful effect on Bishop. As well as writing the poems that would be published in *A Cold Spring* (1955) and *Questions of Travel* (1965), she learned Portuguese and translated a Brazilian classic (*The Diary of Helena Morley*) and Brazilian poetry. Bishop once said that she aimed "to make Brazil seem less remote and less an object of picturesque fancy."

In 1966, Bishop taught for the first time, at the University of Washington. From 1971 on, she taught for all or part of each academic year at Harvard University. Meanwhile, she was writing the stunning poems that would appear in *Geography III* (1976).

Never a very public person, Elizabeth Bishop rarely gave poetry readings, as most of her contemporaries did. In 1976, when she made her acceptance speech for the Books Abroad/Neustadt International Prize for Literature (she was the first American ever to be awarded this prize), she said of herself, "[A]ll my life I have lived and behaved very much like that sandpiper [the one in her poem "Sandpiper"]—just running along the edges of different countries and continents, 'looking for something.' " Three years later, at 68, Elizabeth Bishop died suddenly of a brain aneurysm.

The World of the Poems

Unlike the poetry of Hart Crane and William Carlos Williams, Elizabeth Bishop's poems do not directly reflect a concern with technology or the urbanization of America. For Elizabeth Bishop, growing up sickly and somewhat sheltered in Nova Scotia, Canada, and Worcester, Massachusetts, probably one of the first historical events to have a strong effect on her was the entry of the United States into World War I in 1917. In her prose memoir, "The Country Mouse," she remembers singing "war songs" in school and hoarding barrels of sugar at home. The War also figures in her poem "In the Waiting Room."

By 1927, when Elizabeth Bishop began boarding school, many of the most significant books of modern American poetry had been published, among them Marianne Moore's first collection, *Poems* (1921), T.S. Eliot's *The Waste Land* (1922), Wallace Stevens' first book *Harmonium* (1923), and William Carlos Williams' *Spring and All* (1923).

Two other books, which would also prove to have lasting influence on Elizabeth Bishop, had appeared: the first edition of the poems of British poet Gerard Manley Hopkins and Herbert Grierson's anthology, *Metaphysical Lyrics and Poems of the Seventeenth Century* (1921). The metaphysical poets, who for many generations had been, according to T.S. Eliot, "more often named than read, and more often read than profitably studied," were to have a profound effect on the next generation of American poets because of their merging of intellectual wit and lyricism. Of the metaphysical poets, George Herbert (1593-1633) was Bishop's favorite, partly because of what she called "his absolute naturalness of tone." Her poem "The Weed" is strongly inspired by Herbert's work. You might wish to read Herbert's poem "Love Unknown" along with "The Weed."

In an interview, Bishop spoke of some of the early influences on her writing, such as the fairy tales of Andersen and Grimm. When she was thirteen, she discovered Walt Whitman. Around the same time, she started reading Emily Dickinson, H.D. (Hilda Doolittle), and Harriet Monroe's anthology of modern poets, where she first came across Hopkins' poems.

During the 1930s, Elizabeth Bishop, unlike many American writers, was not much influenced by the Marxist political attitudes of the time. She said she "was always opposed to political thinking as such for writers . . . . Politically I considered myself a socialist, but I disliked 'social conscious' writing." Her own poems of the period are more influenced by the French literary and artistic movement called Surrealism and by the Metaphysical poets than by more politically-oriented writers of the day.

Surrealism, through such techniques as automatic writing and the use of dream images, sought to break down the barriers between sleeping and waking, consciousness and the unconscious. Although Bishop did not use these exact techniques—she was always in conscious control of structure—she did explore the region between dreaming and waking. In such poems as "The Man-Moth," "The Monument," and "Cirque d'Hiver," you can see the influence of Surrealist artists such as Giorgio de Chirico and Max Ernst on Bishop. Art was always very important to Bishop, and several of her other poems are about paintings or sculpture, including two about paintings ("Large Bad Picture" and "Poem") by a great-uncle of hers.

Elizabeth Bishop: The Long Trip Home

Elizabeth Bishop's poetry can be examined in the light of some of the main trends of modern poetry. Her work has affinities with Wallace Stevens' poems of tropical beauty and painterly vision; with William Carlos Williams' poems of the commonplace with their everyday vernacular; and with Marianne Moore's "hybrid compositions," with their naturalist's observations and moral concerns.

Bishop shares with the Modernists, and with the second generation of Modernists of which she is a part, a desire to have the poem itself become an object rather than mere statement, following from Williams' famous command, "No ideas but in things," and Stevens' tenet, "Not Ideas about the Thing but the Thing Itself." Bishop's early poems also show an Imagistic and Surrealistic interest in the yoking together of disparate images and familiar objects to create a new reality in which she minimizes the reference to self in the poetry.

As her poems developed, Bishop began to share with her contemporaries an increasing concern for the role of the self in poetry. While she could never be grouped with the so-called Confessional poets, such as Robert Lowell and Sylvia Plath, Bishop in her later poems becomes more autobiographical and more concerned with a quest for personal identity.

In one of her last poems, "Sonnet," Bishop writes of "a creature divided;/and the compass needle/wobbling and wavering,/undecided." The compass needle wavered all of Bishop's life between the North of Nova Scotia and New England and the South of Key West and Brazil. The titles of her books—North and South, A Cold Spring, Questions of Travel, and Geography III—point to the issues of quest and identity, home and away, exotic and domestic that are at the heart of her poetry.

In the title poem of Questions of Travel, Bishop writes:

> Think of the long trip home.
> Should we have stayed at home
>   and thought of here?
> Where should we be today?

These questions are not rhetorical. They represent a genuine quest for the self and for that nebulous, never-to-be-found place called "home."

This quest often takes the form of a geographical or topographical journey: if only the speaker of the poems can find herself on the map, she may know who she is, both literally and metaphorically, and where she belongs. Even that queer creature, the man-moth—half-man, half-moth—must "investigate as high as he can climb" although the exploration itself is what he "fears most."

The speaker in Bishop's poems often takes on the role of a guide, who, by showing us the physical reality of a place, can help to effect a transformation from sight to insight. This process can be seen in poems like "At the Fishhouses," where the speaker tells us of the dark sea:

> If you should dip your hand in,
> your wrist would ache immediately,
> your bones would begin to ache and
> your hand would burn
> as if the water were a transmutation of fire
> that feeds on stones and burns with a dark
> gray flame.

In other poems, particularly some of the ones set in Brazil, Bishop goes even further to show us what lies beyond the surface description of a place or a person, sometimes writing in an invented persona, as in, for example, "The Riverman," "Manuelzinho," and "Crusoe in England."

These speakers ask questions similar to those that occur in other poems. When Crusoe, speaking of his tendency towards self-pity, asks,

> "Do I deserve this? I suppose I must.
> I wouldn't be here otherwise. Was there
> a moment when I actually chose this?
> I don't remember, but there could have been."

he is echoing the questions in "Questions of Travel." These lines also exemplify the qualities of modesty and understatement in Bishop's poems, her wry humor and self-effacement.

These qualities can also be seen in poems such as "The Moose," where overheard voices on a long bus journey remind the speaker of "Grandparents' voices/uninterrup-tedly/talking in Eternity," and where a moose's sudden appearance in the middle of the road provokes the question: "Why, why do we feel/(we all feel) this sweet/sensation of joy?" The moose, who causes this uncanny feeling, is both alien and familiar, "high as a church,/homely as a house/(or, safe as houses)."

It is characteristic of Bishop's poetry that something like a moose, an armadillo, a mechanical toy, or Crusoe's nicked knife could produce as strong an emotion as "this sweet/sensation of joy." Or that a "crooked box/set up on pilings, shingled green,/a sort of artichoke of a house" (in the poem "The End of March") could function as Bishop's "proto-dream-house,/my crypto-dream-house." Out of these ordinary but significant objects seen in widely-scattered landscapes, Bishop made her enduring, questing poems.

Meet the Speakers

Lloyd Schwartz is a poet and professor of English at the University of Massachusetts in Boston. He met and befriended Bishop while he was writing his dissertation on her, and he has edited and contributed to, along with Sybil Estess, *Elizabeth Bishop and Her Art*.

Margaret Motley lives in Great Village, Nova Scotia, and was a friend of the Bishop family.

James Merrill, whose works have received much critical acclaim, must now be considered to number among our most important and innovative poets. (For further information, please see the **Meet the Speakers** section in the chapter on Wallace Stevens.)

Octavio Paz, poet, critic, and social philosopher, is one of Mexico's most celebrated contemporary writers. He knew Bishop both as a friend and as a translator of some of his poems. A prolific writer, Paz has published books on many diverse subjects, including: *The Labyrinth of Solitude, The Monkey Grammarian* and *Children of the Mire: Modern Poetry from Romanticism to the Avant-garde*. Among his books of verse are *Configurations* and *A Draft of Shadow & Other Poems*.

Mark Strand is a poet whose verse has won him far-reaching acclaim. Like Bishop, he has made several translations of foreign poets, including *The Owl's Insomnia* by Rafael Alberti. (For further information, please see the **Meet the Speakers** section in the chapter on Wallace Stevens.)

Howard Moss, poetry editor of *The New Yorker*, is an accomplished poet and playwright who has been a long-time admirer of Bishop. He is a member of The National Institute of Arts and Letters and received The National Book Award in 1972. Among his many books are *Instant Lives & More, New Selected Poems*, and *Two Plays: The Palace at 4 A.M. and The Folding Green*.

Frank Bidart is a leading figure in American poetry. His bold and unflinching work is innovative both in form and content. His works include *Golden State, The Book of the Body*, and *The Sacrifice*.

Mary McCarthy is a novelist, literary critic, and essayist. She has written on a wide range of subjects, including history, art, political responsibility, and the state of the modern novel. She first met and became friends with Elizabeth Bishop when they were students together at Vassar College and collaborated on a literary magazine. Her many books include *The Oasis, Occasional Prose, The Writing on the Wall and Other Literary Essays*, and her autobiographical works, *Memories of a Catholic Girlhood* and *How I Grew*.

Robert Giroux is one of America's major publishers. Chairman of the board of Farrar, Straus & Giroux, he was Elizabeth Bishop's editor and friend. Besides editing Bishop's *Collected Prose*, he has also authored *The Book Known as Q: A Consideration of Shakespeare's Sonnets*.

Study Plan for This Unit

1. Complete the section **Before Watching the Film: Journal-Writing and Other Activities**.

2. Read the Bishop poems, many of which are featured in the television program.

These poems, among others, will be highlighted in this unit. Read some of the shorter poems aloud, paying particular attention to linebreaks, and patterns of sound (end-rhyme, internal rhyme, alliteration, assonance, etc.) in the poems. Notice the kinds of descriptive imagery Bishop uses.

The Map
The Man-Moth
The Weed
Cirque d'Hiver
At the Fishhouses
The Shampoo
Questions of Travel
The Armadillo
The Riverman
In the Waiting Room
Crusoe in England
The Moose
Poem
One Art
Santarém
Pink Dog

3. Watch the film.

4. Complete the section: **After Watching the Film: Journal-Writing and Other Activities**.

5. Go through the **Guided Reading**.

6. Complete the **Exercises and Assignments** as specified by your instructor.

7. Take the **Self Test**.

Before Watching the Film: Journal-Writing and Other Activities

1. Describe a place you know well from three different points-of-view. For example, you could describe it as if you were seeing it from an airplane, from a passing car, and as if you were right in the middle of the place.

2. In your journal, write down a list of objects and words you associate with the word "North" and then write a list to go with "South."

3. Write down any responses you have to the cliches "Home is where the heart is" and "Travel is broadening."

4. Jot down any striking or unusual words or phrases from the poems you read.

While Watching the Film

1. Pay careful attention to what the landscapes of Nova Scotia, Brazil, and other places look like.

2. Jot down any unusual or confusing images in the film.

After Watching the Film: Journal-Writing and Other Activities

1. Go back to your list of words that you associated with "North" and "South" and write down any new words that watching the film made you think of.

2. After seeing the film, which poems do you feel that you understand better? Why? Which poems still puzzle you?

3. Judging from the poems you heard in the film, is Bishop's style of writing closer to Whitman's public, all-encompassing voice or to Dickinson's private, hermetic voice?

4. Elizabeth Bishop asks a lot of questions in her poems. Does she answer them? Think of a question that you really want to know the answer to and explore the possible answers and implications of the question, using as many concrete images as possible.

5. Think of the way that Bishop used the story of Robinson Crusoe to write her poem, "Crusoe in England." Choose a character from a myth or fairy tale, or a real person from history and write a brief poem in the voice of the character you picked.

Guided Reading

First read "In the Waiting Room" printed below. Then answer the questions and do the activities for each section. Remember to keep referring to the poem as you answer each question. The purpose of the questions is to help you understand the poem. One person's answers to the questions are supplied below the questions, but keep in mind that they are not the only ones. Your answers may differ from the ones below, which is fine as long as you can support your own answers with evidence from the poem.

In the Waiting Room

In Worcester, Massachusetts,
I went with Aunt Consuelo
to keep her dentist's appointment
and sat and waited for her
in the dentist's waiting room.   5
It was winter. It got dark
early. The waiting room
was full of grown-up people,
arctics and overcoats,
lamps and magazines.   10
My aunt was inside
what seemed like a long time
and while I waited I read
the *National Geographic*
(I could read) and carefully   15
studied the photographs:
the inside of a volcano,
black, and full of ashes;
then it was spilling over
in rivulets of fire.   20
Osa and Martin Johnson
dressed in riding breeches,

laced boots, and pith helmets.
A dead man slung on a pole
—"Long Pig," the caption said.   25
Babies with pointed heads
wound round and round with string;
black, naked women with necks
wound round and round with wire
like the necks of light bulbs.   30
Their breasts were horrifying.
I read it right straight through.
I was too shy to stop.
And then I looked at the cover:
the yellow margins, the date.   35

Suddenly, from inside,
came an *oh!* of pain
—Aunt Consuelo's voice—
not very loud or long.
I wasn't at all surprised;   40
even then I knew she was
a foolish, timid woman.
I might have been embarrassed,
but wasn't. What took me
completely by surprise   45
was that it was *me*:
my voice, in my mouth.
Without thinking at all
I was my foolish aunt,
I—we—were falling, falling,   50
our eyes glued to the cover
of the *National Geographic*,
February, 1918.

I said to myself: three days
and you'll be seven years old.   55
I was saying it to stop
the sensation of falling off
the round, turning world
into cold, blue-black space.
But I felt: you are an *I*,   60
you are an *Elizabeth*,
you are one of *them*.
Why should you be one, too?
I scarcely dared to look
to see what it was I was.   65
I gave a sidelong glance
—I couldn't look any higher—
at shadowy gray knees,

trousers and skirts and boots
and different pairs of hands   70
lying under the lamps.
I knew that nothing stranger
had ever happened, that nothing
stranger could ever happen.
Why should I be my aunt,   75
or me, or anyone?
What similarities—
boots, hands, the family voice
I felt in my throat, or even
the *National Geographic*   80
and those awful hanging breasts—
held us all together
or made us all just one?
How—I didn't know any
word for it—how "unlikely" . . .   85
How had I come to be here,
like them, and overhear
a cry of pain that could have
got loud and worse but hadn't?

The waiting room was bright   90
and too hot. It was sliding
beneath a big black wave,
another, and another.

Then I was back in it.
The War was on. Outside,   95
in Worcester, Massachusetts,
were night and slush and cold,
and it was still the fifth
of February, 1918.

Questions

1. After reading the title, what did you expect the poem to be about? What other associations did you have with the title?

2. Who is the speaker of the poem? How would you characterize the speaker when she was a child?

Answers

1. A "waiting room" might evoke feelings of nervousness, dread, boredom, or restlessness. It could be a waiting room in a hospital, a doctor's office, a principal's office, or a railroad station. In a larger sense, a waiting room might refer to a place that is a kind of limbo where you don't know what will happen next.

2. The speaker of the poem is a woman named "Elizabeth" who is looking back to a time many years ago when she was a few days away from turning seven years old. She

185

seems to be a thoughtful, observant, self-reliant child. She is proud of her ability to read, but somewhat shy in the grown-up world of the waiting room. Since the name, place, and dates correspond with the poet's own, it is pretty safe to assume that the speaker is the poet.

Questions

1. What is the effect of beginning the poem with plain, factual details? Why does the poet provide specific names, dates, places?

2. What is the speaker's attitude toward her aunt? Toward the other people in the waiting room? Where does her attitude change in the course of the poem?

3. Point out examples of where you think the speaker uses a child's diction (language or manner of speaking) and where she uses a more adult voice.

4. In line 9, what are "arctics"?

5. In line 26, what is a "Long Pig"?

Answers

1. The specific facts of the first stanza help to establish the waiting room as a real place and set up a contrast with the dream-like state of confusion the speaker enters later in the poem. The descriptions in the first stanza also help to establish the character of the speaker (her combination of shyness and pride) and the child's-eye view of the poem.

2. In the beginning of the poem, the child thinks of her aunt as "foolish" and "timid" (line 42), and the people in the waiting room are scarcely mentioned. After the cry of pain, she feels connected to both her aunt and the people in the waiting room, even though she is still too shy to look at their faces. She realizes her own shyness and timidity are like her aunt's. Lines 77-83 express the speaker's feelings of connection, particularly when she describes "the family voice/I felt in my throat."

3. Examples of child-like diction include phrases such as "It got dark early," "grown-up people," "an *oh!* of pain," and "or made us all just one." The speaker's adult voice is more evident in these descriptions and statements: "dressed in riding breeches, laced boots and pith helmets," "breasts were horrifying," "to stop the sensation of," and "what similarities."

4. "Arctics" are rubber overshoes that reach to the ankle or above. By using this regional and somewhat archaic word, Bishop helps to establish the time frame of the poem. In addition, the word helps to set up a contrast between the cold of Worcester and the tropical heat of Africa.

5. A "long pig" refers to a human being who is killed and eaten by cannibals. The child Elizabeth may not have a full knowledge of what is implied by the name, but the adult Elizabeth looking back in retrospect at the caption has a full awareness of the horrifying nature of the picture.

Questions

1. In lines 17-31, why do you think the poet has described the photographs in the *National Geographic* in this particular order?

2. How does the description of the volcano in lines 17-20 prepare you for later events in the poem?

3. In lines 27-30, what effect does the poet achieve by repeating the phrase "wound round and round"?

4. Why does the speaker identify with her aunt's cry of pain in the second stanza (lines 36-53)?

5. Now look back to line 36. To what does the word "inside" refer?

Answers

1. The photographs are progressively more disturbing to the child. The volcano and the people in pith helmets (Osa and Martin Johnson were married explorers and photographers), while not a part of her everyday reality, arouse manageable emotions. As suggested above, the child may not have a complete understanding of the term "long pig," but when she sees the photographs of the babies and the naked women, she relates them to her own femaleness and is doubly horrified. Will she grow up to have breasts like these?

2. Like the volcano, which in one photograph is "black, and full of ashes" and in the next is erupting, the child's own mind erupts into a whirl of questions after experiencing the photographs and the cry of pain. The image of the volcano erupting is also echoed later in the poem, in the fourth stanza, when the waiting room "was sliding beneath a big black wave" (lines 91-92).

3. Repeating the words emphasizes the child's shock at what she is seeing; it also prefigures the child's sense of dizziness as she tries to keep herself from falling off "the round, turning world" (line 58).

4. She identifies with her aunt's cry because she has been so powerfully affected by the photographs she has just seen, and because she feels a connection both with her aunt and with the people in the magazine who are at the same time both terribly unlike and terribly like herself.

5. The cry, of course, comes from within the dentist's operating room where Aunt Consuelo is. We don't know when we first read the line, however, that it also comes "from inside" young Elizabeth. By planting these words where she has, the poet prepares us for the difficult realization that follows.

Questions

1. In line 66, why does the speaker give a "sidelong glance"? Why, in lines 77-83, does she name only parts of bodies?

2. What happens between stanzas four and five (lines 94-95)? What events are implicit? Why does the speaker repeat information in this stanza that has already been given earlier in the poem?

3. What war is referred to in line 96 ("The War was on.")? What are some other meanings of this phrase?

Answers

1. She is too shy—particularly after encountering the embarrassing and terrifying breasts—to look directly at any of the people in the waiting room. She is also fearful of seeing directly "what it was I was," as indicated a few lines earlier. This perspective of seeing only knees, trousers, skirts, boots, and hands also reinforces the speaker's child's-eye view of the world, and echoes her earlier view of the waiting room as being full of disembodied objects—"arctics and overcoats, lamps and magazines."

2. In the fourth stanza, the speaker feels hot and stifled in the waiting room. She may, perhaps, have even lost consciousness momentarily. The break between the fourth and fifth stanzas indicates her recovery, her coming back to herself and the facts of the external world. She is repeating information to reassure herself that, despite the scariness of her revelation that "you are an I,/you are an *Elizabeth*,/you are one of *them*," the familiar world is still there.

3. The war referred to is World War I. But in another sense the speaker is referring to the battle with self-consciousness she has just gone through. It has been a struggle to realize that she is not just an individual but a person who is like others, despite all their strange and alien qualities. Conversely, looking at it from the "outside," she also realizes that other people are individuals like her. Her suddenly gained ability to swing back and forth between these two perspectives is a large part of what makes her feel dizzy.

Further Question

1. The stanza divisions represent stages in the speaker's experience. What are these stages?

Answer

1. The poem is constructed of five stanzas. The stanza divisions occur at crucial points in the speaker's experience; they indicate changes in time or perception. For example, the first stanza emphasizes the setting of the poem, while the second stanza brings the child out of the world of the waiting room and *National Geographic* and into the process of empathy and self-questioning. The third stanza begins with the speaker trying to reestablish the factual qualities of the first stanza, "to stop/the sensation of falling off/the round, turning world." But the process of trying to make sense of the "awful hanging breasts" and her aunt's "cry of pain" fails, and in the brief fourth stanza, Elizabeth loses her grip on the physical world, becomes disoriented, and perhaps loses consciousness or faints for a moment. In the fifth stanza, the child comes back to reality, but with a changed perception of the world.

Exercises and Assignments

1. Reread "The Map." The last line of the poem states, "More delicate than the historians' are the map-makers' colors." Explain what you think Bishop means by this. Do you agree or disagree with her view? Why?

2. Bishop got the idea to write her poem "The Man-Moth" from a newspaper misprint of the word "mammoth." Find a misprint of your own (or invent one by changing a letter or two in a word or phrase) and write a brief poem based on the misprint.

3. Many of Bishop's poems, particularly those written in the 1930s, are based on dream images or on images from Surrealist paintings. Read "The Weed" and "The Monument," then write a description based on either a dream you've had or a painting you've seen.

4. Reread "At the Fishhouses." Notice how the use of the present tense gives a sense of immediacy to the poem. Bishop said of this poem that "the use of the present tense helps to convey this sense of the mind in action" and that "switching tenses always gives effects of depth, space, foreground, background, and so on." Point out other ways in which Bishop gives an effect of three-dimensional reality to this poem. Which of the five senses are emphasized?

5. In "Questions of Travel," the speaker wonders whether it is worth it to travel: "Should we have stayed at home./wherever that may be?" Giving evidence from this poem and from the other Bishop poems you have read, what do you think Bishop's final answer to that question would be?

6. Like Marianne Moore, Bishop was a poet concerned with writing precisely about nature, and she often focused on animals in her poems. The poetic device of attributing human qualities or emotions to plants or animals is called personification. What is the effect of personification in some of the Bishop poems you have read? Write some examples of personification of your own.

7. In the poem "The Armadillo," why is the armadillo so important?

8. "The Riverman" is a persona poem written in the voice of a man who claims he has had a supernatural experience with the river spirit, Luandinha. What details (descriptions, similes, etc.) do you find in the poem that make you believe that the riverman has actually had this experience? (**Note:** Bishop has been described as a poet who can make the strange seem domestic and the domestic seem strange. Look for places where Bishop yokes the uncommon and the common together.)

9. In a letter to a friend, Bishop once wrote: "What one seems to want in art, in experiencing it, is the same thing that is necessary for its creation, a self-forgetful, perfectly useless concentration." Use this quotation to write about your experience of reading Bishop's poems. How can concentration be "perfectly useless"?

10. "Crusoe in England" is Bishop's retelling of the Robinson Crusoe story (from the novel by Daniel Defoe). Bishop's Crusoe is quite different from Defoe's Crusoe. If you have read *Robinson Crusoe*, describe some of the ways in which Bishop's characterization of Crusoe differs from Defoe's. If you have not read the novel, write about Bishop's use of understatement and humor in the poem.

11. In "The Moose," how does Bishop's sentence structure reinforce the idea of a long bus journey? Why does the appearance of the moose have such a powerful effect on the speaker of the poem and on the other passengers in the bus?

12. A poem that puts forward a philosophy of the art of poetry is called an *ars poetica*. Reread "Poem" and comment on the ways in which Bishop, while writing about her great-uncle's tiny painting, is also remarking on her own methods of composing a poem. How does her attitude about the painting change from the beginning to the end of the poem?

13. Reread "Santarem." Think of a place you visited once that interests you. Try to describe the place and what happened to you there, using vivid sense imagery that will enable someone else to see the place the way you saw it.

14. Reread "Pink Dog." The poem is set in the time of year when Carnival (the festive time before Lent) is celebrated. What are some of the ways that Bishop writes about a serious subject (poverty in Rio de Janeiro, a city in Brazil) in a humorous way? Notice the rhyme scheme of the poem, the use of puns, etc.

Self Test

Read "One Art" and answer the following questions.

One Art

The art of losing isn't hard to master;
so many things seem filled with the intent
to be lost that their loss is no disaster.

Lose something every day. Accept the fluster
of lost door keys, the hour badly spent.   5
The art of losing isn't hard to master.

Then practice losing farther, losing faster:
places, and names, and where it was you meant
to travel. None of these will bring disaster.

I lost my mother's watch. And look! my last, or   10
next-to-last, of three loved houses went.
The art of losing isn't hard to master.

I lost two cities, lovely ones. And, vaster,
some realms I owned, two rivers, a continent.
I miss them, but it wasn't a disaster.   15

—Even losing you (the joking voice, a gesture
I love) I shan't have lied. It's evident
the art of losing's not too hard to master
though it may look like (*Write* it!) like disaster.

Questions

1. List some of the patterns of repetition you find in this poem.

2. How does the form of the poem reinforce the content of the poem?

3. If you were trying to prove to someone that Elizabeth Bishop was the author of this poem, what would you say? Support your answer with evidence from the poem and with references to other Bishop poems that you have read.

Answers to Self Test

Answers to Self Tests begin on page 226.

For Further Reading
Books by Elizabeth Bishop

The Collected Prose. New York: Farrar, Straus, and Giroux; 1984.

The Complete Poems. New York: Farrar, Straus, and Giroux; 1983.

Books about Bishop

Ivask, Ivar, editor. "Homage to Elizabeth Bishop, Our 1976 Laureate." *World Literature Today.* Winter; 1977.

Kalstone, David. "Elizabeth Bishop: Questions of Memory, Questions of Travel." *Five Temperaments.* New York: Oxford University Press; 1977.

Schwartz, Lloyd and Estess, Sybil P., editors. *Elizabeth Bishop and Her Art.* Ann Arbor: University of Michigan Press; 1983.

Robert Lowell (1917-1977)

Robert Lowell could have learned a good deal of American history just by going back through his family tree. His mother was descended from Edward Winslow, who came to America on the *Mayflower*, and from John Stark, a brigadier general of the American Revolution. Robert's father was the scion of the Traill-Spence line of the Lowells, a less well-to-do branch of one of the richest and most powerful families in America. They had made their mark as poets and preachers rather than as statesmen and captains of industry. The best known was Robert's great-great-uncle, poet James Russell Lowell.

As a boy, Robert Lowell did not seem much inclined to uphold either side of this heritage. He fought a lot, dressed carelessly, and, with the exception of history, was not a very good student. About half way through his stay at St. Mark's boarding school, however, he started to work hard, have long and intense discussions with friends and teachers and carry out arduous self-prescribed studies over the summer vacations. During his last year at St. Mark's, he decided to be a poet.

Lowell had been destined for Harvard University since he was a boy growing up on Boston's Beacon Hill. His parents, though not wealthy, were still very much a part of what he would later call "the mob of ruling-class Bostonians," and Harvard was where they sent their sons to college. Lowell enrolled in 1935, but did not find the literary stimulation or recognition he wanted, and after one and a half years he transferred to Vanderbilt University to study with poets Allen Tate and John Crowe Ransom. When Ransom left for Kenyon College before the term began, Lowell followed him. At Ransom's suggestion Lowell studied Classics, a choice that developed both his sense of history and his poetic technique. In 1940 he graduated summa cum laude and was valedictorian of his class. In the same year he married fiction writer Jean Stafford.

In 1941 at the age of 24, Lowell converted to Roman Catholicism and immersed himself in Catholic theology and practice. Soon after the United States entered World War II he tried, unsuccessfully, to enlist. By 1943, however, when he was called up to serve, he had become disillusioned by the conduct of the war, especially by the massive bombing of civilians and the demand for unconditional surrender. He declared himself a conscientious objector and as a result spent five months in prison as a draft evader.

Lowell's first full-length book, *Lord Weary's Castle* (1946), appeared after the war and immediately launched him as a leading poet of his generation. The book was reviewed in dozens of papers and periodicals and won the Pulitzer Prize. Yet this was not a happy time for Lowell. His marriage had broken up not long before and not long after he suffered the first of the manic-depressive attacks that were to plague him throughout his life. Shortly after his recovery, in 1949, he married novelist and critic Elizabeth Hardwick, and after an extended stay in Europe, teaching stints in Iowa and Ohio and two more severe manic-depressive attacks, they settled down in his native Boston.

During the 1950s a number of factors conspired to urge Lowell toward a more open and accessible kind of poetry. He was undergoing psychotherapy and working on an autobiography, seeking to get at the causes of his manic-depression. His father had died in 1950 and his mother in 1954, and these losses added urgency to his desire to understand them and to place himself in relation to them and their illustrious forebears. His *Mills of the Kavanaughs* (1951), had been perceived as a falling-off from *Lord Weary's Castle* and Lowell himself was dissatisfied with writing poems in his old manner. Finally, writers such as Allen Ginsberg were challenging the accepted notions of poetry with open, intense, colloquial poems that dealt candidly with their lives and caustically with the state of the nation. All of these things helped to inspire Lowell to create the new style of his *Life Studies* (1959), one of the most admired, and imitated, books in American poetic history.

During the 1960s Lowell was again moved to political action. He protested the war in Vietnam by publicly refusing President Johnson's 1965 invitation to a White House Festival of the Arts and by speaking at the March on the Pentagon in 1967. He became acquainted with Jacqueline Kennedy and advised her in her efforts to groom Robert F. Kennedy for higher office. In 1968 Lowell campaigned for presidential candidate Eugene McCarthy.

In his late poetry Lowell extended the range of both his historical and autobiographical explorations in books such as *History, For Lizzie and Harriet* and *The Dolphin* (all 1973), for which he won a second Pulitzer Prize. The latter two books were very controversial for their detailed revelations about Lowell's and his family's private lives and for their use of actual quotations from personal letters and conversations. Lowell agonized over whether to publish these poems but finally did, and in his last book of poems, *Day by Day* (1977), he defends his decision to "pray for the grace of accuracy" and "say what happened." Robert Lowell died in September 1977, in Manhattan.

The World of the Poems

Robert Lowell was very much a man of his time, and, since he died just ten years ago, at 60, his time was not very different from ours. The world of his poems, then, is a familiar one. Still, some younger readers may not be well-informed about events that occurred before they were born or about the way of life of their grandparents' generation. Much of this can be looked up in books, but better still would be to talk to people who lived through those years. We all know parents, grandparents, aunts, uncles, teachers and others whose adult lives have, to one extent or another, coincided with Lowell's. An interesting experiment would be to find someone who was born around the same time as Lowell, in 1917, and to compare his or her perception of the events described in the poems with the poet's.

Here is a checklist of some of the major events and phenomena that Lowell considers in poems. There are many others that you might want to learn more about.

- World War II and the massive air raids on cities that occurred during it
- the choice of becoming a conscientious objector during World War II
- the fear of nuclear war in the 1950s
- the Vietnam War and the protests against it
- modern political tyranny, Hitler and Stalin
- the social and aesthetic decline of the major American cities
- racial segregation and the civil rights movement
- destructive commercial exploitation of the environment, such as whaling and air pollution
- the decline of the old New England aristocracy, the "Boston Brahmins," from their former authority and grandeur
- the assassinations of Robert F. Kennedy and Martin Luther King
- mental illness and attitudes toward the mentally ill
- attitudes to marriage and divorce

Robert Lowell: History, Public and Private

Like many boys Robert Lowell went through a time when all he cared about was toy soldiers. This soon gave way to an obsession with great military leaders, and during his teens he gathered and read a shelf full of books on Napoleon. Lowell's youthful interest in history was to become a lifelong passion. The more history he learned, however, the more troubling and complicated a picture he saw. Despite many kinds of progress—the retreat of slavery, the establishment of strong democracies, the spread of material well-being and enlightenment—history's keynotes still seemed to be tyranny, cruelty and devastation. Even the more democratic nations were dogged by dark shadows of intolerance and corruption. And in the age of Hitler and Stalin, Hiroshima and Nagasaki, one feared there was worse to come.

It became a major project of Lowell's poetry to examine history in the light of conscience, and eventually he would extend this examination to his own times and his own life. In this Lowell was like the Puritans, though he was, at the same time, very critical of their legacy in which faith, freedom, Christian charity, and industry coexisted with intolerance and slavery, belligerence and exploitation. Many of his early poems explore this violent underside of the New England tradition, as Melville had done in *Moby Dick* and Hawthorne in *The Scarlet Letter*. Lowell's poem "Children of Light," for example, begins:

> Our fathers wrung their bread from stocks and stones
> And fenced their gardens with the Redman's bones. . .

These early poems give a religious explanation for the persistence of evil in history: man's sinful, fallen nature, on the one hand, and on the other, the incomprehensibility of God's Will. As Lowell turned from his religious perspective in the early 1950s, he increasingly came to understand history in terms of the human psyche. "(U)pward angel, downward fish," he had said of the whalers in "The Quaker Graveyard in Nantucket." To Lowell the "upward," creative forces were those of freedom and openness and the "downward," destructive ones those of oppression and narrowness, and more and more he located this struggle between the creative and the destructive in man's own nature.

Lowell especially relished analyzing the play of these forces in the great men who had fascinated him since childhood. How could he reconcile his admiration for Napoleon, the air of glory surrounding him, with his destructive ambition? What drove Stalin to the top of his bloody heap? Everywhere he looked Lowell saw this moral ambiguity. Even "honest Abe" Lincoln had ordered the shooting of deserters during the Civil War. But in the 20th century in the great democracies a still more urgent problem was the moral ambiguity of the man in the street. The erosion of democracy during his lifetime became a major theme of Lowell's work. In "The Mouth of the Hudson," the corruption which he finds reflected in northeast New Jersey's industrial landscape is not just that of the leaders but of the whole social fabric. And in "For the Union Dead" he sees in the people of Boston a "savage servility" that bodes ill for the future of freedom since you can hardly make people be free.

In the late 1950s pressures from both within and without caused Lowell to turn to another kind of history, his own personal history. In 1959 he collected this new work for publication in a volume called *Life Studies*. Life studies are "drawings from life," "sketches using a living model," and in these poems Lowell drew boldly from his own life and those of his family and friends. As one critic said, he "ripped off the mask" and spoke candidly as himself:

One dark night,
my Tudor Ford climbed the hill's skull;
I watched for love-cars. Lights turned down,
they lay together, hull to hull,
where the graveyard shelves on the town. . . .
My mind's not right.

A car radio bleats,
"Love, O careless Love. . . ." I hear
my ill-spirit sob in each blood cell,
as if my hand were at its throat. . . .
(from "Skunk Hour")

This kind of autobiographical poetry may at first seem purely personal, and Lowell did in fact begin writing it to help him sort out personal troubles. However, looked at more closely, it also reveals important social and philosophical implications. For one thing, it is a logical development of Whitman's call for a poetry of Democracy. It affirms the value of each person's experience as a subject for poetry. The poems are also more than personal because the experiences they dramatize are often representative or, on the darker side, symptomatic of American experience in general. The symptoms Lowell finds in himself are the same ones plaguing society.

In the work of his last ten years Lowell broadened the scope of his look at both public and private history, at the same time becoming more skeptical of his ability to understand them. In *History* (1973) he examined a panoramic range of people and events from prehistory to the present, including his own experiences as the chronicle entered his lifetime. Despite their impressive scope these poems are more tentative, less judgmental. Lowell begins to fear that any pattern he imposes on the facts of history falsifies them. Similarly, he wrote two volumes recounting with almost ruthless realism and open-endedness the break-up of his second marriage and the rocky course of his third. Here too he finds that there is no form or simple story that does not distort what happened.

Amid this confusion and uncertainty he still clings to his sense of conscience, trying to find moral guidelines without clear signposts to go by. He decides that the first duty of conscience is simply to try to see things as they are. "My eyes have seen what my hand did," he writes at the end of *The Dolphin*. And in "Epilogue," the last poem of his last book, *Day by Day* (1977), he "pray[s] for the grace of accuracy." This is now the only "momentary stay against confusion" (to use Robert Frost's phrase) that he can find. But it is some light at least for conscience to see by into the darkness of history or that of his own life.

Meet the Speakers

Elizabeth Hardwick, the former wife of Robert Lowell, has published three novels, several short stories and numerous essays in literary criticism. She is a founding editor of *The New York Review of Books*, and her literary and social criticism have appeared widely. Her latest novel, *Sleepless Nights*, was critically acclaimed.

Derek Walcott is an eminent Caribbean poet and playwright who was a personal friend and admirer of Robert Lowell. (For further information see the Hart Crane chapter.)

Frank Bidart is one of the leading figures in American poetry to emerge from the 1970s. He was a friend of Robert Lowell and assisted him in the revision of some of his later poetry. (For further information see the Elizabeth Bishop chapter.)

John Thompson is a highly regarded writer who was a school friend of Robert Lowell. He is a leading authority on prosody, and among his works are *The Founding of English Metre* and an *Historical Guide to English Prosody*.

Robert Giroux was Lowell's former editor at Farrar, Straus and Giroux. (For further information see the Elizabeth Bishop chapter.)

Anthony Hecht is a poet who shares with Robert Lowell an interest in historical and religious themes and a strong grounding in traditional poetics. (For further information see the Emily Dickinson chapter.)

Robert Hass won the Yale Series of Younger Poets Award for his first book of poems, *Field Guide*. Since then he has published *Praise, Winter Mornings in Charlottesville,* and *Twentieth-Century Pleasures*, a book of essays including one on Robert Lowell's poem, "The Quaker Graveyard in Nantucket."

Study Plan for this Unit

1. Complete the section **Before Watching the Film: Journal-Writing and Other Activities**.

2. Read the Lowell poems, many of which are featured in the film.

The Quaker Graveyard in Nantucket
Beyond the Alps
My Last Afternoon with Uncle Devereux Winslow
Sailing Home from Rapallo
Home After Three Months Away
Memories of West Street and Lepke
Skunk Hour
For the Union Dead
The Mouth of the Hudson
Florence
Marcus Cato 234-149 B.C.
Dolphin
Epilogue

3. Watch the film.

4. Complete the section **After Watching the Film: Journal-Writing and Other Activities**.

5. Go through the **Guided Reading**.

6. Complete the **Exercises and Assignments** as specified by your instructor.

7. Take the **Self Test**.

Before Watching the Film: Journal-Writing and Other Activities

1. If you keep a diary, look over some old passages. Would the events that you describe make a better short story told as they are in the diary, or would you want to

alter and rearrange them? (If you don't keep a diary, you could use old letters instead, or write a brief factual account of some time in your life and consider that as material for a story.) Then write a brief story, trying out the approach you have picked.

2. List all the wars you can remember from reading American history. Which ones do you think were for a good cause, which ones not? Or if you are not sure why most of them were fought, look up a few in an encyclopedia and see what it says.

3. Read in a history book a brief description of some other place and time such as ancient Rome, medieval France or Japan in the 19th century. How do you think historians will describe our place and time, America from World War II to the present?

While Watching the Film

1. Pay close attention to the images of Boston and to what is said about it. Notice how Boston contrasts with the other places in Lowell's life and work.

2. Notice at what points in the film photographs are shown and at what points paintings are shown. Also notice when the cinematography is more like photography and when it is more like painting.

3. Listen closely to the poem "For the Union Dead, " and look closely at the Civil War monument for Colonel Shaw and his Negro regiment. This is the sculpture on which Lowell based "For the Union Dead."

After Watching the Film: Journal-Writing and Other Activities

1. How did you like the film's treatment of "The Quaker Graveyard in Nantucket"? How would you have filmed it?

2. Do you think Lowell went too far in revealing things about his own life and the lives of the people around him? Briefly explain.

3. Did any of Lowell's political actions or opinions particularly offend or please you? If so, pick one and try to take the opposite side of the question; i.e., if you agreed with Lowell, argue against him; if you didn't agree with him, think of ways to defend his position.

Guided Reading

"For the Union Dead" was commissioned for the 1960 Boston Arts Festival, and Lowell read it in June of that year in the Boston Public Garden. At a reading in 1966 Lowell said that the poem was "about segregation and the atomic bomb and what's happening to our cities." It also explores the psychological roots of these problems. Lowell's meditation on these themes was inspired by a Civil War monument near his Marlborough Street home and by other scenes and situations around Boston. Several famous writers had written about Colonel Shaw and his Negro regiment—the subjects of the monument—including Lowell's ancestor James Russell Lowell, John Greenleaf Whittier, Oliver Wendell Holmes, Ralph Waldo Emerson and William James. Robert Lowell's great-great-uncle Charles Russell Lowell, himself a Civil War hero known as Beau Sabreur, was married to Shaw's sister, and this relationship undoubtedly helped stir Lowell's interest.

The poem is very rich, full of crosscurrents and surprising connections, so a few hints may be helpful.

1.) Pay special attention to the wars mentioned and how they are characterized.

2.) Notice all the images of fish and places where people or things are compared with fish or other creatures.

3.) Look for the repetition of words and the use of similar images and statements in different parts of the poem.

4.) There are several lines in the poem that look simple and carry you along well enough, but when you stop to think about them it is very difficult to say exactly what they mean, and in fact it is best not to. These lines are not allusions to information outside the poem nor symbols whose meaning you have to puzzle out. They are more like moving searchlights that point up different associations and implications as they land on different parts of the poem. No one of these associations is definitive but all of them add something to the view of the modern world that Lowell is giving us through his eyes.

Note: "The ditch is nearer" (line 53) is one of these lines that set off a wealth of associations but elude definition. In dealing with it, it helps to be clear about the literal "ditch" in line 50 that makes the speaker think of the word and what it implies. The Confederate officers who defeated Colonel Shaw's regiment would not recognize the black troops as legitimate soldiers and buried them in a mass grave without the usual rites of war. The Confederates also threw Shaw's body into the same grave, a great insult from their point of view. Lowell puts the word "niggers" in quotation marks because it was the word used in the dispatches from the front, not because Shaw's father used it. Shaw's father in fact approved of his son's actions and thought that those Northerners who were outraged by the treatment of his son's body were revealing their own racist thinking. This is why he "wanted no monument/except the ditch." (Lowell was aware that these facts might not be clear from the poem alone and would sometimes briefly explain them before reading it.) The Latin epigraph means "They gave all to save the Republic."

For the Union Dead

"Relinquunt Omnia Servare Rem Publicam"

The old South Boston Aquarium stands
in a Sahara of snow now. Its broken windows
    are boarded.
The bronze weathervane cod has lost half its scales.
The airy tanks are dry.   4

Once my nose crawled like a snail on the glass;
my hand tingled
to burst the bubbles
drifting from the noses of the cowed, compliant fish.   8

My hand draws back. I often sigh still
for the dark downward and vegetating kingdom
of the fish and reptile. One morning last March,

I pressed against the new barbed and galvanized   12

fence on the Boston Common. Behind their cage,
yellow dinosaur steamshovels were grunting
as they cropped up tons of mush and grass
to gouge their underworld garage.   16

Parking spaces luxuriate like civic
sandpiles in the heart of Boston.
A girdle of orange, Puritan-pumpkin colored girders
braces the tingling Statehouse,   20

shaking over the excavations, as it faces
    Colonel Shaw
and his bell-cheeked Negro infantry
on St. Gaudens' shaking Civil War relief,
propped by a plank splint against the garage's
        earthquake.   24

Two months after marching through Boston,
half the regiment was dead;
at the dedication,
William James could almost hear the bronze
    Negroes breathe.   28

Their monument sticks like a fishbone
in the city's throat.
Its Colonel is as lean
as a compass-needle.   32

He has an angry wrenlike vigilance,
a greyhound's gentle tautness;
he seems to wince at pleasure,
and suffocate for privacy.   36

He is out of bounds now. He rejoices in man's lovely,
peculiar power to choose life and die—
when he leads his black soldiers to death,
he cannot bend his back.   40

On a thousand small town New England greens,
the old white churches hold their air
of sparse, sincere rebellion; frayed flags
quilt the graveyards of the Grand Army of the
        Republic.   44

The stone statues of the abstract Union Soldier
grow slimmer and younger each year—

wasp-waisted, they doze over muskets
and muse through their sideburns . . .   48

Shaw's father wanted no monument
except the ditch,
where his son's body was thrown
and lost with his "niggers."   52

The ditch is nearer.
There are no statues for the last war here;
on Boylston Street, a commercial photograph
shows Hiroshima boiling   56

over a Mosler Safe, the "Rock of Ages"
that survived the blast. Space is nearer.
When I crouch to my television set,
the drained faces of Negro school-children
              rise like balloons.   60

Colonel Shaw
is riding on his bubble,
he waits
for the blessèd break.   64

The Aquarium is gone. Everywhere,
giant finned cars nose forward like fish;
a savage servility
slides by on grease.   68

Lines 1-11

1. Lowell describes the Aquarium as standing in a kind of desert, "a Sahara of snow." To what feature of a real desert does the Aquarium correspond?

2. About how old was the speaker when he had the experience that he recalls in the second stanza?

3. Read lines 5-11 aloud, giving some thought to how you would say "My hand draws back."

4. Notice that the speaker has switched back to the present tense in line 9. What psychological process or emotional response is suggested by the change of tense? Or, to put it differently, what goes through the speaker's mind between lines 8 and 9?

5. What is the human equivalent of the "dark downward and vegetating" tendency that the speaker sees in the animals?

Answers

1. The Aquarium is like an oasis; or rather, it was: now it is "boarded" up and "dry."

2. He was a child, probably quite a small child. If we assume the speaker to be a

dramatic representation of Lowell himself (as is often the case in his poems), we can be more precise. Lowell was born in 1917, so the Aquarium visit would have occurred in the Twenties.

4. It may be that the speaker actually reached out a hand toward the remembered fish—as we sometimes do in a dream or daydream—and then caught himself. While common enough in dreams, this could be a disturbing experience outdoors on a cold, bright day. More likely, though, it is an imagined or symbolic gesture: he felt as if his hand had pulled back, or the gesture symbolizes the difference between then and now. Now he is more cautious, indrawn, "cowed" perhaps by society's expectations, all too aware that adults are not supposed to reach out and touch.

5. The speaker sees in the animals an image of his own tendency to escapism, inertia and regression. Like all of us he sometimes retreats into the "dark" of unconsciousness, sometimes surrenders to the "downward" pull of inertia and becomes depressed, sometimes indulges in childishness. This is why he fears giving in to this rich and seductive "kingdom."

Lines 11-24

1. The words "new" in line 12 and "old" in line 1 are redundant as far as their denotations go. The description of the Aquarium makes it clear that it is old, and the fences put up around construction sites are always new, in the sense of temporary, even if old materials are used. But what connotations and implications of "old" and "new" does Lowell point up by using the words in this redundant way?

2. Which meanings of "gouge" and "underworld" come into play in line 16?

3. How does line 24 imitate what it describes? Read lines 19-24 aloud.

Answers

1. The word "old" is often used to connote endearment or nostalgia as in "my old pal" or "the old hometown," and that is how Lowell uses it here. The word "new" is neutral in itself but is linked to "barbed," suggesting that new things are dangerous or sinister. By specifying "old" and "new" Lowell is implying that the contrast between the Aquarium and the construction site is not just an isolated instance but marks a trend. Our cities are becoming more stressful and dangerous, less attractive and inspiring.

2. There are, of course, the physical gouging out of the hole and that the garage will be below ground. But there are also the notions of price gouging and the construction industry's connections with the "underworld" of organized crime. The "underworld" also suggests Hades or Hell.

3. The phrase ends the longest sentence in the poem. The line itself is like a "plank" propping up the heavy, shakily piled-up sentence on top of it.

Lines 25-40

1. Why does the monument "stick like a fishbone in the city's throat"?

2. There are many comparisons Lowell could have used to give an image of Colonel Shaw's leanness. Why a "compass-needle"?

Answers

1. Because it confronts the city with a truth about itself that it finds hard to swallow, namely its hypocrisy about race. Boston, which had been a leading center of abolitionism and which was still one of the most liberal cities in America, was also a strictly segregated one. In the 1950s it resisted court orders to integrate its schools as fiercely as many areas of the South. The monument, then, is a vivid reminder that the city had sent black soldiers off to die for a freedom that it was still not fully granting to their descendants. Before the sixties were over this tension between image and reality had erupted into terrible riots. In 1974 the U.S. First Circuit Court of Appeals quoted this line of Lowell's in its opinion upholding Boston's school desegregation order.

2. The compass-needle suggests Colonel Shaw's purposefulness and sense of direction. Like a compass-needle that always points north, he was able to guide himself by his principles through all the twists and turnings of criticism and doubt. The formation of the black regiment was very controversial. Some thought the blacks wouldn't make good soldiers; some thought they were being needlessly sacrificed to make a point. Colonel Shaw took all this in but did not let it sway him from his own sense of what mattered most.

Lines 41-68

1. Contrast Lowell's description of more recent Civil War statues (lines 44-48) with his description of Saint Gaudens' monument to Colonel Shaw and his men. Lowell not only prefers the Saint Gaudens' monument, the others worry him. What is it that bothers him about the more recent memorials?

2. Which is the "last war" referred to in line 54?

3. Reread lines 55-58. What do you think about this use of an image of nuclear war to advertise a safe?

4. What visual effect is created in lines 59-60 by the opposing verbs "crouch" and "rise"?

5. Look up the word "crouch." One of its meanings mirrors images that occur right near the beginning and the end of this poem. What meaning, and which images does it recall?

Answers

1. What worries Lowell about the statues is that they romanticize and prettify the war so that people won't have to think about why it was fought and how much suffering and destruction it caused. The statues represent a dangerous forgetfulness of history.

2. This must be the Korean War (officially a "conflict,"—war was never declared) since there were surely World War II memorials in Boston by 1960 when Lowell was writing. Also, the Korean War was the first American war in which black and white soldiers were not assigned to separate units.

3. Once introducing this poem at a reading, Lowell said that he really saw the sign he described and that it made him think of mankind being survived by its money and of the biblical admonition to "put up treasure where it lasts."

4. The two verbs combine to suggest a view from an awkwardly high and oblique angle, as in a fish-eye mirror. Lowell is probably suggesting that this is how many whites see their black neighbors, as small, distorted, anonymous figures passing behind a clear but impenetrable screen.

5. "Crouch" can mean "to bend or bow servilely, to cringe." This recalls the "cowed, compliant fish" in line 8 and the "savage servility" of the fishlike cars in line 67. Notice that, since it is the speaker doing the crouching, this word choice implicates him in the complacency and slavishness that he sees around him.

Further Questions

1. The image of the urban "desert" in lines 1-2 is one that Lowell quietly develops in other parts of the poem. For example, what is the connection between the children's "drained faces" and the drained Aquarium tanks of line 4?

2. There is another, larger image of emptiness and desolation in the poem. Lowell doesn't explicitly compare it with a desert but he doesn't have to; the desert is a natural and common image for this larger desolation. What is this other kind of "desert"?

3. When the speaker says, "The ditch is nearer," he is associating the ditch where Shaw and his men were left with some of the other things he has been seeing and thinking. This line has many associations throughout the poem. Find at least three developments or situations that the speaker associates with "the ditch," things that are growing "nearer," i.e., becoming more imminent, closing in, contributing to a trend.

4. Why does the line "There are no statues for the last war here" (line 54) follow right after "The ditch is nearer"? What do the two statements have to do with each other? Similarly, why does Lowell join lines 55-56 to line 54 with a semicolon instead of starting a new sentence? What does the advertising image have to do with there being no statues for the Korean War?

5. Colonel Shaw's "bubble" in line 62 is another image that resonates strongly throughout the poem but is hard to define. Look through the poem for ways in which Colonel Shaw might be said to be "riding on" a "bubble," ways in which he is suspended or left in limbo, "riding on" a false hope or illusion. (**Hint**: Can you recall the monument from the film? Up to this point, when Lowell speaks about Shaw and the regiment in the past tense, he is remembering things he has learned from history. When he uses the present tense, he is describing the memorial on Boston Common. Lines 61-64 are again in the present tense.)

6. What does Colonel Shaw's bubble have to do with the nuclear image in lines 55-58?

7. Which meanings of "break" does Lowell employ in line 64?

8. What does Lowell mean by "savage servility"?

Answers

1. "Drained faces" is a vivid way to capture the children's confusion and terror at being thrust into the middle of a frightening situation. However, it also suggests that living in an empty, desolate place (the urban "desert") "drains" them, gradually makes them empty and desolate.

2. The advertising image Lowell describes in lines 55-58 makes him think about nuclear weapons. The desolation left by such weapons would be a man-made "desert" more deathly than any natural one. All the images of desolation and loss in the poem are haunted by this possibility of a much greater disaster.

3. The excavation for the "underworld garage" is a kind of ditch and represents a trend in urban development that Lowell finds ugly and inhumane. The schoolchildren of line 60 are in the news because they are involved in a program to desegregate the schools. The program created great tension, and people feared there would be violence. This rising danger makes the speaker consider the possibility of racial bloodshed in Boston, of blacks and whites again falling in battle over equality. (And Boston was in fact the scene of serious racial violence before the sixties were out.)

The image of a safe surviving a nuclear blast reminds the speaker of the people who wouldn't. This would be another mass grave in which black and white would lie together and might be another case where there would be "no monument/except the ditch." The ditch has still further associations such as Shaw's suffocating "for privacy" in line 36, but no one of these is predominant. Part of the scariness of this image is that it is convincing—we tend to believe that "the ditch is nearer"—despite our not really knowing what the ditch is. Not being able to define the forces of doom is part of our predicament.

4. One of the reasons "the ditch is nearer" is that "there are no statues for the last war." As much as the romanticized war memorials disturbed the speaker, having none is worse. Only being able to remember the war in a touched-up version is better than trying to forget it entirely. Lowell is afraid that those who forget history will be "condemned to relive it." The ad for the safe is another example of ignoring history or not taking it seriously enough. By joining the two clauses with a semicolon, Lowell reminds us that a nuclear war could be "the last war" in a different sense also.

5. The monument shows Shaw and his men on the march in 1863. Shaw is very much in suspense. He doesn't know how his hastily trained troops will do against Confederate regulars and must have some fear that things will turn out badly. From our point of view, knowing how things do turn out, we could well say he is "riding on his bubble," since they are marching to slaughter. Similarly, if he imagined in 1863 that America was close to achieving racial equality, he was "riding on" an illusion or false hope. Since the cause for which he gave his life is still "up in the air," he remains in a kind of limbo waiting for history to decide whether his death, and those of his men, were in vain.

6. In the nuclear age the earth itself is like a fragile bubble on which Colonel Shaw and each of us are riding.

7. Lowell is using at least three meanings of "break": 1.) a sudden or violent rupture 2.) an interruption from work or duty for rest or relaxation 3.) a stroke of good luck. The puns on "break" point up Shaw's ambivalence: his ability to be hopeful and doubtful at the same time, to feel the criticisms of his position while still maintaining it. Even his most heroic quality, his ability "to choose life and die," is ambivalent since death would be a relief from his lack of privacy, from the responsibilities of his rank and from the danger and fatigue of battle. Shaw too feels the tug of the "dark downward and vegetating kingdom."

8. The word "savage" tells us that this "servility" is both fierce and primitive, a throwback, a kind of social regression. The Merriam-Webster dictionary gives these

meanings for "servility": 1.) a slave's condition: the state of slavery: servitude 2.) a mean or cringing submissiveness, obsequiousness 3.) lack of independence or spirit—undue dependence or deference 4.) slavish imitation: want of originality, inspiration, invention. In the course of the poem Lowell has presented images and planted suggestions that bring all of these senses of "servility" into play. One important implication is that the citizens of Boston no longer place a very high value on freedom. This is not a simple criticism, though. The people are not simply "cowed, compliant fish" in "giant finned cars." Poet and critic Alan Williamson has written that "man's lovely,/ peculiar power to choose life and die" stands in contrast to "man's equally peculiar, less lovely ability to choose death and live." This was a power that Lowell saw increasing frighteningly fast in modern life, but it was also one that he felt from within. The speaker of the poem understands that the people of Boston feel the same kinds of internal and external pressures that he does; his indictment is tempered with sympathy. But clearly he identifies more with the troubled heroism of Colonel Shaw than with the untroubled complacency of those who just want to get by.

Exercises and Assignments

1. Read "Memories of West Street and Lepke." How many different kinds of "connections" has Lepke lost? Briefly explain each one.

2. Read "Skunk Hour" and answer the following:
    a. What impression do you get of the poem's speaker? How is each of the three persons described in the first four stanzas like or unlike him?
    b. What does the speaker see in the skunks that helps him to take heart and get "on top of" his situation?

3. Read "Epilogue."
    a. In what ways can a painting be more accurate than a snapshot?
    b. How would you answer the question "Yet why not say what happened?"

4. Read "Dolphin" and give two or three reasons Lowell may have had for saying "My eyes have seen what my hand did" instead of "I have seen what I did."

5. a. To whom is the speaker talking in the first three lines of "Marcus Cato, 234-149 B.C."?
    b. How could deafness make Cato a stronger ruler?
    c. The last line of this poem plays off the saying "Rome was not built in a day." Which version do you agree with more? Write a paragraph backing your choice.

6. a. The final line of "My Last Afternoon with Uncle Devereux Winslow" is very surprising but very effective. It is prepared for by much more than the black earth and white lime that the young Lowell is mixing. Throughout the poem Lowell develops a series of bright and warm images and an opposing series of cold and dark images. These are so woven into the scenes that you don't especially notice them as you go along. On a large piece of paper list these words, putting the cold/dark ones to the right (the colder and darker the further right they go) and the warm/bright ones to the left (as above the warmest and brightest go furthest left) After doing this, explain the phrase "the one color."
    b. Compose a verbal portrait of one of your relatives the way Lowell does of his Uncle Devereux.

7. In the first stanza of "Sailing Home from Rapallo" Lowell addresses his dead mother. Then for the rest of the poem he turns to the reader, telling about the trip home, the burial arrangements and the family cemetery. But can you find at least two places where Lowell again seems to be speaking to her, sharing the story with her, though he does not explicitly do so?

8. a. Find the three places in "The Mouth of the Hudson" where Lowell brings something to eat or drink into close contact with some dirty or noxious industrial by-product. In this way he coaxes us into tasting and smelling (in our imaginations, of course) the industrial wastes and realizing how they affront our senses. Now look once more at the end of the poem. How does the phrase "sulphur-yellow sun" expand upon this realization?

   b. In the Bible sulphur is called brimstone and is listed among the torments waiting for sinners in Hell. By choosing this word Lowell likens the industrial landscape to Hell. Look again at the words "ledges," "tan" and "unforgivable." What does each of these words suggest in light of the implied comparison between the landscape and Hell?

9. a. One critic compared the sound of the language of "The Quaker Graveyard in Nantucket" to organ music. Pick three lines to illustrate this comparison.

   b. Many readers have remarked on the violence of the verbs in this poem. Find three verbs that convey violence both through their meaning and their sound. These powerful verbs give motion to the poem's heavily stressed lines (lines that contain a high percentage of strongly accented syllables, such as "Seaward. The wind's wings beat upon the stones . . . " in part II). Find three more of these heavily stressed lines. How is this combination of violent verbs and heavily stressed lines appropriate to the poem's theme?

   c. "For the Union Dead" and "The Quaker Graveyard in Nantucket" both dramatize contradictions between America's ideals and the realities of her history. How do they differ in their handling of this problem?

   d. Why do you think Lowell uses the words "blue-lunged" in the next to last line of the poem? What physical properties of the waves does "blue-lunged" suggest? What associations does this image have with whales and whaling? What associations does it have with Lowell's variation on the biblical tale of the creation of man in the three preceding lines? (For the actual biblical account, see Genesis 2.)

10. Lowell once explained why he dedicated "Skunk Hour" to Elizabeth Bishop. " 'Skunk Hour' is modeled on Miss Bishop's 'The Armadillo' . . . Both [poems] use short line stanzas, start with drifting description and end with a single animal." Read (or reread) both poems and then write your own using the pattern that Lowell describes.

11. We don't usually think of ourselves as living in history but, of course, we do, and we are affected everyday by circumstances and events that will later be discussed as "history." Write a poem or story in which you deal with the way some large external situation or major event has affected you or your family. Experiences like living through an economic recession, or growing up in a highly technological age, or serving in the military, or moving from one country to another are all examples of our lives crossing with history.

Self Test

Reread "Home After Three Months Away." List four or five ways in which Lowell identifies with the tulips in stanza three. Briefly explain each one. (**Note**: In the first line of the stanza Lowell alludes to Christ's parable of the lilies of the field. See Matthew 2:28-30 or Luke 12:27-28.)

Answers to Self Test
Answers to Self Tests begin on page 226.

For Further Reading
Books by Robert Lowell

Day by Day. New York: Farrar, Straus and Giroux; 1977.

Life Studies. New York: Farrar, Straus and Giroux; 1980.

Lord Weary's Castle. San Diego: Harcourt Brace Jovanovich; 1983.

Selected Poems. New York: Farrar, Straus and Giroux; 1982.

Books about Lowell

Berryman, John and Nims, John Frederick and Wilbur, Richard. "A Symposium on Robert Lowell's 'Skunk Hour.'" *The Poet and His Critics*. Orloff, Anthony, editor. Philadelphia: JB Lippincott; 1962.

Hamilton, Ian. *Robert Lowell: A Biography*. New York: Random House; 1983.

Jarrell, Randall. "The Kingdom of Necessity." *Poetry and the Age*. New York: Ecco Press; 1980.

Sylvia Plath (1932-1963,

Sylvia Plath has been labelled a "confessional poet" and a "spokeswoman for the feminist movement." But neither label accurately sums up the extraordinary craft or range of subject she displayed in her work. Her poems have been admired not only for their technical brilliance, but also for their emotional force. The critic Elizabeth Hardwick once said "Her [Plath's] work is brutal, like the smash of a fist . . ."

Born on October 27, 1932, Plath spent the first years of her life in Winthrop, Massachusetts, near the ocean. In spite of the Depression, the Plaths had a fairly stable life. Otto Plath, Sylvia's father, was a biologist, German teacher and beekeeper (Sylvia was later to take up her father's hobby); Aurelia Plath, 21 years younger than her husband, a traditional wife.

Plath was a precocious child, gifted in painting and drawing as well as writing. (She published her first poem at the age of eight in *The Boston Traveller*.) Her idyllic childhood was shattered, however, by her father's death, in 1940, from an advanced case of undiagnosed diabetes. Plath was then eight years old and her father's favorite. "I'll never speak to God again," she said to her mother upon hearing of her father's death. Indeed, she never completely recovered from her grief and rage over the loss of her father, the subject of some of her best poems.

Throughout high school, she diligently pursued the craft of writing fiction and poetry. With her mother, Plath conspired to write "hack stories" to make money. After 45 rejections, she published her first story in *Seventeen* magazine in her senior year. In 1951, Plath entered Smith College on full scholarship. From the outset she was an extremely ambitious and competitive student. She won poetry prizes, a guest editorship at *Mademoiselle*, and graduated summa cum laude in 1955. In the early years, her ambitions were the traditional, conventional ones of post-World War II teenagers.

In the summer of her junior year at Smith, however, Plath suffered a nervous breakdown. She had returned home from her summer position as guest editor at *Mademoiselle* deeply exhausted and overcome with doubts about her self-worth. These feelings were accompanied by an increasing sense of isolation and entrapment: "I've gone around for most of my life as in the rarified atmosphere under a bell jar." Later that summer, she took an overdose of sleeping pills and hid herself in the basement of the family house. She was found after three days; it was considered a miracle that she was still alive. She later wrote about the events of these years in the autobiographical novel *The Bell Jar* (1963).

In 1955, she won a Fulbright Fellowship to Newnham College, Cambridge, where she received her M.A. in 1957. At Cambridge, she met the British poet Ted Hughes whom she married after four months. He was a romantic figure, larger than life, and their courtship was passionate. In her journals, Plath describes drawing blood on their first kiss, getting wildly drunk with this "God-like" man whom she felt was her counterpart, her equal at last.

They returned to Northampton, Massachusetts where Plath taught at Smith College. Afterward they moved to Boston where Plath audited Robert Lowell's poetry seminar at Boston University and where she met the poet Anne Sexton. The Hugheses returned to England, and in 1960 Plath gave birth to her daughter, Frieda. This was the same year her first book of poetry, *The Colossus*, was published, receiving critical acclaim for its range of language and stylistic virtuosity.

After *The Colossus* she began to work on the poems that were later to appear in *Ariel* (published posthumously in 1965). Ted Hughes has noted that Plath abandoned her old laborious process of composing poems during this period. Instead she wrote poems at "top speed, as one might write an urgent letter."

In 1962, Plath had a second child, Nicholas. Shortly thereafter, the marriage fell apart. In the ensuing months, Plath began writing poetry at an intense rate. As she wrote in her poem "Kindness": "The blood jet is poetry,/There is no stopping it." These poems reflected her struggle with the feelings of abandonment first experienced as a young girl at the death of her father and now relived with the departure of her husband. In these poems her rage is expressed in horrifying visions of violence. Through writing out her pain, Plath attempted a process of renewal, a peeling away of the old, false selves (the selves dependent on father, mother, and husband) in an attempt to gain a true sense of herself. She failed. On February 11, 1963, she committed suicide.

Aside from *Ariel*, her posthumous works include: *Uncollected Poems* (1965), *Crossing the Water* (1971), *Winter Trees* (1972), and the *Collected Poems* (1981). *The Journals of Sylvia Plath* was published in 1982. Plath wrote to her mother almost daily after she left home for Smith College and throughout her life. These letters have been collected in *Letters Home* (1975).

The World of the Poems

After World War II, Americans sought a return to "normalcy." There was pressure on women to return to their domestic roles after having proven themselves independent and competent in a number of unusual situations during the wartime crisis. But there were women in the 1950s who wanted to have a career as well as a husband and family. Plath, was, without a doubt, one of these women. She once described herself as a "triple threat woman; wife, poet and teacher." Indeed the tension between these roles continued throughout her life and surfaced in places as a theme in her work.

Plath went to college in the 1950s when the expectations for women were to be pretty, fun, and "not go too far." Primarily, women were expected to get married and fulfill the duties of wife and mother. This meant a woman should provide moral and emotional support for her husband, keep a clean house, present a nice table, entertain well, have the right manners, and above all, take care of the children. Status for a woman meant making a good marriage to a steady wage-earner, preferably someone capable of climbing the success ladder. Many young women panicked if they were not engaged by their senior year. To add to the pressures, some young men were intimidated by intelligent women. The thinking went, if a girl was smart, she probably wasn't fun—or marriageable.

Plath was aware of the prejudice against "brainy" women. She was once pleased when, after telling a date she got all A's, he didn't believe her. Smith College, however, was committed to fostering academic excellence and a sense of independence in women. Plath was torn between her commitment to academics and to her writing and her desire to be a "popular, red-blooded, all-American girl."

Plath did not reject the conventions of her day, despite the outward "bohemianism" of being and marrying a poet. In fact, she embraced them, working hard to achieve and fulfill all of the expected roles. She married a brilliant poet, and as his adoring wife, typed all of his manuscripts and sent them out. She once wrote to her mother: "I am so happy his (Ted's) book is accepted first . . . I am more happy than if it was my book published!" (Probably because this relieved a good deal of the pressure of achieving success before he did.) Yet, she also recognized that she was a genius in her own right. The guilt and anxiety over this conflict was with her until the final spurt of writing after the marriage failed. Only then did Plath attempt to become entirely true to herself, finally casting out the "good girl" who tried to please everyone.

Plath was an avid reader. Among the poets who count as influences are (in no particular order): Dylan Thomas, Emily Dickinson, Theodore Roethke, W.H. Auden (once her teacher), Robert Lowell (another teacher), William Butler Yeats, and Adrienne Rich. She was particularly influenced in her later work by Robert Lowell's *Life Studies*, a so-called "confessional" work because of its basis in autobiography. These poems, like poems by Anne Sexton, Plath's contemporary and fellow auditor of Lowell's seminar, introduced a new intimacy and directness into poetry, a style Plath called in a review, "uniquely American." In an interview, she said that she considered *Life Studies* an "intense breakthrough into very serious, very personal emotional experience, which I feel has been partly taboo." Lowell's (and others') breakthrough allowed Plath to experience a similar breakthrough in writing about "peculiar, private and taboo subjects"—namely, the life of the psyche.

Earlier influences such as Dylan Thomas, Yeats, and Auden helped her to concentrate on mastering form, particularly the use of cadence—the rhythm of the line beyond metrical rhythm that produces the "music" of the line. Later she was able to explode these forms to create her own unique style.

Sylvia Plath: the Mythology of Self

In his introduction to *The Journals of Sylvia Plath*, Ted Hughes wrote: "A real self, as we know, is a rare thing. The direct speech of a real self is rarer still . . . When a real self finds language, and manages to speak, it is surely a dazzling event—as *Ariel* was." Sylvia Plath's "real self" experienced passion, rage, and pain. Yet she managed to transform her experience from mere autobiographical "confession" into art. To do so, she had to mythologize her own experience to make it significant to others. Plath linked her private experience to public experience through the use of Greek mythology, Freudian psychology, folk tales, fairy tales, religious analogies and world history. (She was a voracious reader in all of these areas, as well as of other poets.) The speaker of the poem "Lady Lazarus," for example, shares many of the actualities of Plath's life, particularly her first suicide attempt. Yet Plath mythologizes herself in "Lady Lazarus"—through the title itself, with its references both to Lady Macbeth and to Lazarus, the man Jesus raised from the dead, and through the multiple transformations, the speaker goes from a Holocaust victim to a phoenix reborn "out of the ash." Even the language of the poem goes through various transformations, evoking towards the end the folk or fairy tale witches' incantation: "Ash, ash—/You poke and stir./Flesh, bone, there is nothing there—."

In an interview for the BBC, Plath said:

> I think my poems come immediately out of the sensuous and emotional experiences I have. I believe that one should be able to control and manipulate experiences, even the most terrifying, like madness, being tortured . . . I want to be able to manipulate these experiences with an informed and intelligent mind. I think that personal experience is very important, but certainly it shouldn't be a kind of shut box and sort of mirror-looking narcissistic experience. I believe it should be relevant, and relevant to larger things, the bigger things, such as Hiroshima and Dachau and so on.

210

Thus we see the "relevant" topic of the Holocaust linked to the daughter's terrible pain in "Daddy," and the bombing of Hiroshima linked to the woman's passion in "Fever 103°."

Like Dickinson, Plath explores emotional and psychological boundaries. But unlike Dickinson, her persona is always a dual "I"—she steps forward to speak as her "real" self. At first glance, this persona seems narcissistic; when we look more closely we see the mythic transformation at work. She does not say, "My husband left me so now I want to kill myself," or "My father died so I'm furious at him." She discards facts in order to transform the experience into art, to make it resonate. In doing so, she allows her actual father in both "The Colossus" and "Daddy" to become a Freudian father image. Critic Sandra Gilbert points out that the father in "The Colossus" is a "vehicle through which she [Plath] can think about history and the world." (The daughter in the poem says, "O father, all by yourself/You are pithy and historical as the Roman forum.")

Plath wrote from events in her life. Exploiting the present, she is breathtakingly original in transforming domestic subjects such as parent/child relationships, birthdays, motherhood, wifehood, and biological realities into the psychologically charged subjects of poems. She even manages to transform nursery language into the stuff of art in "Daddy" to express her insight into the relationship between father and daughter.

Although Plath was not a feminist in the contemporary sense, she did use some traditional female symbols in the mythologizing of her experience. These symbols included the moon and blood. (Look, for example, at the images of the moon in "The Moon and the Yew Tree," and in "Edge.") She also transformed the conventional image of the witch into a symbol of female power. In "The Disquieting Muses," for example, Plath transforms the traditional image of the male poet's muse, a beautiful woman, into an image accessible to women, three "disquieting" witches whom she calls her "travelling companions."

In her final extraordinary spurt of writing, Plath exploded her own craft and subject matter to write powerfully, almost brutally of what she knew.

Exercise: Look at a domestic experience such as your birthday. Explore in prose or in a poem what you and others go through during such an event. You may want to begin by reading Plath's poems "Balloons" and "Cut."

Meet the Speakers

Wilbury Crockett was the teacher of Plath's advanced English class in high school. Crockett introduced Plath to the great classics of English and American literature and encouraged her to continue writing.

Margaret Shook was a fellow honors and scholarship student with Plath at Smith College.

A. Alvarez is an English critic and anthologist who was a friend of Ted Hughes and Sylvia Plath. He edited *The New Poetry* and has written *The Savage God: A Study of Suicide* and *Stewards of Excellence: Studies in Modern English and American Poets*.

Aurelia Plath is the mother of Sylvia Plath and has edited a volume of her daughter's letters, *Letters Home*.

Clarissa Roche is the wife of Paul Roche, the noted English poet and translator. She and Plath were close friends.

Dido Merwin is the former wife of the acclaimed American poet W.S. Merwin. She was a good friend of Sylvia Plath during the years she spent in England.

Sandra Gilbert, a professor of English literature at Princeton University, is an acclaimed critic as well as a poet. With Susan Gubar she has written *The Madwoman in the Attic: The Woman Writer and the Nineteenth Century Literary Imagination*, and edited *Shakespeare's Sisters: Feminist Essays on Woman Poets*. Her books of verse include *The Summer Kitchen* and *Emily's Bread*.

Study Plan for this Unit

1. Complete the section **Before Watching the Film: Journal-Writing and Other Activities**.

2. Read the Plath poems below, many of which are featured in the film. These poems will also be highlighted in this unit. Plath's poems are often admired for their stunning aural effects and interesting rhymes, among other things. Listen for these aspects of her poetry when you read the poems aloud.

The Disquieting Muses
Daddy
The Moon and the Yew Tree
Tulips
Edge
Ariel
The Beekeeper's Daughter
Lady Lazarus
Fever 103°
Stings
The Stones
The Colossus
Ocean 1212-W (personal essay)

3. Watch the film.

4. Complete the section **After Watching the Film: Journal-Writing and Other Activities**.

5. Go through the **Guided Reading**.

6. Complete the **Exercises and Assignments** as specified by your instructor.

7. Take the **Self Test**.

Before Watching the Film: Journal-Writing and Other Activities

1. In her autobiographical essay "Ocean 1212-W," Plath wrote about her "childhood landscape" of the New England seashore. She said, "I sometimes think my vision of the sea is the clearest thing I own." Write a page about your "childhood landscape" and how it affected you.

2. After reading the poems listed above, write a brief description of how you imagine the poet.

3. Plath's poem "Blue Moles" was inspired by the following entry in her journal:

October 22, 1959: Two dead moles in the road. One about ten yards from the other. Dead, chewed of their juices, caskets of shapeless smoke-blue fur, with the white, clawlike hands, the human palms, and the pointy corkscrew noses sticking up. They fight to the death Ted [Hughes] says. Then a fox chewed them.

Read the poem. Then record in your journal a detailed description of an animal. Turn your description into a poem.

While Watching the Film

1. Jot down images of women's roles in the film.

2. Listen carefully to Plath's reading of her own work.

After Watching the Film: Journal-Writing and Other Activities

1. Look back at your entry for 2. in **Before Watching**. How has your impression of Plath, the person and the poet, been altered by viewing the film?

2. Were you surprised by the way Plath read her work? If yes, how will it affect your reading of the poems? If no, why not?

3. Plath once said in an interview that the poems in her first book were not meant to be read aloud. Her "recent" poems, she said, had to be read aloud. Compare the poem "The Colossus" to "Lady Lazarus." Can you tell which one should be read aloud? How? (Then check the dates!)

4. Plath's early death has created a myth of her as a martyr or suicide, a tragic female victim over whom death finally triumphed. Some critics say that Plath's reputation is based more on this myth than on her poetry. How would you answer the critics?

Guided Reading

The poem "Tulips" was published in Plath's second book *Ariel*, (1965) widely regarded as her most important volume. The poem itself was written in March, 1961, shortly after Plath underwent surgery for an appendicitis. As you go through the **Guided Reading**, keep in mind that this is one reader's interpretation.

Tulips

The tulips are too excitable, it is winter here.   1
Look how white everything is, how quiet,
   how snowed-in.
I am learning peacefulness, lying by myself quietly
As the light lies on these white walls, this bed,
   these hands.

I am nobody; I have nothing to do with explosions.   5
I have given my name and my day-clothes up to
    the nurses
And my history to the anesthetist and my
    body to surgeons.

They have propped my head between the pillow
    and the sheet-cuff
Like an eye between two white lids that will
    not shut.
Stupid pupil, it has to take everything in.   10
The nurses pass and pass, they are no trouble,
They pass the way gulls pass inland in their
    white caps,
Doing things with their hands, one just
    the same as another,
So it is impossible to tell how many there are.

My body is a pebble to them, they tend it as water   15
Tends to the pebbles it must run over, smoothing
    them gently.
They bring me numbness in their bright needles,
    they bring me sleep.
Now I have lost myself I am sick of baggage—
My patent leather overnight case like a black pillbox,
My husband and child smiling out of the
    family photo;   20
Their smiles catch onto my skin, little smiling hooks.

I have let things slip, a thirty-year-old cargo boat
Stubbornly hanging on to my name and address.
They have swabbed me clear of my loving
    associations.
Scared and bare on the green plastic-pillowed
    trolley   25
I watched my teaset, my bureaus of linen,
    my books
Sink out of sight, and the water went over my head.
I am a nun now, I have never been so pure.

I didn't want any flowers, I only wanted
To lie with my hands turned up and be utterly
    empty.   30
How free it is, you have no idea how free—
The peacefulness is so big it dazes you,
And it asks nothing, a name tag, a few trinkets.
It is what the dead close on, finally;
    I imagine them

214

Shutting their mouths on it, like a Communion
    tablet.   35

The tulips are too red in the first place,
   they hurt me.
Even through the gift paper I could hear them breathe
Lightly, through their white swaddlings,
   like an awful baby.
Their redness talks to my wound, it corresponds.
They are subtle: they seem to float, though they
   weigh me down,
Upsetting me with their sudden tongues and
   their color,
A dozen red lead sinkers round my neck.

Nobody watched me before, now I am watched.
The tulips turn to me, and the window behind me
Where once a day the light slowly widens
   and slowly thins,   45
And I see myself, flat, ridiculous, a cut-paper
   shadow
Between the eye of the sun and the eyes of
   the tulips,
And I have no face, I have wanted to efface myself.
The vivid tulips eat my oxygen.

Before they came the air was calm enough,   50
Coming and going, breath by breath,
   without any fuss.
Then the tulips filled it up like a loud noise.
Now the air snags and eddies round them
   the way a river
Snags and eddies round a sunken rust-red engine.
They concentrate my attention, that was happy   55
Playing and resting without committing itself.

The walls, also, seem to be warming themselves.
The tulips should be behind bars like dangerous
   animals;
They are opening like the mouth of some great
   African cat,
And I am aware of my heart: it opens and closes   60
Its bowl of red blooms out of sheer love of me.
The water I taste is warm and salt, like the sea,
And comes from a country far away as health.

Lines 1-7
1. Where is this poem taking place?

2. Which details give us a clue to the speaker's state of mind in this stanza? How would you describe the speaker's state of mind?

Answers
1. The poem takes place in the speaker's hospital room after she has undergone an operation.

2. Clearly, the speaker is in a state of heightened awareness—she is particularly sensitive to colors and inanimate objects such as the tulips which appear "too excitable." The phrase "I have nothing to do with explosions" implies that formerly, the speaker was feeling "explosive." The tulips are so bright in contrast to her mood that they seem "explosive" to her. The speaker's vulnerability has led her to dissociate herself from her "self." She discards aspects of her identity ("name," "day-clothes," "history," "body") so that she becomes "nobody."

Lines 8-14
1. What is the significance of the pun on "Stupid pupil" in line 10? How does the sound of these words place emphasis on the pun?

Answer
1. "Stupid pupil" refers to the simile of the previous lines, in which the speaker's head resting on the pillow is compared to a staring eye that continually "has to take everything in." However, when you read "stupid pupil" aloud, the strong accents on the first syllables of "stupid" and "pupil" and the repeated sounds make the phrase accusatory—as though an angry teacher were berating a dull student. Indeed, it's the "stupid pupil" that takes everything in dully and without full comprehension.

Lines 15-21
1. Read lines 15 and 16 aloud. How do these lines reflect their meaning?

2. What is the impact of the metaphor in line 21?

Answers
1. Through repeated sounds, stress, and enjambment, Plath makes the line flow like the stream over the pebble. Notice that the flow of words, like the stream, eddies just a little on "pebble." The word "pebble" also recreates the burbling sound of the stream. The line break at the word "water" runs the sentence over into the next line as the water runs over the pebbles.

2. The image of "smiling hooks" is a little sinister. For the first time in the poem, we get a clear sense that the speaker is a little deranged. It's as though the speaker has transformed herself from pebble to fish and is only kept from swimming away by her family photo. Ordinarily, a photograph of one's smiling husband and child would be regarded as comforting: to the speaker, however, the photo is an irritating reminder of her former life—her "baggage."

Lines 22-28

1. What events are being described here?

Answer

1. The speaker recalls both the experience of being wheeled out of her hospital room and of going under anaesthesia. Notice that the speaker's experience of "letting things slip" is not so much a terrifying experience as a purifying one.

Lines 29-35

1. What do the "flowers" in line 29 signify to the speaker?

2. What is the speaker describing in this stanza?

3. What do lines 34-35 refer to?

Answers

1. The flowers in this line (note the generalization from "tulips") signify the speaker's responsibility or obligation to the outside world. If you receive flowers, you have to write a thank-you note—you have to acknowledge those "loving associations."

2. Still experiencing the aftereffects of the anaesthesia, the speaker describes her own death and even her funeral. She "didn't want any flowers," and she knew exactly how she wanted her body arranged— "my hands turned up and . . . utterly empty." In line 31, when the poem shifts back to present tense, the speaker again addresses us from the realm of the dead: "How free it is, you have no idea how free—." The anaesthesia gives the speaker the opportunity to imagine her own death and, rather than this being a frightening experience for her, she wants to remain in this realm.

3. What the ancient Greeks "close[d] on" was a coin placed in the mouth to pay the ferry ride over the river Styx, the river of death. Plath overlays on this image the Christian image of the communion tablet, referring to line 28: "I am a nun now, I have never been so pure." She imagines death as communion with the world, a release from being herself, from her own identity.

Lines 36-42

1. What shift takes place between the end of the previous stanza and the beginning of this one?

2. In line 39, how do the tulips "correspond" to the speaker's wound?

3. What does the speaker compare the tulips to in this stanza?

Answers

1. As the speaker resurfaces from the anaesthesia, the tulips (the outside world) begin to assert themselves again. The first line, "The tulips are too red in the first place, they hurt me" reads as though it is a response to the question "What bothers you so much about those tulips?" Against her will, the speaker is forced to acknowledge the existence of the outside world again, and to collect some of her identity.

217

2. The "redness" of the tulips is like the redness of the speaker's wound, now stitched up by the surgeon. The tulips also "correspond" in the sense of communicating across a distance; the redness crosses the gulf of the speaker's detachment to "talk to" her wound. Finally, the tulips "correspond" in a negative sense because they are opening up while the wound is closing.

3. The speaker compares the tulips to "an awful baby," "sudden tongues," and "lead sinkers."

Lines 43-49

1. What two natural processes are alluded to in this stanza?

2. Read the stanza aloud. Then count the number of first-person pronouns ("I," "my," "myself," "me"). Include the homonyms in your count. What is the effect of these pronouns?

3. Look up the word "vivid" in your dictionary. Why did Plath select this word to describe the tulips?

4. How does this stanza contrast with the second stanza?

Answers

1. The speaker refers to phototropism and to photosynthesis. However, the tulips would turn to the sun, not to the speaker; and they would not "eat" oxygen, but produce oxygen. Ironically, the more the speaker attempts to be "scientific" or rational, the more she appears to be paranoid and deranged.

2. There are twelve first person singular pronouns in this stanza. The repeated use of the pronouns places emphasis on the speaker's self-absorption. Paradoxically, the more the speaker wants to "efface" herself, the more the self intrudes. The speaker projects "eyes" (I's) onto the tulips and the sun while she would like to disappear in their eyes (the eyes of the outside world).

3. "Vivid" describes the color of the tulips, but it also comes from the Latin *vividus*, full of life, from *vivere*, to live. The tulips are a call to life.

4. In the second stanza, the speaker's face is compared to an eye ("stupid pupil") propped between the "pillow and the "sheet-cuff." In this stanza, the "face" has been "effaced." The speaker sees herself as a "cut-paper shadow/Between the eye of the sun and the eyes of the tulips." Before she watched the nurses passing to and fro, now she feels she is being watched.

Lines 50-56

1. What does the speaker mean in line 55 when she says, "They concentrate my attention"?

Answer

1. She means that the tulips force her to pay attention to them. She is feeling so passive that the tulips act on her like a magnet.

Lines 57-63

1. The tulips are opening up in this stanza. How does the poet reinforce this event through sound? (**Note**: Read line 59 aloud.)

2. When does one ordinarily become "aware" of one's heart? What makes the speaker in the poem aware of her heart?

3. What is the significance of the "water" in line 62?

Answers

1. You can literally experience a sense of opening when you pronounce "opening," "mouth," and "African."

2. One ordinarily becomes aware of the pounding of one's heart when one is either scared or excited or has just finished some strenuous exercise. The speaker experiences an intense, irrational fear as she realizes that life is opening again for her.

3. The "water" refers to her tears, coming from the "country far away as health," they are harbingers of her recovery. The tulips have worked their health on her. The tulips are life and have brought her life—like her heart that "blooms" in spite of everything.

Further Question

1. Go back over the poem and list all the images and references to water. What is the significance of the water imagery?

Answer

1. The first reference to water is implied in the second stanza where the nurses are compared with gulls. Even when they are passing inland, gulls make us think of the sea and "white caps." In the next stanza, the nurses themselves have become like water "tending" the pebbles on the bottom of the river. Water in this stanza is soothing, even numbing. We're reminded of the river Lethe, the river of forgetfulness in Hades, from Greek mythology. Indeed, the speaker begins to forget her associations to her identity. In the fourth stanza, she has "let things slip." She is now a cargo boat "swabbed clear" of her "loving associations." Finally, she sinks out of sight underwater, where she experiences a complete detachment. The water becomes baptismal, leaving her without the cumbersome bother of an identity. Yet in the sixth stanza, when the speaker has begun to resurface, the tulips threaten to sink her and, unlike the sinking in the fourth stanza, this sinking is a threat: " . . . they weigh me down . . . A dozen red lead sinkers round my neck."

Another river appears in the eighth stanza. This time the river is a river of air, a noisy, active river that, unlike the river Lethe in the third stanza, "snags and eddies" around the tulips—"a sunken rust-red engine." This river seems to be an ordinary industrial river, a river of the real world, filled with abandoned cars and other debris.

In the final stanza, the speaker is linked through her tears to the sea. Her link to the sea is symbolically a link to health. Yet that sea is located in a far-off land—"a country far away as health." Throughout the poem, the water imagery underscores the process the speaker undergoes from sickness and a letting go, back to reality and the road to health.

Final Exercise
  Compare the patient in "The Stones" to the patient in "Tulips."

Exercises and Assignments

  1. Plath wrote a number of poems that used beekeeping as the central metaphor. Aside from the important autobiographical allusions inherent in the metaphor—Plath's father was an avid beekeeper—she mined the ritual aspects of the activity, transforming the details of beekeeping into symbols. Read "The Beekeeper's Daughter" and "Stings." Then list some occupations or hobbies that could be viewed as metaphor. Choose one of these activities and write out the steps and details that make up the activity. Finally, write a poem based on the activity as an extended metaphor.

  2. In the poem "Daddy," Plath uses rhyme to enhance the meaning of the poem. Read the poem aloud and then answer the following questions: How does the rhyme work with the sense of poem? How does the rhyme contribute to the tone of the poem? (**Note:** There is a very conspicuous rhyme in the poem, "Daddy." What impact does it have?)

  3. Make a list of the fairy tales, folk tales, and myths alluded to in "The Disquieting Muses." Reread the poem. What societal myths or conventions are also alluded to in the poem? Write a brief essay discussing how your childhood was affected by fairy tales, folk tales, and family and societal myths.

  4. In the poem "Lady Lazarus," the speaker adopts a number of theatrical voices and styles. Read the poem aloud and make a note of the changes the voice goes through. Is there a section in the poem that reveals the "true" voice of the speaker? If yes, explain. If no, explain.

  5. Plath's poems often give you the feeling that you're making your way through a dark and ominous landscape. "This landscape," to quote Stephen Spender, "is a mental one in which external objects have become converted into symbols of hysterical vision." Read "The Moon and the Yew Tree." Explain how the speaker fuses with the landscape and what vision this produces.

  6. In the poem "Ariel," how does Plath make the presence of the horse felt without actually describing the horse?

  7. The symbol of the queen was important both to Plath and to Dickinson. Read "I'm ceded—I've stopped being Theirs—," and "Stings." Compare the two poets' use of the queen symbol.

  8. "Ariel" and "Fever 103°" both relate sexual passion to a wish for death and to violence. How do they differ in the way they relate these themes?

  9. Plath published the poem "The Colossus" three years before she wrote "Daddy." How does the earlier poem anticipate the later one on the same subject?

  10. Go through some of the "women's" magazines such as *Mademoiselle*, *Vogue*, *Cosmopolitan*, etc. and make a list of the kinds of values, roles, and attitudes that are being promoted for women. How much have these values changed since Sylvia Plath's day?

11. Imagine that Plath did not commit suicide, that she's alive and well and living in London. How does this affect your reading of the poems?

12. How does Plath link her personal history to public history in "Fever 103°"?

13. One of Plath's powerful themes was the unleashing of violence. Compare Plath's treatment of this theme in "Daddy" and "Lady Lazarus."

Self Test

How many references can you find to Plath's work in the following parody? Note references to style as well as to actual poems.

Godiva

I wear a cobra's black bonnet,
A granite
Grin,

With an acetylene
Tongue
Behind the row of headstones.

Don't touch, Herr . . .
Just look.
Look. Look. Look.

A jacket of ashes,
Ragged umbrellas for hands,
The shadow of this lip a pit,

Just look at it.
Good God!
A mole in a spotlight of knives,

A puppet with no strings
Attached. Nothing.
Lady Godiva on a nag, nag, nag.

Suck this living doll's
Last tear if you will,
But beware

I eat in
Like Hiroshima ash.
I sizzle,

Herr Love, Herr Lucifer,

Your flash
In the pan.

—D.C. Berry (From the *Brand-X Anthology*)

Answers to Self Test
Answers to Self Tests begin on page 226.

For Further Reading
Books by Sylvia Plath:

Ariel. New York: Harper and Row; 1965.

The Bell Jar. New York: Bantam Books; 1981.

The Collected Poems. Hughes, Ted, editor. New York: Harper and Row; 1981.

Johnny Panic and the Bible of Dreams: Short Stories, Prose and Diary Excerpts. New York: Harper and Row; 1979.

The Journals of Sylvia Plath. McCullough, Frances, editor. New York: Dial; 1982.

Letters Home: Correspondence 1950-1963. Plath, Aurelia Schober, editor. New York: Harper and Row; 1975.

Books about Plath:

Alexander, Paul, editor. *Ariel Ascending: Writings About Sylvia Plath.* New York: Harper and Row; 1985.

Hardwick, Elizabeth. "Sylvia Plath." *Seduction and Betrayal, Women and Literature.* New York: Random House; 1974.

Lane, Gary, editor. *Sylvia Plath: New Views on the Poetry.* Baltimore, Johns Hopkins; 1979.

Newman, Charles, editor. *The Art of Sylvia Plath: A Symposium.* Bloomington and London: Indiana University Press; 1970.

Uroff, Margaret Dickie. *Sylvia Plath and Ted Hughes.* University of Illinois; 1979.

GLOSSARY

alliteration   a sound pattern within the line created by the repetition of a consonant at the beginning of words or syllables. For example, "weathered the winter, wretched outcast." (Ezra Pound)

allusion   an indirect reference to something the poet assumes is known by the reader. Poetic allusion may refer to another poem, or to something from myth, religion, or art, or to an historical event. Poetic allusions enrich the poem through bringing about a connection to the world outside the poem.

anaphora   the repetition of the same word or phrase at the beginning of each line.

apostrophe   the rhetorical device of speaking to an absent or dead person, or to an object or an abstraction, as though it were present and could hear and understand.

assonance   a sound pattern within the line created by the repetition of similar vowel sounds. For example, "Winding across wide water, without sound." (Wallace Stevens)

blank verse   lines in iambic pentameter that are unrhymed.

connotation   the meanings we associate with words beyond their dictionary (denotative) definitions. For example, the word "home" connotes warmth, security, comfort, whereas it denotes "a place where one lives; residence; habitation." Compare denotation.

consonance   the repetition of a sequence of consonants in nearby words with a change in the intervening vowels. For example, "bland/blind," "flash/flesh," "breed/bread."

denotation   the dictionary definition of a word. Compare connotation.

ellipsis   the leaving out of words which in prose syntax would be necessary to make sense but which do not need to be there for the poem to make sense. For example, "Unmoved—an Emperor be kneeling/Upon her mat—" (Emily Dickinson). The missing words might be: [She is] Unmoved [that] an Emperor [should] be kneeling upon her mat. There are other possibilities. (Note: an ellipsis is a mark [. . .] indicating an omission of a word or series of words.)

end-rhyme   the rhymes that occur at the ends of lines in rhymed poems.

enjambed   a line of poetry that breaks without a pause created by punctuation or syntax. For example, "mottled clouds driven from the/northeast—a cold wind. Beyond, the/waste of broad muddy fields." (William Carlos Williams)

figurative language   any use of words not meant to be taken literally.

free verse   a piece of writing that is divided into lines, but that does not adhere to a strict metrical pattern. Poems in free verse usually have irregular line lengths and are usually unrhymed. Although free verse is free of strict metrical patterns, it is as controlled as other forms.

haiku   a Japanese poetic form composed of three lines of five, seven, and five syllables exactly in that order. Traditional haiku convey the poet's impression of a natural scene.

iambic pentameter   See meter.

iambic tetrameter   See meter.

iambic trimeter   See meter.

internal rhyme   any rhyme that occurs within a line of poetry.

inversion   a change in the normal word order. For example, "My mother I love" is an inversion of "I love my mother."

level of diction   the choice of words depending on the audience or occasion. A State of the Union address requires a formal level of diction; a stand-up comedian's monologue usually requires an informal level of diction.

metaphor   a figure of speech which usually demonstrates how one thing is like another through an implied comparison. For example, "My Life had stood—a Loaded Gun—" (Emily Dickinson). Notice that slang is usually metaphoric: "Let's split," or "Life's a drag."

metaphoric comparison   See metaphor.

meter   the regular recurrence of some rhythmic pattern or pulse. The pattern is usually analyzed by the number of pulses (called "beats" or "feet") per line. The basic beats of English verse are: the iamb, the trochee, the anapest, and the dactyl. (See the Introduction for examples of these feet.) The usual number of recurrences is three (trimeter), four (tetrameter), five (pentameter), or six (hexameter). Thus, a line containing five iambs is said to be in "iambic pentameter," a line containing four iambs is in "iambic tetrameter," and a line containing three iambs is in "iambic trimeter."

metonymy   a figure of speech one thing is called by the name of another thing with which it is closely associated. For example, a "jock" for a male athlete.

ode   a meditative poem of some length. It is usually formally elaborate, but the term does not refer to a specific organization. The irregular ode is made up of stanzas of different patterns. For an example, read Robert Lowell's "To the Union Dead."

onomatopoeia   word sounds that imitate the sounds of the thing being described or mimic the thing in some other way. For example, "Chieftain Iffucan of Azcan in caftan/Of tan with henna hackles, halt!" (Wallace Stevens) used to depict the blustering of a bantam rooster.

oxymoron   a phrase that links, in one unit, words that usually appear as contraries: "cold fire," "terrible beauty," "sweet sorrow."

paradox   any statement that seems contradictory, yet may, nonetheless, turn out to be true.

parody   a poem which humorously imitates the style or content of another poem or of a poet's work in general.

pastoral   a poem that depicts an idyllic natural landscape and nostalgically evokes the beauty and peace of nature.

persona poem   a poem in which a character other than the poet is the speaker.

personification   a figure of speech in which some human characteristic or motive is attributed to an animal, an abstraction, or an inanimate object. For example, "April is the cruellest month."

quatrain   any four-line stanza.

repetition   one of the simplest forms of rhythm.

rhyme scheme   the pattern of end-rhymes that characterizes a stanza or poem. Rhyme schemes are indicated by letters which indicate which lines rhyme. For example, abab indicates that the first and third lines rhyme and the second and fourth lines rhyme. See Introduction for further examples.

sestina   one of the oldest and most complicated fixed forms used in English. It has six six-line stanzas and a three-line envoy (concluding stanza). The same six words that end the lines in the first stanza reappear in the other stanzas as line-end words (at least three of them have to appear in the envoy). Their arrangement is different in each stanza, according to a set pattern.

simile   a form of comparison using such words as "like," "as," or "as if." For example, "The aquarium is gone. Everywhere,/giant finned cars nose forward like fish . . . " (Robert Lowell)

slant rhyme (or off rhyme)   a rhyme with vowels slightly "off," but with the final consonants as expected. For example, "gate/mat," "June/men," or "port/chart."

soliloquy   a poem in which the speaker seems to be speaking an inner monologue aloud. For an example of a soliloquy, read "The Widow's Lament in Springtime." (William Carlos Williams)

sonnet   a lyric poem in 14 lines, normally in iambic pentameter, and rhymed according to one of a number of set forms. These forms include the Petrarchan sonnet (abbaabba cdcdcd or cdedce or cdecde); the Shakespearean sonnet (abab cdcd efef gg); and the Spenserian sonnet (ababbcbccdcd ee). The content of the sonnet is mirrored in its form. When the rhyme scheme changes (for example, with the closing couplet of the Shakespearean sonnet), the poet makes a shift, often from a proposition to a conclusion. For an example of this shift, read Shakespeare's "Sonnet 30."

syllabic verse   verse which contains a constant number of syllables in a line, but does not contain regular stresses.

synecdoche   a figure of speech in which a part or characteristic of something represents the whole. For example, "All hands on deck!" or "I should have been a pair of ragged claws/Scuttling across the floors of silent seas." (T.S. Eliot)

synesthesia   the perception or interpretation of one sense in terms of another. For example, "sweet face," "bitter tone," or "sour look."

tercet   any three-line unit.

villanelle   an Old French form in six stanzas and two rhymes, usually in iambic pentameter. The first and last lines of the opening tercet alternate as the closing line of the following four tercets, and the two lines together conclude the final quatrain.

Self Test Answers

Robert Frost

1. C

2. B

3. a. We've found "Mending Wall," "The Death of the Hired Man," and "Mowing." There may be others!

   b. (1.) The parody is written in blank verse. (2.) The parody uses the sound of sense. (3.) The parody uses Frost's understatement.

4. Line 5: "Her tone of meaning but without the words." The poem works metaphorically to convey the concept of the sound of sense; for example, a bird's song often seems to echo a given listener's mood or a specific phrase. In New England, for instance, the song of the white-throated sparrow is often translated as "Old Sam Pea-body Pea-body."

Ezra Pound

In this passage, Pound suggests that he can now see some important truths, but that it is beyond his power to communicate these truths by putting them into words in his poetry. He suggests that communicating these truths would be a hard task for anyone—("I have brought the great ball of crystal;/who can lift it?"). It is possible to see that there is truth ("the great acorn of light") and divine order ("it coheres all right") but it is hard to enter into that state of mind which allows a person to experience the conviction of this truth with complete certainty and assurance.

As in "Canto 81," the poet is here still criticizing himself, referring to his "errors and wrecks" and to madness. Also, as in "Canto 81," he sets a limit to his self criticism. He says "Charity I have had sometimes," and he wants to blame himself for what he has done wrong, but also to give himself credit for having been correct in some of his actions and views and insights—("To confess without losing rightness").

"What thou lovest well remains,/The rest is dross" is echoed in, "If love be not in the house there is nothing," and where in "Canto 81" the apparitions of three women appeared to comfort him in his tent, here he remembers how two beautiful women had raised his spirits and "saved" him from the "blackness" of despair by visiting him at St. Elizabeths. Where, in "Canto 81," he had watched the ant and had learned humility from studying "the green world" of nature, here he has been saved from despair "by squirrels and bluejays."

In "Canto 116," Pound emphasizes his feeling of having little power of his own to bring order back into his "wrecked" life. He cannot lift the ball of crystal or enter the acorn of light. He says "my notes do not cohere" and "I cannot make it flow thru," yet ultimately he has hope. He says "it [i.e. the physical and spiritual world] coheres all right" and implies that even the faintest possible glimpse of the truth, which he is comparing to a very weak candle or "rushlight," will be enough to lead him "back to splendour." (It is worth noting, in addition, that he also includes in this passage, in "The voice of famine unheard," a reminder that economic injustice and the sufferings of the destitute are still with us.)

Langston Hughes

The modern black poet seems to have answered Hughes' call in "The Negro Artist and the Racial Mountain" to create an art free from white literary standards, an art that speaks directly to a black audience. Lee's poem, like Hughes', is in the oral tradition although the tone is more coolly defiant than Hughes' usual tone. However, like Hughes' tone, Lee's contains a touch of ironic humor. Like Hughes, Lee captures the rhythms of jazz to convey the experience of being black.

Lee's jazz is more modern than Hughes' jazz, probably John Coltrane is an influence rather than the be-bop jazz musicians. Another reflection of Hughes' influence can be seen in Lee's use of the black idiom. Lee goes even farther than Hughes did in using slang, using nonstandard spelling to transcribe black English and its intonations. For Lee, as for Hughes, the use of the idiom is a way of celebrating the black identity.

Finally, Hughes' influence is seen in Lee's choice of the urban black as the subject of his poem. Lee's "cool" dude is as sharply delineated as any of Hughes' portraits of the black working class. Hughes' legacy allowed the modern black poet to explore racial themes and to use black language and culture as the basis of art.

Walt Whitman
See the answers to the Hart Crane Self Test.

Hart Crane
"I Saw in Louisiana a Live-Oak Growing" was written by Whitman, and "Royal Palm" was written by Crane.

You can tell that "Royal Palm" is Crane's poem for a number of stylistic reasons. One is his use of synesthesia: "Green rustlings," "Drift coolly," "whispered light" (there are others). Two, is his use of unusual modifiers: "blazed asperities," "deathward breath," and "azured height." The difficult vocabulary and condensed images are also characteristic of Crane's poetry. Finally, Crane explores the almost cosmic, metaphysical dimension to human experience in his juxtaposition of feeling words with words that connote time and space: "Forever fruitless," "Its frondings sighing in aetherial folds," "ascending emerald-bright."

"I Saw in Louisiana a Live-Oak Growing" is identifiably Whitman for both stylistic and thematic reasons. The long lines with their lilting cadences are typical of Whitman's poems as is the use of the first person. Repetition and lists are also characteristics of Whitman's poetry. Finally, the themes of "manly love" and the celebration of nature are important ones in Whitman.

William Carlos Williams
Like Williams', Ammons' implicit advice in the poem is "nothing is lost" so pay attention to detail. The form of the poem on the page creates a visual image of the shore (or the narrow parking lot by the shore) just as Williams' "Between Walls" creates visually the narrow space between two buildings. Ammons, like Williams, experiments with line breaks to create rhythm and impact. For example, we get the effect of the wind blowing hard "hitting me hard/side the head." And the almost comic interruption "what a/way to read/Williams!" is characteristic of Williams who doesn't hesitate to comment on the scene the way you would if you were there. We also hear the American idiom in words like "scrappy," "side of the head," and "piss." The "way to read Williams" turns out to be to pay close attention to the seemingly unimportant details of a woman walking her dog. Ammons has clearly paid attention to Williams' advice "you can make a poem out of anything."

Emily Dickinson
1. Poem 1: White, chill, heart very still, does not know you, quiet bed, tears will not wake her.

Poem 2: soldered mouth, awful rivet, hasps of steel, cool forehead, listless hair, adamantine fingers, shall never wear a thimble, indolent. (One could add the flies, the freckled pane, and the cobweb to the second list under "indolent" because, alive, the dead housewife was an industrious one who would have shooed the flies, washed the panes, and swept away the cobwebs.)

The details in the first list are general, conventional and expected; those in the second, concrete, vivid and surprising. The contrast is more dramatic in the second poem because of these details. Dickinson provides the reader with specific comparisons that are quite surprising but are also clearly appropriate and easy to visualize. This causes the reader to attend to a sight that is not an easy one to look at—one that we would normally hurry over or cover with cliches as the first poet does.

2. For the second poem: low, staggered, hot so often, thimble, and housewife.

All we learn about the woman in the first poem is that she "mourned and died" for the person being addressed. We know so little else that we don't know how to take this. Mourned over what? Died literally? And as a direct result? Or in some other sense?

In the Dickinson poem, we learn that the woman is a humble ("low") housewife who worked very hard, so hard that she "staggered." "Hot so often" might also indicate bouts with fever, possibly fevers associated with childbirth. She sewed and kept a clean house—the flies and cobwebs and spotted panes flourished only after her death. In this poem, we can picture the woman in her daily life and venture some educated guesses about her circumstances.

In contrast, the first poem tantalizes us with a glimpse of a major conflict that would reveal a lot about the woman if it were developed. But it is not developed and all we know is that some woman underwent some painful situation or lived with some painful burden for which the person being addressed bears some responsibility. We cannot picture her or imagine her feelings distinctly enough to feel real sympathy.

3. The commands in the first poem are spoken to a person whom the dead woman used to know and for whom she "mourned and died"—however we take that. Those in the other poem are addressed to a person imagined as being in the same room with the body and the speaker. This room could be the one where the wake is being held and the other person imagined as being there could be you the reader or just some other mourner.

"Put" is concrete but general, whereas "Stroke" and "Lift" tell you more precisely how to move your hand. "Handle," though general, is a word usually used for things, not people, and so emphasizes the lifelessness of the fingers, perhaps even suggesting (through the pun) that they are like handles. "Weep" and "Mourn" tell the listener what to feel. The imperatives in the second poem merely propose actions, leaving the implications to speak for themselves.

4. Essentially, the first poem asks for pity for the dead woman and righteous indignation at the person who "wrought her woe." The pity is hollow though because we cannot picture the woman and do not know what she suffered or how it felt to her. The indignation is similarly shallow, but it is tempered by the platitude in the last two lines. Anyone can identify with the experience of learning too late, so we feel some pity for the remorseful perpetrator too. But the platitude at the end is so broad that it takes us far outside the dramatic situation we've barely had a chance to get into. We see it as if from miles away and can't make out enough to do more than whet our curiosity.

Dickinson's poem also shows compassion for the woman and expresses indignation at her lot, but its main focus is the terror of being with a corpse. All three of these responses are heightened because the poem brings us in close and lets us discover things for ourselves. We've seen above how it seduces us into looking at this painful sight and reveals through casual details the difficulty of the woman's life. The indignation is also expressed quietly and indirectly, rather than through direct accusation and commands. The word "indolent" ironically assumes the voice of someone who is displeased with the housewife for neglecting her chores. However, the last word of the poem reminds us that the housewife is not lying in daisies out of indolence but has been "lain" there. This brings us back to the main focus of the poem, the terrible image of the corpse. Dickinson knows that, if she can draw this true, it will evoke more terror and pity and indignation than any outcries or challenges could.

Marianne Moore

The early version, with lines that stretch across the page, is a sequence of abstract ideas, the unit of attention being the sentence rather than the line. The relationship of the ideas to each other is confusing: after Moore likens the snail's compression to a graceful style, she states that contractility is not a real virtue but modesty is; then, she concludes that there are "things . . . infinitely more worthwhile than style." Like what, for example? It appears that she has, in the course of the poem, contradicted herself. In addition, her sentences are awkwardly constructed; the repetition of "virtue" and "things" is distracting; the verb "is" is used too many times.

In the later version, the line, not the sentence, is the unit of attention, with each word earning its place on the line. Strong end words such as "style," "virtue," and "horn," contrast with "is," "the," and "in" used in the earlier version. Moore also edited any phrasings that obscured her meaning so that we are left with a poem that acknowledges the value of style throughout. At the end, rather than contradicting herself, she brings the poem back to its original image of the snail, with its "absense of feet" and "curious occipital horn." This calls our attention to the play on feet (as poetic meter) which emphasizes the relationship of the snail's virtue to what Moore sees as a virtue in writing.

T.S. Eliot

Prufrock refers to Marvell's poem indirectly at first, with the insistence "There will be time" (a response to "Had we but World enough and time"). This insistence on there being enough time is repeated in various forms 11 times in the sections beginning on line 23 and ending on line 48. "Prufrock" then refers directly to "To His Coy Mistress" in lines 91-93: "To have bitten off the matter with a smile,/To have squeezed the universe into a ball/To roll it toward some overwhelming question."

The two poems are similar in that they both at first appear to be about love but are at least as much about time and how we deal with the inevitable decay of our physical selves. Both poems frequently take an ironic or humorous tone that makes us at first take their argument less seriously; e.g., "I grow old . . . I grow old . . ./I shall wear the bottoms of my trousers rolled" and "The grave's a fine and private place/But none, I think, do there embrace." Prufrock, however, laments the difficulty of attaining love given the, to him, sordidness and artificiality of the real world.

Marvell's theme of the unrelenting passage of time that we continuously hear at our backs is responded to in many of Eliot's poems and particularly in the *Four Quartets*, which set out to demonstrate that time is a continuum and that past, present and future all exist simultaneously.

Wallace Stevens

"To Autumn" influenced Wallace Stevens throughout his life and references to it can be found in many of his poems. The two poems that most obviously refer to Keats' poem are "Sunday Morning"—particularly in the final section—and "The Auroras of Autumn." The following are just a few of the similarities.

"Sunday Morning" is written in a series of sonnet-like sections and a nameless female persona is the vehicle for the poet's philosophical inquiry. Both poems address nature and feature animals as part of the answer to the poem's questioning: in Keats' ode, the animals form part of a pastoral landscape in which lambs bleat and redbreasts (robins) whistle; in "Sunday Morning," the animals are seen in a wilderness landscape where deer walk in the mountains and quail whistle. Read aloud the final sections of each poem and note the similarity of sound in Keats' lines about the "small gnats" and Stevens' lines about the "flocks of pigeons." Notice how in both poems the structure of the lines imitates the movement of the animals.

In "The Auroras of Autumn," Stevens depicts a much wilder season than the one Keats describes. Note that the Aurora Borealis is only seen in the extremely northern parts of the United States, where autumn is likely to be a harsher season than in the temperate climate of England. Instead of Keats' "light wind" which "lives or dies," we are given a "cold wind" which "chills the beach" and later "knock(s) like a rifle butt against the door." Instead of "gathering swallows," we are shown birds that fly like "wild wedges, as of a volcano's smoke." Keats nostalgically looks back to spring and then dismisses this nostalgia; Stevens suggests that "in the midst of summer" one can stop to "imagine winter." In general, there is an air of menace to the autumn season that was not present in Keats' poem: form is seen "gulping after formlessness" and the question is asked: "Shall we be found hanging in the trees next spring?" In this poem, Stevens personifies nature—as Keats does in many of his poems—although Stevens has both father and mother as personifications of nature, and other dualities are present to remind us that the North American seasons are not as idyllic as the one Keats' ode presents us with, that our earthly paradise is "harridan, not hushful."

Elizabeth Bishop

1. The form of this poem is called a villanelle. A villanelle is an old French form, consisting of five tercets (three-line stanzas) and one quatrain (four-line stanza), for a total of nineteen lines. The first and third lines of the first stanza alternate as the closing line of the following four tercets, and serve as the concluding lines of the quatrain. The poem is built on two rhymes; the rhyme scheme looks like this: aba aba aba aba aba abaa. Most villanelles are written in iambic pentameter. Bishop varies the form by changing the repeating lines somewhat as the poem progresses, rather than repeating them exactly.

2. The speaker of the poem is trying to convince herself (and the reader) that losing things you love is not a disaster. The emphatic quality of the repeating lines helps to reinforce this "lesson" she is trying to teach. By the end of the poem, however, the repetition has taken on an ironic quality, and by the last line, we know that she has not really convinced herself that losing isn't a disaster. Bishop emphasizes this point by interrupting herself and inserting the parenthetical phrase, "Write it!," as if to force herself to bring the form to its conclusion. Notice how she starts with small things—door keys, a watch—and moves to greater and greater losses.

3. Some of the ways by which you could recognize this as a Bishop poem might be through the references to travel and homelessness, as in "Questions of Travel," "Crusoe in England," and "The Moose." Other things that might earmark this poem are its spareness and precision of language, the wry understatement (no self-pity about these losses!), and the parenthetical asides, which tie it stylistically to other Bishop poems, such as "The Moose" and "Poem."

Robert Lowell

Like the tulips Lowell is exhausted, "bushed," and his "enervation," like theirs has "snowball-[ed];" i.e., it is a cumulative effect, in his case, of a series of attacks of mental illness. The tulips are a special, certified variety, and Lowell too has his "pedigree" as the scion of several old New England ruling-class families. He is a "cultivated" man but in his manic state he regresses toward more of a "wild" condition like the "pedigreed" tulips that cannot now be distinguished "from weed."

He feels flattened ("horizontal") both in the sense of worn out and in the sense of being ashamed or afraid to lift his head. Also, think of how tulips look: a weighty and impressive "head" (the flower) on a relatively fragile and simple "body" (the stem). Lowell may feel that his disturbed mental life has become more than his aging body can bear. The tulips grow in a "coffin's length" of soil. This comparison has several associations one of which is simply that Lowell feels dead tired. Also he has just returned from a mental hospital and must have had some doubt as to whether he would get out. If he hadn't, the hospital would have been like a coffin in which his former life was interred. This image may also be meant to suggest how his sane life looks to him when he is manic—he feels confined like the plants that grow in narrow strips around urban buildings or like a live man lying in a coffin.

Sylvia Plath

The parody contains direct references to: "Ariel," "The Moon and the Yew Tree," "Fever 103," "Lady Lazarus," "Gulliver" (This poem was not featured in the study guide or the film.),"Blue Moles."

References to Sylvia Plath's style include the word choices of "tongue," "suck," "doll," "lip"—words Plath often used in her poems. Another reference to Plath's style is the use of the three-line stanzas which she uses in such poems as "Ariel," "Fever 103," and "Lady Lazarus." The parody also makes reference to Plath's harsh aural effects often achieved through alliteration: "I wear a cobra's black bonnet,/A granite/Grin,." The repetition of a word three times is another stylistic reference: "nag, nag, nag" and "Look. Look. Look."

There may be other references we've missed!

Copyrights and Citations